Textual Contraception

• • • •

Textual Contraception
Birth Control and Modern American Fiction

• • • •

BETH WIDMAIER CAPO

THE OHIO STATE UNIVERSITY PRESS
Columbus

Copyright © 2007 by The Ohio State University.
All rights reserved.

Library of Congress Cataloging-in-Publication Data

Capo, Beth Widmaier, 1973–
Textual contraception : birth control and modern American fiction / Beth Widmaier Capo.
   p. cm.
Includes bibliographical references and index.
ISBN: 978-0-8142-1059-8 (cloth : alk. paper)
1. American fiction—20th century—History and criticism. 2. Abortion in literature.
3. Birth control in literature. 4. Motherhood in literature. 5. Eugenics in literature.
6. Race in literature. 7. Literature and science—United States. I. Title.
PS374.A24C37 2007
810.9'436346—dc22
            2007016126

This book is available in the following editions:
Cloth (ISBN: 978-0-8142-1059-8)
CD-ROM (ISBN: 978-0-8142-9139-9)
Paper (ISBN: 978-0-8142-5713-5)
Cover design by Janna Thompson-Chordas
Text design and typesetting by Jennifer Shoffey Forsythe
Type set in Adobe Fairfield

Contents

····

List of Illustrations vii
Acknowledgments ix

1   "Lewd and Lascivious" Literature 1

2   "As Red and Flaming as Possible"
Radical Rhetoric of the 1910s 20

3   "For Married Women Only"
Birth Control and Modern Marriage 53

4   "Conscious Makers of People"
Achieving a Free Motherhood 85

5   Reading the Body, Controlling the Race
Birth Control and the Eugenic Impetus of the
1920s and 1930s 110

6   The Economics of Desire and Despair
Birth Control and the Depression Era 145

7   Conclusion
Textual Contraception 168

Bibliography 191
Index 213

Illustrations

Figure 1	Candie's fragrance. Advertisement. *Mademoiselle*, December 1999: 49.	2
Figure 2	K. R. Chamberlain, "Breed! We Need Men," *Birth Control Review*, April/May 1917: 5.	33
Figure 3	Lou Rogers, "The New Vision," *Birth Control Review*, December 1918: 8–9.	34
Figure 4	Lydia Gibson, "The Boss's wife can buy information to limit her family," cover of *The Blast*, February 12, 1916.	36
Figure 5	Lou Rogers, "Mrs. Poor Patient," *Birth Control Review*, June 1918: 5.	37
Figure 6	Cornelia Barns, "Remember, Mrs. Judd," *Birth Control Review*, August 1919: 9.	45
Figure 7	Lou Rogers, "Must She Always Plead in Vain?," cover of *Birth Control Review*, July 1919.	50
Figure 8	Warren Wheelock, "Mother and Child," cover of *Birth Control Review*, December 1931. Reprinted with permission of Alexander Sanger.	83
Figure 9	"Dedicated to Voluntary Motherhood," cover of *Birth Control Review*, February 1921.	89
Figure 10	Arthur Young, "Hell on Earth," *The Masses*, March 1915.	129
Figure 11	Advertisement for *Seed: A Novel of Birth Control* by Charles Norris, back cover of *Birth Control Review*, September 1930. Reprinted with permission of Alexander Sanger.	136
Figure 12	"Bread! Bread! Bread! Hungry all the time," *Birth Control Review*, May 1932: 6. Reprinted with permission of Alexander Sanger.	148
Figure 13	Ruth Rozaffy, "We want another as soon as we can afford it," *Birth Control Review* 12.1 (1937): 12. Reprinted with permission of Alexander Sanger.	167
Figure 14	"I'll need to see a marriage license," *Ms.*, Summer 2005: 31. Reprinted with permission by the National Family Planning and Reproductive Health Association.	170

Acknowledgments

I HAVE MANY PEOPLE to thank for making this book possible. My first thanks belong to Deborah Clarke, whose unflagging encouragement and insightful commentary have shaped this project since its inception. Colleagues and teachers who have read and commented on this work at various stages include Susan Squier, Mark Morrisson, Sanford Schwartz, Julie Vedder, Erika Spohrer, Janet Holtman, Kristin Jacobson, Lisa Udel, Kelly Dagan, Jennifer Brown, Margaret Marek, Almut Spalding, and Caryn Riswold. My gratitude goes to Eckhart Spalding for his technological expertise and to Claire Brackel for preparing the index. Thanks also belong to the readers and editors at The Ohio State University Press for their thoughtful readings and suggestions.

Finally, I owe a tremendous debt to my parents, Nancy and Robert Widmaier, for their continued love and support. And perhaps most importantly, to my partner Nick Capo, an exceptional writer and editor, thank you for sharing the joy and frustration of this long journey.

Chapter 7 has been adapted from "Inserting the Diaphragm In(to) Modern Fiction: Mary McCarthy, Philip Roth, and the Literature of Contraception," *Journal of American Culture* 26.1 (March 2003): 111–23. Parts of chapters 3, 4, 5, 6, and 7 appeared in a different form in "'Can This Marriage Be Saved?': Birth Control and Marriage in Modern American Literature," *Modern Language Studies* 34.1–2 (Spring/Fall 2004): 28–41. Brief pieces of chapters 1, 2, 3, 4, and 6 have appeared in a different form in "'How Shall We Change the Law?': Birth Control Rhetoric and the Modern American Narrative," in *Literature and the Law*, edited by Michael J. Meyer (Kenilworth, NJ: Rodopi Press, 2004), 119–44.

1

"Lewd and Lascivious" Literature

TODAY, MAGAZINES AND television openly advertise and discuss birth control. Birth control pills are the most commonly prescribed drug for women ages 15–44, with an estimated 16 million American women on "the Pill," and recent legislation requires health insurance companies to cover it as a prescription drug.[1] Indeed, the Pill is so ubiquitous to today's media-savvy culture that the Ortho Tri-Cyclen brand distinguishes itself in the crowded market by asking, "If you decide to take the Pill, why not take the only one that helps your skin look better too?"[2] (This hormonal contraceptive, developed by Gregory Pinckus at the urging of Margaret Sanger in 1951, was the first truly new contraceptive device.) Makers of various oral contraceptive brands prominently advertise in magazines focusing on beauty, fashion, health, and "female interests" aimed at women ages 18–35. These ads feature attractive young models and use slogans to highlight the ease and efficiency of their products to appeal to today's busy woman ("Take birth control off your mind and just keep it on you" reads an ad for Ortho Evra, the contracep-

---

1. The seemingly automatic coverage of the male impotence drug Viagra in the late 1990s spurred "Contraceptive Equity" (see Goldberg A1). Individual states have passed bills mandating that employee-sponsored insurance plans cover FDA-approved prescription contraception, while the Equity in Prescription Insurance and Contraceptive Coverage Act (EPICC) slowly works its way through the federal government. According to *Shape* magazine, one year's supply of the birth control pill can cost more than $300, yet it is not covered by the majority of insurance plans and HMOs (Moriarty 24). Indeed, one way or another, women are still "paying" for their reproductive choices.

2. According to Lara V. Marks, the pharmaceutical company Johnson & Johnson tripled their sales of Ortho Tri-Cyclen when it was approved as an acne treatment (6). See also Oudshoorn and Asbell on the history of the birth control pill; see Gossel on the marketing of the pill.

FIGURE 1. Candie's fragrance. Advertisement. *Mademoiselle,* December 1999: 49.

tive patch, while an Estrostep pill ad reads, "One part complexion, one part protection. Your pill. For more reasons than one.") The open marketing of female contraceptives demonstrates birth control's transition from an illegal and "obscene" idea to a popular product marketed through glossy advertisements.

In 1938 Margaret Sanger predicted that in the future "birth control will have the position that the tooth brush has today, and people will think no more of it than they do of the tooth brush as an essential to good health" ("Quotable Quote"). Have we reached that point? Birth control is big business in the United States, both for pharmaceutical companies and for advertisers. Analysts have estimated the U.S. market for Depo-Provera alone in 1996 exceeded $850 million a year. Birth control has entered the realm of commercial advertising for mainstream products such as Candie's fragrances, which shows bra-clad actress Alyssa Milano opening a medicine cabinet overflowing with brightly wrapped Trojan condoms and two bottles of Candie's fragrance—one for men, one for women (fig. 1). The colorful fragrance bottles evoke youthful sexuality from their surroundings and an aura of risqué excess, although seeing sex linked here to responsible practices is refreshing. Indeed, is the woman's "Mona Lisa smile" for the fragrance or the condoms—which is she reaching for? And is this her medicine cabinet, displaying signs of a sexually active woman, or is she in the bathroom of her partner?

The Candie's fragrance ad also points to the continued assumption that birth control is a female responsibility. Although condoms have been used for hundreds of years, as both a prophylactic and contraceptive device, birth control has long been the domain of women. Currently, men can choose from withdrawal, condoms, and vasectomy as methods with varying degrees of effectiveness. Although a male hormonal contraceptive is in clinical trials, funding and public interest, at least in the United States, have been erratic. Women face a much longer list of available methods, such as the diaphragm, sponge, intrauterine device (IUD), pill, Norplant, Depo-Provera, female condom, and Ortho-Evra patch. And pharmaceutical company researchers are testing new forms of contraception for women, including a seven-year IUD, a film that dissolves inside the vagina, a disposable diaphragm, and a vaccine. These developments have not been without controversy, however. Plan B, the emergency contraceptive "morning-after" pill, has not received Food and Drug Administration (FDA) approval in the United States (although over thirty other countries, including Canada, have approved it), and two officials at the FDA resigned in protest over what they saw as the intrusion of politics into science (Kaufman). Some pharmacists have invoked a moral right to refuse to sell Plan B, which former Wisconsin Senator Tom Reynolds has equated with abortion, and Illinois Governor Rod Blagojevitch issued an emergency order that pharmacists must stock and fill any contraception prescription (Brackett).[3] The sense of social immediacy is as alive among reproductive rights activists now as it was during the early years of the twentieth century when the birth control movement began.

How did birth control infiltrate the American consciousness on social, economic, and personal levels? Contraception was not always such a widespread and visual part of popular culture. Indeed, for a long time contraception was illegal and widely considered immoral, linked

---

3. See also Shorto.

to prostitutes and "fallen women." The birth control movement in the United States, roughly from 1914 to 1940, was a time of social upheaval as the public acceptance of contraception tangled with World War I, the passage of the Nineteenth Amendment and changing roles for women, the growing power of the medical profession, the economic crisis of the Depression, and controversy over immigration.

The birth control movement, often remembered for the political agitation of Margaret Sanger, was a vital part of this social ferment in modern American history.[4] Dorothy Day, a young activist and journalist, covered the birth control movement for the socialist *New York Call* and later served as assistant editor of *The Masses*, another radical periodical supporting birth control. In her 1924 novel, *The Eleventh Virgin*, Dorothy Day describes the fevered atmosphere of political and social change experienced by young radical journalists:

> There was much to do—meetings to attend of protest against labor, capital, the high cost of living, war-profiteering. . . . There were meetings to start strikes, to end strikes, to form unions, to fight against other unions. Food riots came. The city hall was stormed—if you can call it storming (as the papers did) when a crowd of fat Jewish women from the East Side with babies in their arms stood in front of the city hall and scolded that institution. . . . There were birth control meetings—trials of birth control leaders, meetings of the Anti-Conscription League, the Emergency Peace Federation—and interviews galore. (113–14)

This autobiographical novel, written while Day was recovering from a traumatic abortion, captures the excitement of activism and the paradoxical position of radical women, fighting for social justice while still trapped by conventional gender roles and their own fertile bodies. Day's story further captures the complex and evolving emotions individual women have toward reproduction and contraception: she later founded the Catholic Worker Movement and attempted to find and destroy all copies of *The*

---

4. I use the terms birth control and contraception interchangeably as any deliberate effort to prevent conception. The term birth control, as defined by Margaret Sanger in 1914, referred to "the conscious control of the birth rate by means that prevent the conception of human life" (*My Fight for Birth Control* 84). Thus, from the start Sanger and others were careful to distinguish the contraceptive methods they advocated from abortion. This distinction was made repeatedly to gloss the birth control movement with the patina of respectability and enable it to argue from a position of morality. As Frederick A. Blossom writes, "by 'birth control' is meant the regulation of conception by harmless means, with a view to preventing the birth of undesired children. By no stretch of the wildest imagination can it be made to spell abortion or any form of infanticide" (12).

Eleventh Virgin.[5]

Like Dorothy Day, other American authors, male and female, canonical and forgotten, captured the issues and tone of the birth control movement in their fiction, contributing their narratives to social discourse on the morality and economics of legal contraception. In the novels of authors from Theodore Dreiser to William Faulkner, plays from Susan Glaspell to Lorraine Hansberry, and stories from Ernest Hemingway to Angelina Grimke, birth control and its attendant controversies implicitly or explicitly influenced the narrative. Whether authors consciously saw their writing as enacting a social as well as aesthetic role, these works together compose a rich and valid site to examine the birth control movement and its historical implications for female sexuality and reproductive control.[6] Placing these works in the context of the birth control movement, and the social discourse of economics, marriage, motherhood, and eugenics, this study traces the ways American authors took up and influenced dominant cultural discourses. As V. F. Calverton argued in 1926, "One of the best methods of discovering the theories of sex behavior which have prevailed in any generation is by examining the literature of the period" (*Sex Expression in Literature* xxv). This study, then, establishes the important role of fiction in shaping the birth control movement and the effects of contraception on modern narrative.

Birth control occupies an interesting social position. It is ostensibly within the realm of the private, of the female body and the tension between motherhood and independence, choice and biology. But little in the female "private sphere" remains a matter of individual choice untouched by social norms. Contraceptive practice was illegal during the early years of the twentieth century, but social forces as diverse as radical socialism, an incipient women's movement, and corporate profit

---

5. See Day's autobiography, *The Long Loneliness* (1952).

6. While authors such as Theodore Dreiser took an active role in the birth control movement, others touched more subtly on the debate. Many modernist writers, especially those who published in "little magazines" such as the *Little Review* and *The Masses*, "tended to see the social role of art as an issue related to the nature of public discourse" (Morrisson 6). Frederic Jameson argues persuasively that making strong distinctions between "high" aesthetic literary value and "low" political literature limits our ability to fully understand a text. Jameson writes, "From this perspective the convenient working distinction between cultural texts that are social and political and those that are not becomes something worse than an error: namely, a symptom and reinforcement of the reification and privatization of contemporary life. Such a distinction reconfirms that structural, experiential, and conceptual gap between the public and the private, between the social and the psychological, or the political and the poetic, between history or society and the 'individual,' which—the tendential law of social life under capitalism—maims our existence as individual subjects and paralyzes our thinking about time and change just as surely as it alienates us from our speech itself" (20).

seeking were introducing contraception to the public vocabulary under more acceptable guises, such as "voluntary motherhood" and "feminine hygiene." Advertisements for drugs to "regulate the female menses" circulated in newspapers and magazines. These same periodicals acted as a forum for public debate over the moral and legal implications of birth control. The public battle over companionate marriage, women's role in the public sphere, the declining birth rate and growing poverty, were fought not only in newspapers and magazines but also in fiction.

My purpose in this study is a dual one: to place previously unexamined literary material alongside canonical modernist fiction in the context of American and feminist history, and to explore the process of the circulation and exchange of contraceptive issues within contemporary literary production. The resulting narrative is not intended to be exclusionary but rather to introduce new material into an interdisciplinary understanding of modern literary and American cultural history. This methodology owes a debt to several recent works, including Michael Trask's *Cruising Modernism: Class and Sexuality in American Literature and Social Thought* and Daylanne English's *Unnatural Selections: Eugenics in American Modernism and the Harlem Renaissance*. Such a methodology can illuminate the relationship between modern American social thought and literature. This study takes as a given that literature is not separate from the public sphere, and that, while shifting aesthetic criteria may separate "high" and "low" art, the written word can have a powerful rhetorical effect and play an integral role in popular culture.

As a vehicle for information exchange and normalization, fiction both is influenced by and has a powerful influence on social acceptance of cultural norms. As Rachel Blau DuPlessis argues, "any literary convention—plots, narrative sequences, characters in bit parts—as an instrument that claims to depict experience, also interprets it. No convention is neutral, purely mimetic, or purely aesthetic" (*Writing beyond the Ending* 2). Consider, for example, the development of the "bodice-ripping" romance and its current popularity. These works openly portray female (hetero)sexuality and the sex act itself through lines such as "[h]is whole weight rested on me now as he upped and raised me for still greater penetration" (Gabaldon 437). The explicit sexual description allows readers to contextualize and normalize their own feelings of desire, in turn influencing their acceptance of sexual expression in the broader popular culture.[7] At the same time, however, these depictions often leave out the

---

7. While most contemporary romance novels still portray heteronormative sexuality, a growing number of works depict lesbian sexuality. While recognizing the existence of multiple sexualities during all periods of history, this study focuses on reproductive hetero-

unromantic features of sex, the awkward, unseemly, and messy bits.

While sex appears more openly in current mainstream fiction than it did previously, fiction still rarely describes the ritual act of birth control. No scene in Gabaldon's novel shows the narrator slipping in her diaphragm prior to "savag[ing] each other in desperate need" (437). When birth control does appear, it is often the site of comedy or potential disaster. Ann Beattie mentions a son pricking a pinhole in his mother's diaphragm in her 1980 novel, *Falling in Place*, and Don DeLillo sets a scene of his 1997 opus, *Underworld*, in Condomology, an urban condom boutique. If the media now openly advertises birth control, and it is an important part of many women's lives, why is it still largely absent from fictional plots? Could this gap be due to reticence in discussing a "private issue," or some sense that the topic is obscene, or the objection that contraception is not a legitimate authorial concern?

According to Suzette Henke, female authors of the twentieth century have failed to discuss "the profound connection, for fertile women of every age, between sexuality and reproductive potential" because they still are trapped by cultural myths of femininity (46).[8] These myths include those perpetuated by romance novels of an effortless and romantic sexual encounter. Henke asks, "What works of modern literature portray a woman inserting a diaphragm? Vertiginous from morning sickness? . . . All these physiological events are, perhaps, too messy, violent, or indelicate to be part of women's literary consciousness" (52). However, this surface absence is not a void of female experience. As Henke further notes, "The perpetual connection of female desire to anxieties attendant on reproductive potential" has not been so much "erased, as it were, from the semiotic code" as written into the very structure of that code (52). It is a silence that speaks the reasons for its condition, the issues that shape this persistent anxiety. In critically analyzing fiction we can trace out the social forces impinging on public and literary consciousness, adding depth to our narrative of history. As Nancy Armstrong states, "a text may serve, in other words, as a drop of amber which preserves a complex social dynamic that cannot be contained within the text in question" (355).

No single work provides a definitive understanding of the movement for birth control, but as an intersecting network these texts reveal the social forces at play. They "construct the frameworks, fashion the

---

sexuality. The birth control movement upheld heteronormative sexuality in its discourse.

8. See also Susan Koppelman Cornillon, who argues that "certain types of feelings and experiences common to women in our culture are not represented in our fiction by male or by female novelists, or, if these phenomena are mentioned, it is in a context that reinforces our alienation from ourselves and the mystification of our humanness" (114).

metaphors, create the very language by which people comprehend their experience and think about their world" (Lauter 11). Consider two cases. The popular sitcom *Seinfeld* aired an episode entitled "The Sponge" in 1995. Upon learning that her preferred contraceptive method, the Today Sponge, has been removed from the market, Elaine performs a "hard-target search. Of every drug store, general store, health store and grocery store in a 25-block radius" because, as she says, "women are really loyal to their birth control methods." To conserve these valuable commodities, Elaine screens every date to see if he is "sponge-worthy" (Mehlman). This episode had real-world effects, prompting Allendale Pharmaceuticals to reissue the Today Sponge in 1999. A second incident provides an additional example of the interaction of fiction and fact in popular media culture. Candace Bushnell, "chick lit" author and creator of *Sex and the City*, helped launch a new oral contraceptive, Seasonale, which lowers the number of menstrual cycles from thirteen a year to four. Bushnell's turn as spokeswoman reveals the permeable barrier in today's popular culture between author and celebrity, between novel and television, and between a fiction of the sexually emancipated woman and technological innovations that make that emancipation possible.

Accounts of the need for and use of birth control, especially from the perspective of the contracepting woman herself, do not dominate contemporary fiction, nor do they dominate the fiction of the 1910s through 1930s when the political movement to legalize birth control occurred. Rather, these accounts infiltrate texts through the many issues that tied the birth control movement to other social concerns: economics, eugenics, women's roles, the falling birth rate, and America's place in the international sphere. Since birth control was marginalized in the private sphere until Margaret Sanger and others made it a matter of public debate, we should not be surprised that it has also been marginalized as a fictional subject.[9] Instead, fiction explores the conditions that necessitate birth control, including the physical facts of repeated pregnancy on a woman's body. Birth control appears within these narratives as a subtext. Because birth control was a private issue in women's lives, it is a hidden issue in the lives of female characters: Charlotte Rittenmeyer's douche bag may get brief textual space in Faulkner's *If I Forget Thee, Jerusalem* (1939), yet its failure shapes the narrative. Nella Larsen's Helga Crane may have

---

9. Because she was a single-issue reformer after 1916, Margaret Sanger is often considered the public face of the movement. Many other reformers were involved, however, including Emma Goldman, Mary Ware Dennett, Agnes Inglis, Jessie Ashley, Ida Rauh Eastman, Rose Pastor Stokes, Carl Rave, and Carlo Tresca (see Gordon, *Moral Property of Women*).

no explicit knowledge of birth control, yet it is her very ignorance that leads to the final scene in *Quicksand* (1928).

While many scholars have explored abortion and motherhood in literature or in history, *Textual Contraception: Birth Control and Modern American Fiction* begins to close the gap between disciplinary accounts.[10] While valuable, previous studies of motherhood or abortion in literature reaffirm, through repeated accretion of scholarly attention, the "naturalness" of the pregnant female body. But what of contraception, of the premeditated, conscious decision to control one's reproductive life? What is missing from current scholarship is an investigation of deliberate attempts to avoid such a state, of woman-with-womb but not woman-as-womb. This study also provides an analysis of works from popular and radical periodicals and reads them in the context of historical developments and other literature. Historical studies of the birth control movement ignore the cultural work done by fiction and other popular forms, focusing instead on leaders and organizations, dates and legal struggles. For example, historian Norman Himes writes of the "increasing diffusion, democratization or socialization" of birth control knowledge, but he ignores two critical venues for this democratization: popular media and fiction (*Medical History of Contraception* xvii). Too often historians ignore fiction, assuming that its created reality is far removed from the "factual" history they are attempting to ascertain. Yet literature provides a rich social artifact that can track cultural change on multiple levels, most obviously in the events selected to move the plot along and the character types as reflections of social norms. Written as well as oral methods have

---

10. The birth control movement began to receive significant scholarly attention in the 1970s. Linda Gordon (*Moral Property of Women*), Carol McCann, James Reed (*Birth Control Movement and American Society*), and Andrea Tone (*Devices and Desires*) have written comprehensive social and political histories of contraceptive technology in the United States. Bernard Asbell, Elizabeth Siegel Watkins, and Lara V. Marks have written specifically on the development of the birth control pill. Adele E. Clarke, Nellie Oudshoorn, and Merriley Borell discuss the scientific approach of biologists and researchers in the development of hormonal contraceptive methods. Lynne Masel-Walters and Ellen Chesler are representative of writers placing Sanger squarely at the center of the movement, while Constance M. Chen, John M. Craig, and Robyn Rosen focus on Mary Ware Dennett's contributions to the American Birth Control League.

Many feminist scholars consider abortion as a legal, psychological, and technological issue, including Mary Boyle, Janet Farrell Brodie, Kristin Luker, and Rosalind Pollack Petchesky. Literary scholars such as Judith Wilt, Irene Dash, Joy Castro, and Donna Hollenberg have examined fictional representations of abortion.

While the birth control movement has been extensively discussed by historians, less examined is the literary and artistic response to the inherent drama of birth control. Anne G. Balay has written briefly on birth control in Katherine Norris's *Mother*, and Sheryl Stevenson identifies opposition to motherhood in Djuna Barnes's *Ryder*. On British authors, see Mary Lowe-Evans, Jerome Meckier, and Christina Hauck.

been important to the retention and circulation of contraceptive knowledge among women even up to the present, and women were as likely to find accurate information in fiction as in nonfiction, from a friend as from their doctors. Indeed, as one anonymous reader told me, "Most of us learned about all this [contraception] from the novelists, not from any health care clinic. And our mothers were hopelessly uninformed and afraid." Wendy Wasserstein's 1978 play *Uncommon Women and Others* echoes how a novel by Mary McCarthy provided a contraceptive education. The character Leilah muses, "Do you know the first time I ever really understood about diaphragms or sex was from reading *The Group*" (28).

Today, women have a variety of options offering up to 99 percent effectiveness. But what did women who wanted to control their fertility use earlier, and what social as well as scientific developments led to the variety of methods we enjoy today? A brief look at the historical and literary developments leading up to the early twentieth century is necessary before more closely examining the relationship between literature and the political movement for birth control.

Birth control is not a new idea. Historian Norman Himes claims "the *desire* to control conception is a universal social phenomenon" (*Medical History of Contraception* 209). The title of chapter 3 of Dr. Charles Knowlton's 1832 *Fruits of Philosophy*, "Of Promoting and Checking Conception," concisely describes a concern of humanity since earliest recorded history.[11] The Egyptians, early Hebrews, Greeks, and Romans had knowledge of early contraceptive techniques, and in these societies women used herbal concoctions, prolonged lactation, interruption, pessaries (vaginal suppositories used to support the uterus or rectum), the rhythm method, condoms, and other barriers.[12] Textual evidence of effective chemical and herbal birth control exists since the second century B.C., and contraception and abortion are mentioned by Aristotle, Plato, and Socrates. The Berlin Papyrus, circa 1300 B.C., commands, "You should [make] for her a prescription to loosen semen," and in the fifth century B.C. Aristotle wrote of "smearing the cervix with cedar oil, or lead with olive oil" to prevent conception (Riddle, *Contraception and Abortion from the Ancient World to the Renaissance* 66). The Ebers Papyrus, written between 1550 and 1500 B.C., contains medical prescriptions for

11. See Chandrasekhr on Charles Knowlton. Other marriage manuals of the period include Dr. Frederick Hollick's *Marriage Guide*, which had gone through dozens of editions by the 1870s.

12. Race, class, geography, and other factors complicate women's access to and relationship with contraception. Dorothy E. Roberts argues, "Race completely changes the significance of birth control to the story of women's reproductive freedom" (*Killing the Black Body* 56). See also Solinger (*Pregnancy and Power*).

birth control. Plants such as pomegranate seed, silphium, acacia, Queen Anne's lace, juniper, willow bark, pennyroyal, and rue could be taken by mouth or used as a pessary.

Methods of contraception and abortion hold a prominent place in the classical and medieval medical records. But who had access to this knowledge, and how widely was it practiced? Many scholars, such as Norman Himes, have argued that this knowledge was limited to physicians and was not spread among the populace. This supports the general belief that birth control was not a regular or conscious practice in the ancient and classical world. More recently, however, John M. Riddle has refuted this claim, arguing that although early herbal methods were largely ineffective by today's standards and linked to "superstitious" charms, the low birth rate can be explained by the conscious practice of birth control. Based on little evidence of male-dependent methods, such as coitus interruptus, condoms (sheaths of animal skin or linen), or the rhythm method, Riddle concludes that as early as antiquity birth control has depended on the actions of women, who had both effective contraceptives and a female network to transmit the needed information, passing knowledge orally from one generation of women to the next (*Contraception* 5).

Women lost access to much of this knowledge when male physicians replaced midwives and social attitudes towards women's bodies and reproductive duties spawned laws against contraception. Christianity's growth in the Middle Ages led to increased opposition to fertility control, which became associated with witchcraft and magic; indeed, Riddle argues that the rash of midwives killed as witches was due to the threat they represented as practitioners of and as circuits of knowledge of birth control and abortion (*Eve's Herbs* 113). Both church and law argued that sex was only for procreation, and recipes for herbal contraceptives were confiscated. The position of midwives degenerated into mere birthing assistants, and medical curriculums excluded birth control during the Renaissance. Published herbal recipe books contained minimal information on contraceptive and abortifacient recipes, and apothecaries sold mixtures under "the cloak of false labels," a practice that continued through the early twentieth century (Riddle, *Eve's Herbs* 165).

Historians of sexuality note that ideas of marriage and family changed in the late eighteenth century from a family-centered view of marriage that focused reproduction as the purpose for sex to an idea of companionate marriage.[13] Attitudes toward contraception continued to develop due to "altered attitudes and habits in sexuality and the role of the church;

---

13. *Intimate Matters*, by John D'Emilio and Estelle B. Freedman, is an excellent study of America's changing attitudes toward sexuality.

the development of embryology and the dissemination of debates about fetal development; the awareness of and, in some cases, alarm over the relationship between population size and political and economic power" (Riddle, *Contraception* 213). The 1820s–1850s saw a movement for "free love"—not advocating promiscuity, but the belief that love, not marriage, should be the basis for sexual relations. The social purity movement advocated "voluntary motherhood" through continence and abstinence, rejecting the necessity for birth control by other means but emphasizing human control of family size. Although these reformers recognized female sexuality and eroticism within marriage, they argued that women gained social and moral power through self-denial. The middle class read marriage manuals and listened to speakers on physiology and health, while the lower classes looked to almanacs and newspaper advertisements for insight into sexual health.

But social attitudes regarding birth control were slow to change, and the 1800s witnessed the legalized suppression of contraceptive information. In England, Lord Ellenborough's 1803 crime bill declared it murder to "administer to, or cause to be administered to or taken by any of his Majesty's subjects any deadly poison, or other noxious and destructive substance or thing, with intent [for] . . . his Majesty's subject or subjects thereby to murder, or thereby to cause and procure the miscarriage of any woman, then being quick with child" (qtd. in Riddle, *Contraception* 207). In colonial America laws began to mirror this phrasing, and a wave of statutory laws based on the wording of the Ellenborough bill attacked abortion, which had been treated on the basis of common law.[14] In 1829 the New York state legislature passed a law stating, "Every person who shall wilfully administer to any pregnant woman, any medicine, drug or substance whatever, or shall use or employ any instrument of other means, with intent thereby to destroy such child, unless the same shall have been necessary to preserve the life of such woman . . . shall, upon conviction, be punished by imprisonment in a country jail not more than one year, or by a fine not exceeding five hundred dollars, or by both such fine and imprisonment" (qtd. in Harper 247).

Information that had once been available vanished from the published record as pharmaceutical guides deleted information on the contraceptive usages of many drugs, and marriage manuals omitted their discussions of sexuality. Marital guides such as Charles Knowlton's *Fruits of Knowledge; or, the Private Companion of Young Married People* (1832) and Robert Dale Owen's *Moral Physiology; or, A Brief and Plain Treatise on the*

---

14. See Mohr.

Population Question (1831) had contained basic and often conflicting information on contraception. For instance, Owens's tract, in print for forty years, included a brief and rather vague discussion of birth control methods. It recommended coitus interruptus as the best method, citing the vaginal sponge as ineffective and the skin condom as too expensive. Knowlton, who later was prosecuted for obscenity for *Fruits of Knowledge*, wrote a much more specifically useful tract, which included a chapter with detailed descriptions of human genitalia as well as a chapter on birth control methods. The purpose of *Fruits of Knowledge*, which had gone through ten printings by 1877, was "to obtain and disseminate a knowledge of means whereby men and women may refrain at will from becoming parents, without even a partial sacrifice of the pleasure which attends the gratifications of their productive instinct" (8). Knowlton not only advocated post-coital douching as the most effective method but also recommended douching solutions containing alum or salt, gave approximate dosages, and informed women on how and where to obtain a syringe.

The Comstock Act of 1873 made it illegal to distribute through the U.S. mail "any article or thing designed or intended for the prevention of conception or procuring of abortion" as well as "advertisements" or "information" regarding birth control.[15] The act, named for New York reformer Anthony Comstock, was part of the Progressive Era's attempt to wipe out vice.[16] This national obscenity law ignored distinctions between pornography and medical information and treated any printed material discussing contraception, including fiction and advertisements, as illicit. When a publisher reprinted Knowlton's *Fruits of Philosophy* in 1876, he was fined under the Comstock Act for publishing such a "dirty, filthy book," and had to withdraw the book from the U.S. market. (In England, Bradlaugh and Besant republished it and used their indictment in that country for publicity for birth control.) The Comstock Act limited what could pass through the mail and, in consequence, influenced what would be published and read. Sellers advertised contraceptive materials such as syringes and douches under the guise of "feminine hygiene products"; however, many of these ads were for ineffective sugar pills and powders.

15. While feminist critics such as Janet Farrell Brodie and Carol Smith-Rosenberg have argued that the purpose of the Comstock Act was in part to control female sexuality, Nicola Beisel argues that Comstock himself was motivated by a desire to protect children: "children, not women, were Comstock's concern, although he assumed that the rearing of morally pure children required women devoted to home and family" (9).

16. Marge Piercy's 2005 historical novel *Sex Wars: A Novel of the Turbulent Post–Civil War Period*, is an interesting fictional account of Comstock, Victoria Woodhull, Elizabeth Cady Stanton, Susan B. Anthony, and a fictional immigrant woman who goes into the condom-making trade.

While the message of the advertisement may have been innocent enough to get by Comstock, the inherent message was clear enough to women in need. What these "Preventative Powders" were meant to prevent, clearly, was pregnancy.

By the late nineteenth century, contraception and abortion were illegal and unavailable to any but a few wealthy women, and the concept of "birth control" went against social and religious ideas of woman's proper role. The American Medical Association, founded in 1847, opposed contraception and abortion to differentiate professional doctors from midwives. The new field of gynecology equated women's health with their reproductive function.[17] Indeed, not until 1936 did the majority of the nation's medical schools train students in contraceptive methods.

Even as moral and legal sanctions stripped information on birth control from the public record, scientific and technological advancements improved methods, enabling birth control to be "inexpensive, reliable, and available" (Bullough 104). Condoms made of fish bladder and other materials had been available, but at $5.00 a dozen in New York City in 1860, only the wealthiest could afford them. Then, the vulcanization of rubber in 1843 and 1844 led to the growth and development of the condom industry, enabling the mass production of cheap condoms marketed for prophylactic rather than contraceptive purposes. The vulcanization of rubber also enabled the development of the rubber diaphragm and pessary, which became the recommended device in Dutch contraceptive clinics. In 1846 a diaphragm patented as "The Wife's Protector" emphasized both the place of sex within marriage and the mysterious question of what the device would protect her from. In the United States, rubber pessaries were developed, patented, and advertised strictly as medical devices to support a prolapsed uterus. Madame Restell (also known as Anna Lohman) sold her "Portuguese Female Pills" for "suppression of the menses" for five dollars per box, advertising in New York newspapers from 1840 to 1845. Sold under the guise of a "certain cure for married ladies," Restell hid her product under mystery (what disease is being cured?) and respectability (for married women only, of course). Although the product's actual purpose was not stated as contraceptive, the rhetoric accompanying it surely leads to that idea, asking, "Is it desirable, then—is it moral—for parents to increase their families, regardless of consequences to themselves, or the well being of their offspring, when a simple, easy, healthy and certain remedy is within our control?" (qtd. in Olasky 51).[18]

17. See Kapsalis for a fascinating look at the history of gynecology.
18. On Madame Restell, see also Browder. See Tone, *Controlling Reproduction*, for an edited collection of original newspaper advertisements and articles. See Tone, *Devices*

Although she may have been the most (in)famous advertiser, she was by no means alone: ads also appeared for "Dr. Vandenburgh's Female Regeneracy Pills," "Portuguese Female Pills," "French Lunar Pills," and "Madame Costello's Female Monthly Pills."

The Comstock Act was challenged by doctors, publishers, and social activists. Dr. Edward Bliss Foote challenged the act in "A Step Backward" and advertised contraception in his medical encyclopedia, *Plain Home Talk*, in 1875. But authorities seized and destroyed Foote's pamphlets recommending his "Womb Veil," thus ensuring that such effective devices would only be available to women wealthy enough to have private doctors who would diagnose them with a prolapsed uterus. Despite the promise of the Mensinga pessary, "Womb Veil," and diaphragm, most Americans in the nineteenth century continued to practice abstinence, withdrawal, and the misunderstood rhythm method (E. Katz, "History of Birth Control in the United States" 87).

Critics disagree on how effective the Comstock Act was in suppressing birth control information.[19] Population studies demonstrate that the decision to limit family size preceded the official birth control movement in both the United States and England. The average family size dropped throughout the 1800s and 1900s. According to Esther Katz, "white marital fertility rates dropped from an average of 7.04 births per woman in 1800 to 3.56 births in 1900" ("History" 82). Among the African American population, fertility dropped sharply during the latter years of the nineteenth century until about 1940 (McFalls and Masnick 89). Scholars have found an increasing body of evidence suggesting that "it was the result not of natural physiological changes, but of deliberate efforts to limit the number of children born" (E. Katz, "History" 82). Contemporary surveys support this conclusion. Katherine B. Davis conducted a survey of 1,000 women who were of marriageable age before the onset of World War I. Seventy-four percent of respondents practiced some form of contraception, while an even larger number surveyed believed that it was morally right. Dr. Clelia Mosher found that 84 percent of the Victorian women she surveyed practiced some form of fertility control. In *Middletown*, a sociological study of the changing trends from 1890 to 1925 in the "life of a small American city," the Lynds noted that, despite an earlier marriage age, family size was shrinking (from 4.6 in 1890 to 3.8 in 1920) due in

---

and Desires, on the contraceptive industry's transformation from illicit trade to legitimate business.

19. Himes argues that the Comstock Act was effective, but later historians such as Esther Katz have noted veiled news of contraception in newspaper medical columns and penny circulars.

part to "the diffusion of knowledge of means of contraception" (111). The Lynds described the distribution of contraceptive knowledge across class as a pyramid: "At the top, among most of the business group, the use of relatively efficacious contraceptive methods appears practically universal, while sloping down from this peak is a mixed array of knowledge and ignorance, until the base of ignorance is reached" (125). The working class in urban northern areas and in the South did not have easy access to birth control, and evidence of effective contraceptive use outside of the middle class only surfaces in the 1930s.

This study concentrates on the turbulent political and social context of the United States in the years between the World Wars.[20] During these years a cogent movement to legalize birth control began, and fiction contributed to this fight even as it underwent fundamental stylistic changes. Bolstered by increased urbanization and technological advancement, American society sought rationality and order, and the birth control movement marketed its wares as a means to bring science and logic to reproduction.[21] In literature, naturalism's interest in social shaping of the human character gave way to modernism's experimentation and alienation during the 1910s and 1920s, which in turn gave way to the social realism of the 1930s.

Why posit a link between literature and birth control, between the aesthetic and the sociological? What is needed to gain insight into these factors is a cultural analysis of the literary discourse that surrounded and sustained the topic of birth control. As Esther Katz notes, "Clearly, analyses using census data and statistical records can track important links between economic variables and fertility rates, but they cannot adequately incorporate the complex weave of factors that may have gone into so fundamental a decision as whether or not to have a child" ("History" 87). Literary representations published during the period not only reflected social values but served to influence the terms and outcome of the birth control debate itself. How was female sexuality represented with regard to pregnancy and childbearing, duty and freedom? How were women's bodies depicted? How were birth controllers portrayed, and how were these texts used rhetorically to forward or oppose the cause? In what ways did contraceptive ideology affect narrative structure itself, enacting a form of

---

20. Birth control movements were happening in other countries as well. See Rose on Marie Stopes's battle for birth control in Britain, Grossmann on the movement in Germany, and Ramirez and Seipp on Puerto Rico.

21. Bauman argues that modernity's "task of order" was accomplished via the strategies of exoticizing, segregating, scientific management, and assimilation (4); see Banta on managerial science and narrative.

literary or "textual contraception"?

To answer these questions, chapters 2 through 7 explore fictional representations of women's lives, the economic and ethical implications of birth control, and eugenic and feminist arguments. Because "causal claims are notoriously difficult to verify, as they often rely on associative rather than empirical proofs," I consider the fiction within the rhetorical arguments of the birth control movement and in the matrix of reader letters, demographic studies, historical events, and literary theory (Rado 4). Rather than assuming that the birth control movement and its outcome are universally positive, I hope to expose the complicated nature of the movement, the negative as well as the positive effects it had on women's (and men's) lives.

Authors suffered under the same censoring restrictions that the Comstock Act of 1873 imposed on birth control information, and endured the monitoring of their work for any sign of "lewd and lascivious" implications. This prohibition limited the openness with which authors could write about sexuality and contraception. Despite this censorship, American writers contributed to the changing public sentiment that overturned the Comstock Act. For example, in his 1922 novel *The Beautiful and the Damned*, F. Scott Fitzgerald lampoons the old-fashioned reformist impulse of Anthony Comstock in his description of the protagonist's grandfather: "He became a reformer among reformers. Emulating the magnificent efforts of Anthony Comstock, after whom his grandson was named, he leveled a varied assortment of uppercuts and body-blows at liquor, literature, vice, art, patent medicines, and Sunday theatres" (4).[22] Fitzgerald attributes this lengthy string of "immoral" practices, conflating literature with vice, to an older, dying generation. The novel's protagonist views his grandfather as "a rabid monomaniac," "a prig, a bore, and something of a hypocrite" (4, 71). By poking fun at the old-fashioned morality of Anthony Comstock, artists and writers led readers to question the relevance and efficacy of a law so obviously a ban to progress. This sentiment echoes the basis of the birth control movement as articulated in Margaret Sanger's 1917 trial testimony: "I cannot respect the law as it exists today" ("Sanger on Trial").[23]

The following chapters create a rough chronology to highlight how the

22. British writer George Orwell also invokes Anthony Comstock, ironically naming a character who sells erotica in a seedy bookstore "Gordon Comstock" in his 1936 novel *Keep the Aspidistra Flying*.

23. Arrested October 1916 for operating a contraceptive clinic in the Brownsville section of Brooklyn, Sanger was brought to trial for violating Section 1142 of the New York State Penal Code. The trial took place in January 1917 and Sanger was found guilty, serving a thirty-day prison sentence. See *New York v. Sanger*.

birth control movement evolved alongside literary developments. Over the course of this discussion, key themes emerge as prevalent at certain periods. Chapter 2 examines the early years of the movement and the more radical feminist and socialist rhetoric that underlay the call for birth control during the 1910s. Chapter 3 examines how women and writers negotiated the ideas of the New Woman alongside traditional views of marriage and motherhood during the 1920s, as the movement sought increased public legitimacy. Chapter 4 discusses this growing conservatism and its calls for a modern scientific motherhood, while chapter 5 considers how increasing social anxiety over immigration and racial tension during the 1920s led to an alignment with the growing field of eugenics. During the Depression Era economic arguments came to the fore of the movement's rhetoric, and these developments are considered in chapter 6. In 1936 the birth control movement won the *U.S. v. One Package* decision, which legalized the prescription of contraceptives by a licensed physician for the purpose of preventing pregnancy. The study concludes with a consideration of the continued legacy of the birth control movement in American fiction.

Each chapter discusses fiction alongside historical documents and letters from readers of the *Birth Control Review*, published from 1917 to 1940. In tone, character type, and narrative the letters and the literature often sound interchangeable, demonstrating the dialogue between women's lived reality and fiction. In her 1928 introduction to *Motherhood in Bondage*, a collection of letters she had received, Sanger asks, "What writer of fiction has more briefly or more heart-breakingly revealed the tragedy of a whole life?" (xiv). While the letters tell a heartrending tale, the fiction adds a depth of detail and dialogue, effectively recreating a realistic, rounded drama that may invite and affect a different audience. The following chapters analyze a wide range of works by early-twentieth-century American authors, including Theodore Dreiser, Meridel LeSueur, Djuna Barnes, Ernest Hemingway, William Faulkner, Kay Boyle, Ellen Glasgow, F. Scott Fitzgerald, and Nella Larsen.

Not simply by censorship were authors restricted; they were constrained by a limited range of narrative possibilities for female characters that reenacted the narrow range of roles available to women. Some texts engaged with the struggle to rewrite the traditional biological narrative of women's lives. These chapters investigate the relationship between developments in the social rhetoric of birth control and developments in fictional technique and content. The historical period of the birth control movement covers several currents in literature: naturalism's focus on the real and lower class brought franker discussion of the social consequences of too many pregnancies; radical writers demonstrated the female body as capitalist commodity; popular magazine writers forwarded a sentimental vision of femininity and motherhood; and modernist authors experimented with narrative as they discussed sexuality. How could the traditional biological plot of women's lives—virginity to marriage to pregnancy to motherhood and domesticity—be narratively interrupted? This textual contraception, an interruption of the reproduction of the traditional plot(s), allowed for new conceptions of women and sexuality.

Taken together, these works help to break the silence that surrounded social perceptions of birth control. Did these authors intend to engage in an ongoing social and political debate? Did they create works of literature or of propaganda? Such a distinction is at best arbitrary. While many of the stories published in the *Birth Control Review* overtly influenced readers by illustrating points made in the rest of the journal, and thus may be characterized by some critics as "propaganda," all texts may serve a didactic function in the use that the reader makes of them. As Susan Rubin Suleiman and others have noted, texts are read in a cultural context, and often take on rhetorical as well as aesthetic functions.[24] These texts range from sentimental drama to political agitprop to experimental fiction, but all respond to the issues of the birth control movement.

---

24. On the rhetorical uses of fiction, see also Booth and Lauter.

2

"As Red and Flaming as Possible"
Radical Rhetoric of the 1910s

> The Rebel Women claim:
> The Right to be lazy.
> The Right to be an unmarried mother.
> The Right to destroy.
> The Right to create.
> The Right to love.
> The Right to live.
> —*The Woman Rebel*, March 1914: 3

THE FIRST THREE decades of the twentieth century witnessed great changes, both in American life and in American fiction. The push for women's suffrage and increased employment for women outside the home helped to change long-held ideas about female roles and the capabilities of their bodies. Sigmund Freud's *Three Essays on the Theory of Sexuality* appeared in English in 1905 and contributed to growing discussions about the need for sex education and the idea that women and children were sexual beings.[1] New roles for women opened in the years between the World Wars, and female sexuality gained wider social acceptance. Young women smoked cigarettes, danced, and cut their hair. They "made necking America's favorite pastime, and 36 percent of them engaged in premarital intercourse" (James Reed, "The Birth Control Movement before *Roe v. Wade*" 28). Reformers for birth control, including Emma Goldman, Margaret Sanger, and Mary Ware Dennett, read

---

1. According to Julian B. Carter, sex education began in the 1910s in America as a response to the growth of venereal disease.

progressive theorists and sexologists who warned that abstinence and withdrawal were dangerous to the development of both men and women. The subject of sex, and of female desire, entered public discourse. Press coverage of the early birth control movement's challenges to the law contributed to debates over the purpose and morality of sex. In turn, this dissemination aided the movement by accustoming people to "shocking" or radical ideas. Leslie Fishbein argues that this "repeal of reticence" in the pre–World War I years "led to increased recognition of sexuality, although many still worried that people would become sex-obsessed" (35). The time was right for birth control.

American fiction also underwent many changes during this period. During the late nineteenth century, literature generally conformed to the genteel code embodied in a statement by the 1897 U.S. Commission of Education: literature "educates man's insight into the distinction of good from evil, reveals to him his ideals of what ought to be, and elevates the banner of his march toward the beautiful good and the beautiful true" (Boyer 16). The 1873 Comstock Act also policed literature for its moral lessons. However, by the turn of the century many authors were challenging these precepts. Naturalism, with its emphasis on environmental forces shaping and limiting individual opportunity, was a natural fit with the birth control movement, as was a muckraking journalistic impulse. In its attempts to expose life's harsh nature, this literature explored taboos such as violence and the darker side of marriage. This critique offered implicit support for contraception.

Potentially radical ideas implicating birth control in a social rather than sexual revolution ran through articles and fiction published in radical periodicals and also, although perhaps more subtly, in mainstream novels. A common belief in freedom and social change linked journals such as the *Blast*, *The Masses*, *Mother Earth*, *The Woman Rebel*, *Birth Control Review*, and *New York Call*. They were also united, at least briefly, geographically and through a host of shared contributors. Emma Goldman, Max Eastman, Floyd Dell, Mary Heaton Vorse, Inez Haynes Gillmore, Susan Glaspell, Theodore Dreiser, Sinclair Lewis, Margaret Sanger, and other artistic and political leaders all lived for a time in the Greenwich Village area of New York City.[2] Greenwich Village was a hotbed of radical thought. Villagers read Havelock Ellis's *Psychology of Sex*, underwent

---

2. Floyd Dell, *The Masses'* editor, contributed a humorous six-part series on "The Outline of Marriage" to the *Birth Control Review* in 1926, and the *Review* positively reviewed his novels. Mary Heaton Vorse and the artist Cornelia Barns contributed to both periodicals, and Vorse, Elsie Clews Parson, and Rose Pastor Stokes supported Margaret Sanger in her legal battles. See Fishbein.

Freudian analysis for their sexual repression, and joined discussion groups such as the Heterodoxy Club. Their influence reached far beyond the confines of the Village, thanks in part to *The Masses* (1911–17) and other periodicals. Women often led the sexual rebellion in the Village. Mabel Dodge Luhan used her Fifth Avenue salon as a forum for taboo topics such as birth control and free love, and credits Margaret Sanger as the one "who introduced to us all the idea of Birth Control. . . . She was the first person I ever knew who was openly an ardent propagandist for the joys of the flesh" (Luhan 69). Indeed, Sanger met Emma Goldman, one of the first advocates for birth control as part of a socialist program, at Dodge's salon in 1911.

Discussions of sexuality reached outside of private forums such as the Heterodoxy Club and fed the impulse toward realism present in authors such as Theodore Dreiser and Ellen Glasgow. Sherwood Anderson recalled, "I do not think that any of us, at that time, wanted to over play sex. We wanted in our stories and novels to bring it back into its real relation to the life we lived and saw others living" (qtd. in White, *Sherwood* 343). As the media began to cover the public face of the birth control movement, such as the trials of Margaret Sanger, William Sanger, Emma Goldman, and Ben Reitman, the fiction and art in journals such as *The Masses* and *Birth Control Review*, Sanger's second attempt at magazine publishing begun in 1917, dramatized the debate, bringing the radicalizing social reality of poverty before the public in another form.[3]

Many historians credit Margaret Sanger as the founder and driving

---

3. Sold through subscription and street sales, the *Birth Control Review* gained a circulation that fluctuated between 15,000 and 30,000 (as compared to the *Woman Rebel*'s more modest 2,000). Judging from the readers' letters, this audience included doctors, clergymen, reform-minded society ladies, and poor women from rural and urban settings. To challenge the sanction against "lewd and lascivious" material, the *Birth Control Review* used rhetorical appeals to prove why birth control information was necessary, not titillating. It contained detailed and impassioned arguments on eugenic sterilization, birth control abroad, child labor, poverty, religion, medicine, and state and national laws. In addition, it reported on legal trials, birth control league meetings, the opening of birth control clinics, reports from nurses and social workers, press clippings, and letters from readers. Poetry extolling motherhood or praising Sanger and other leaders littered the pages, as did cartoons and drawings reminiscent of *The Masses*. Although well-known British and American authors such as Theodore Dreiser, Upton Sinclair, Agnes Smedley, H. G. Wells, Julian Huxley, Vera Brittain, and Charlotte Haldane contributed articles in support of the birth control movement, the fiction that appeared in its pages was by lesser-known authors. The *Review* often contained book reviews of novels that it deemed as adding to the conversation surrounding contraception, including novels by many of the above-named authors. Overall, the fiction in the pages of the *Birth Control Review* corresponded with and contributed to the message of the articles and art. The literature presented the issues in another form, a dramatic genre that offset the didactic tone of the articles, injecting life into the statistics on child mortality and providing "case studies" to the impassioned arguments.

force behind the American birth control movement.[4] According to her autobiography, after seeing the devastating physical, social, and economic effects of multiple pregnancies on the poor women of New York City's East Side from 1900 to 1902, Sanger decided to campaign for birth control. Sanger is a controversial figure, with critics and biographers alike disagreeing on her role. Her forceful personality and "flamboyant defiance of the law" unquestionably helped to push birth control as a term and concept into public circulation (Reed, "Birth Control Movement before *Roe v. Wade*" 31). However, Sanger was not the first to make birth control a public issue. Emma Goldman viewed birth control as a vital part of the larger issue of freedom. She, too, had witnessed the devastating effects of uncontrolled pregnancy on poor women while working as a nurse. Both women began their crusades as part of a larger call for social justice, both established and wrote for radical periodicals, and both challenged the Comstock Act by writing and lecturing about birth control. Goldman, an immigrant anarchist, socialist, and feminist, traveled the country speaking on free love, birth control, modern drama, conscription, and other topics, and published her ideas in *Mother Earth* from 1906 to 1917, selling it at her lectures and by subscription. She made "The Limitation of Offspring" a regular topic of her lectures beginning in 1910, and in 1915 she

---

4. This study discusses Sanger more than other leaders due to her role in publishing *Woman Rebel* and the *Birth Control Review*. Scholars such as D'Emilio and Freedman credit Sanger as the mover behind the movement, as do Himes, Reed, Gordon, and others. Mary Ware Dennett was perhaps more radical than Sanger; when Sanger fought for a "doctors only" bill Dennett persisted in arguing for the complete repeal of the Comstock Act. Dennett lobbied state and national politicians and unsuccessfully tried to find a sponsor for her bill. Birth control reformers found themselves split between supporting Sanger's "doctors only" bill and Dennett's "clean repeal" bill. Dennett argued that a medical monopoly on birth control information would not help the common people, and that it actually reinforced the idea that birth control was somehow shameful. The two reformers publicly disagreed, and in 1921 Sanger, openly hostile to Dennett and the Voluntary Parenthood League, organized the American Birth Control League. Constance Chen makes a powerful case for the importance of Dennett's presence in the movement and her strategies in *"The Sex Side of Life": Mary Ware Dennett's Pioneering Battle for Birth Control and Sex Education*. Chen portrays Sanger as a latecomer and publicity hound: "Like other unthinking people, whether liberal or conservative, Sanger was myopic and intolerant" (162). Chen also describes Sanger as jealous, subversive, hypocritical, egomaniacal, and "shrill and hysterical" (163), while depicting Dennett as a spotlight-avoiding saint who just wanted to improve "the lives of all women" (166). See also Dennett's 1926 tract, *Birth Control Laws: Shall We Keep Them, Change Them, or Abolish Them?*, and Rosen.

Archival information on Sanger is available through the Margaret Sanger Papers Project (http://www.nyu.edu/projects/sanger/). A series of books containing her papers, edited by Esther Katz, is in progress, with the first volume published by the University of Illinois Press in 2002. On Goldman, whom *The Masses* lauded "as the woman who had done the most in the country to champion the cause of birth control" (Falk 153), see Falk and Shulman.

explained "how to practice birth control," "the first time the subject had been publicly discussed anywhere in America" (Shulman 169). Sanger's first periodical, *The Woman Rebel*, openly proclaimed her radical purpose in its title, and she moved from writing and speaking to establishing birth control clinics and organizations.

This chapter examines the radical writings of Goldman, Sanger, and other authors and social activists from 1910 to 1920. Their early ties to the Socialist Party led to rhetoric and literature depicting birth control as a vital part of social and economic revolution.[5] The birth control movement had its roots in Progressive Era reform and "was part of a general upswing in activism. Joining that resistance, birth controllers appealed for support, particularly to women and to working-class and poor people in general, because they believed that lack of control over reproduction helped perpetuate an undemocratic distribution of power" (Gordon, *Moral Property of Women* 139). The socialist emphasis found its equivalent in fiction, some of it published in radical periodicals, which depicted an oppressive class divide, the inadequacy of the current philanthropic system, and a critique of marriage. Using a variety of tactics, from sentiment to humor, writers in the 1910s introduced birth control in the context of an emancipatory movement for social justice.

Goldman and Sanger were entering into a new public debate about contraception, which intersected with a complexity of other issues including economic inequity and its effects on women. The status quo can perhaps best be seen with a brief analysis of Kathleen Norris's 1911 novella, *Mother*, a work that some have called anti-birth-control propaganda.[6] The protagonist, Margaret, hears the gossip of her wealthy employer's friends, none of whom has more than three children. Ironically, these women discuss their reasons for not having more children in terms of money. Mrs. Carr-Boldt, married to a millionaire, states, "People—the very people who ought to have children—simply cannot afford it!" (112). She goes on to list the many things children simply must have, including a trained nurse for each child. Her friends agree, "You don't want to have them

---

5. The first two decades of the twentieth century were full of labor radicalism, including the International Workers of the World. The widespread support for this worker-centered message is evidenced by the 1912 presidential election, in which nearly one million Americans voted for Socialist candidate Eugene Debs. The Socialist Party of America split into three groups, including the American Communist Party, in 1919. This split is symbolic of the larger fragmentation of leftist political organizations. Although their propaganda attempted to forward a univocal message, the Left had no coherent party doctrine. Mari Jo Buhle reports that the "new intellectuals" of the Socialist Party supported birth control, while the old guard party loyalists were hostile or apathetic. For a more general history of the American Left, see Paul Buhle.

6. See Balay.

unless you're able to do everything in the world for them" (114). While wanting to provide for your offspring is a laudable sentiment, Norris uses these leisure-class mothers to argue against birth control at several levels. She undermines a class-based eugenic argument, that only certain people "ought to have children," by contrasting the idle rich women with Margaret's own mother, who provides a loving home for her seven children. Norris also deconstructs as selfish the idea that family size should be based on economic conditions via her characterization of Margaret's Mother. The family lives in a shabby poverty that young Margaret finds embarrassing, yet provides the material basics for each child, thus showing that children need love alone, not nurse and nanny.

While Norris argues against birth control by canonizing Mother, a refusal to depict real poverty and its consequences, such as overcrowding, disease, and despair, weakens her argument. That is, Norris assumes homogeneity of class such that all poverty is genteel, and ignores differences within economic classifications. Family size is part of a consumer economy, with the wealthy able to make lifestyle decisions. Economists view the number of children as "an individual consumption decision bounded by constraints, tastes, and preferences. The principal idea, which stems from the theory of consumer choice, is that the demand for children reflects the way a household balances its subjective tastes for a number of goods, including children, against externally determined constraints in order to maximize its satisfaction or 'utility'" (Katz and Stern 66). Margaret's ultimate decision that these wealthy women are selfish because they do not have more children erases the very real economic concerns that many women had.

Other writers, such as Theodore Dreiser, supported birth control but carefully veiled their support within their fiction. As a naturalist writer, Dreiser was concerned with examining how external conditions such as economics shaped people's lives. In 1911, also the year of *Mother*'s publication, Dreiser published *Jennie Gerhardt*. The protagonist, Jennie, is tempted to engage in premarital sex to help support her family. Jennie's body, her sexuality, is her most valuable asset, and she agrees to exchange it for her family's security. Here, Dreiser acknowledges the uncomfortable reality of the female body in the labor market and the sexual marketability that led to prostitution. Increased urbanization at the end of the nineteenth century contributed to a growth in prostitution. Viewed as both a moral threat and a menace to public health by spreading venereal disease, prostitution was outlawed by the Progressive Era's 1910 Mann Act and later state laws. Yet Dreiser's Jennie is a wholly sympathetic character who belies seamy popular depictions of diseased whores.

Prostitutes also were suspected of having illicit knowledge of birth control. In keeping with Dreiser's portrayal of Jennie as innocent, her second lover, Lester Kane, introduces knowledge of birth control. He tells her, "But don't worry about that. You don't need to. I understand a number of things that you don't yet. It can be arranged. You don't need to have a child unless you want to. And I don't want you to" (158). What is particularly interesting here is that Lester controls the knowledge, and in doing so controls Jennie's reproductive body. It is his desire, not Jennie's, that she remain unimpregnated, as her infertility increases her value is as a sexual object.

Dreiser consistently supported birth control in his writing: in "A Word Concerning Birth Control," in the April 1921 issue of *Birth Control Review*, he advocates birth control for the poor and is suspicious of efforts to keep this knowledge illegal. He writes, "I sometimes suspect the wealthy and powerful of various persuasions and interests, especially those who might hope to profit from the presence here of vast and docile hordes, of having more of an interest in blind unregulated reproduction on the part of the masses than they would care to admit" (12–13). Reading the novel *Jennie Gerhardt* alongside Dreiser's commentary clarifies his understanding of gender and class in the political economy.

Dreiser's subtext of birth control in *Jennie Gerhardt* coincides with Margaret Sanger's more explicit print campaign in the socialist newspaper the *New York Call*. Beginning in 1911, Sanger published two series of articles, "What Every Mother Should Know" and "What Every Girl Should Know." Both attempted to educate children about sex, touching on topics such as masturbation and desire. By 1913 the series had attracted the censorship of Comstock, and the postal authorities suppressed the last column, "Some Consequences of Ignorance and Silence—Part III." To publicize this censorship the *Call* left a column with only "What Every Girl Should Know. NOTHING! By order of the Post Office Department" as its text. The column never mentioned specific contraceptive method—simply the suggestion was enough for the postal service to deem it in violation of the Comstock Act against "lewd and lascivious" literature.

This publicity, as well as personal experience, helped inspire other activists such as Mary Ware Dennett. Dennett believed strongly in civil liberties and saw the repression of birth control knowledge as a death sentence to many women. Indeed, the mortality rate is truly astonishing: "In 1913 more women between the ages of fifteen and forty-four died in childbirth than from any other cause except tuberculosis, and the mortality was three times that of typhoid fever" (Chen 151). Doctors told Dennett, after her own three difficult labors, not to risk another pregnancy. They would not, however, tell her how to accomplish this. The suppression of contraceptive knowledge had very real and potentially deadly effects for women, and much of the radical fiction that follows used the tragedy of women's broken bodies for dramatic effect.

Margaret Sanger continued her feminist and socialist crusade to push the boundaries over birth control in 1914 by confronting Comstock on two fronts: through the publication of *Family Limitation*, a pamphlet containing "socialist and feminist arguments for contraception with pictures and descriptions of birth control devices then available—the douche, vaginal suppository, condom, sponge and pessary," and with the launch of a new journal, *The Woman Rebel* (Masel-Walters 6).[7] Although *The Woman Rebel* contained no explicit information, the first issue implied that future editions would discuss contraceptive methods: Sanger wrote, "It will also be the aim of *The Woman Rebel* to advocate the prevention of conception and to impart such knowledge in the columns of this paper" ("The Aim" 1). Readers certainly expected and wanted this information. According to *My Fight for Birth Control*, Sanger had received over 10,000 requests for contraceptive information within six months (81). Goldman sold copies of *Woman Rebel* on her lecture tours—indeed, Goldman told Sanger that *The Woman Rebel* "sells better than anything else we have"—and handed out *Family Limitation* and *Why and How the Poor Should Not Have Many Children* by Dr. William Robinson when asked for specific information (Falk 132, 141).

The Woman Rebel was a simple eight-page, three-column monthly newspaper with a range of content—indeed, the one consistent factor is an underlying tone of anarchy. As Sanger wrote in her autobiography, "I worked day and night to make it as red and flaming as possible" (80). *The Woman Rebel* quickly met its objective: the postal service deemed it "unmailable," a fate that had earlier met the January 1910 edition of Goldman's *Mother Earth*. Authorities confiscated four of the seven issues of *The Woman Rebel* and arraigned Sanger for violating the law. Alex Baskin notes, "*The Woman Rebel* was largely a crimson burst of anger. It was an unburdening of emotion, of pent up feelings, of hatreds and of discontent. It was anarchist in expression, direct actionist in tone and woman liberationist in its aspirations. Years later, a less disputatious, more socially respectable Margaret Sanger would refer to the *Woman Rebel* as a little 'sass box'" (ix). Goldman supported Sanger throughout

---

7. "What Every Mother Should Know," "What Every Girl Should Know," and "Family Limitation" are available online through Michigan State University's Digital Collections (http://digital.lib.msu.edu/).

this brush with the law. In the February 1915 edition of *Mother Earth*, Leonard B. Abbott wrote of William Sanger's arrest for distributing *Family Limitation*. Abbott opined that the arrest was "an outrage and should be resented by every fair-minded man and woman" (379). Margaret Sanger fled to Europe after being arraigned for violation of the Comstock Act and returned in 1915, a month after Anthony Comstock's death; the case never came to trial.

While the birth control movement was a frequent topic in Goldman's journal, *Mother Earth*, *The Woman Rebel* was unique in publishing fiction alongside its articles. This fiction largely sought to counter the myths of romance and gentle motherhood by reminding readers of economic imperatives. Emile Chapelier's 1914 article entitled "To Working Girls," for example, destroys the romantic self-perceptions of the "working girl" by depicting the harsh realities of a working-class woman's life: "Every one of you makes yourself the heroine of a novel: you are going to love and be loved by a handsome, fine chap, your life is going to be spent in one beautiful love story! Oh! a fine dream . . . all filled up with tender caresses, passionate embraces, inexpressible pleasures, and undreamt of happiness! For most of you the reality is going to be a nightmare" (12). Chapelier indicts popular fiction, specifically novels, for creating false consciousness among young women. This direct address to working girls was part of the early alignment with socialism and recalls Sanger's dedication of "What Every Girl Should Know" to "the working girls of the world." *The Masses*, a Socialist Party–affiliated periodical known for its political cartoons, in April 1912 used its trademark satire to mock hysterical arguments that socialism and birth control were twin threats to traditional morality.[8] A drawing by Alexander Popini entitled "The Happy Home" depicts a wrinkled woman in a shabby cloak leaving four young children in a bare room. The caption asks facetiously, "Dear Reader, do you know what the above pretty picture is? . . . Is it not too bad of Socialism to try and break up such a Happy Home?" By contrasting the harsh reality of poverty with the satiric caption, the illustration sends the message that socialism is the friend, not foe, of family. Cartoons, articles, and stories presented birth control as a commodity that the wealthy do not want to share with the poor.

8. *The Masses* also differed from other Socialist-affiliated periodicals in its liberal editorial policy, its refusal to endorse coherent party lines, and unified support for birth control. See Fishbein and W. O'Neill; see Morrisson on race/ethnicity and *The Masses*, and R. Fitzgerald for biographies of artists Art Young, Robert Minor, John Sloan, and K. R. Chamberlain.

"Breed!"

THE FEMALE AS FACTORY

The first several decades of the twentieth century saw a transformation in American society that firmly fixed mass production, labor unionism, and a growing "culture industry" in the economic landscape. Social and political unrest circulated throughout public discourse, generating a mechanistic language that the birth control movement took up in its persuasive arguments. Contraceptive rhetoric employed the metaphors and images of the industrial economy, including the trope of the salt-of-the-earth laborer and the dehumanizing factory. The early, and more consciously radical, arguments of the 1910s recognized multiple sites of female production in the labor economy: the female body as a commodity of value either for sex (notably prostitution) or for reproduction (as a factory to reproduce the working class). According to Lindy Biggs, "The machine became a powerful symbol in the early United States. . . . A machine was predictable and perfectible; it was controllable, nonidiosyncratic, easy to routinize and systematize" (5). Similarly, writers figured the female body as machine under the control of the capitalist system. Emma Goldman uses this tactic in an excerpt of "Love and Marriage," reprinted in *The Woman Rebel*, when she asks, "Who would fight wars? Who would create wealth? . . . The race, the race! Shouts the king, the president, the capitalist, the priest. The race must be preserved, though woman be degraded to a mere machine" (3). Women's labor inside the factory and their reproductive bodies outside the factory were subject to the demands of capitalism. Female factory workers joined labor unions to protest unsafe conditions, but with mixed results: although almost 20,000 shirtwaist workers struck for better conditions in New York in 1909 and 1910, over 140 died in the Triangle Shirtwaist Factory fire in 1911.

Regaining control of the female body thus became part of a social revolution. Margaret Sanger, briefly a paid organizer and lecturer for the Socialist Party's Women's Committee in 1911, left in 1912 for the more radical direct action of the International Workers of the World. She aimed her early calls for birth control at working-class women and had distinct revolutionary tones. Sanger established a classic adversarial relationship between proletariat and aristocracy, and saw birth control as a weapon in the hands of the workers: In *Family Limitation* (1914), she wrote, "The working women can use direct action by refusing to supply the market with children to be exploited, by refusing to populate the earth with slaves" (3). This early appeal advanced birth control as a means for women to gain control over their reproductive bodies and firmly situated those bodies within the labor economy.

One common trope in the radical press was equating the female reproductive body with a factory. Rather than producing machinery, the material good at issue is babies to be used by the wealthy. The November 1912 issue of *The Masses* featured a satiric advertisement calling for "Increased Opportunities for Babies" and offered them positions in factories, slums, railroad wrecks, insane asylums, or jobs as white slaves or war casualties. This piece implies that uncontrolled fertility among the poor benefits the wealthy (who need workers and soldiers) but only keeps the poor enchained by poverty. In the context of the birth control movement, contraception becomes a tool empowering the poor while depriving the wealthy of cheap labor.

Sanger's early language envisioned capitalism and sexism as a totalizing system of enslavement, a machine of the master class. In "Why the *Woman Rebel?*," an explanatory editorial in the first issue, she writes, "I believe that woman is enslaved by the world machine by sex conventions, by motherhood and its present necessary child-rearing, by wage-slavery, by middle-class morality, by customs, laws and superstitions" (8). Mechanistic metaphors dissociate motherhood from any human emotion or bond; it becomes simply another mode of production, figuring the female body as doubly laboring, doubly invested in the maintenance of the capitalist economy. As Katherine Stubbs notes, "the rhetorical construction of women as analogous to machines seemed to make possible the supervision, manipulation, and control of women throughout the economic sphere, for the flexibility of this discourse meant that it could be used both in the sphere of production (where working-class women could be represented as "mechanical" workers) and in that of consumption" (142). The discursive invocation of the female as machine justifies the treatment of women as an instrumental object, depersonalizing the woman as worker.[9]

The birth control movement's early rhetoric used this cold, anti-sentimental language as a shock mechanism to argue that capitalism destroys poor families and women. Writing directly to the working class in 1918, Sanger warned, "Do not be deceived. Your children are commodities—they are bought and sold in industry. And the price of infants like the price of everything else, goes up when the commodity grows scarce" ("When Should a Woman Avoid Having Children?" 7). This trope reap-

---

9. Later works, such as Aldous Huxley's *Brave New World* (1932), foresaw a future in which technology would replace the inefficient human body, even in reproduction.

pears in later socialist-oriented feminist literature of the Depression, such as Meridel Le Sueur's "Anunciation." In this story, the pregnant protagonist states, "I remember I kept thinking to myself that a child should be made by machinery now, then there would be no fuss" (128). The body's unruly mess would be removed, making pregnancy and childbearing another antiseptic, mechanistic process of capitalism.

This pessimistic, antagonistic tone was also evident in the visual rhetoric. *The Masses* published a double-page cartoon entitled simply "Breed!" in the December 1915 issue. The political cartoon depicts a fat, rich white man pointing to an empty cradle to the young woman standing behind him. In the background, workers stand outside a factory while a cloud labeled "war" looms overhead. This cartoon appeared six months after the death of 124 American passengers aboard the *Lusitania*, sunk by a German submarine, when Americans were debating a possible entrance into World War I. But the image is prescient in its portrayal of the looming conflict, foregrounding economic and gender divisions and the link between capitalism and militarism. Capital needed poor bodies to fill the ranks of soldiers that die to protect the system and to work in the factories producing the mechanism of war. The wealthy owner is overweight, a visible sign of his wealth in contrast to the mass of workers behind him. His central position is another visual cue to his power over the other figures. The simple command to "Breed!" tells the story of a woman's role: her body is the factory producing labor and cannon fodder. Read in this frame, a subtext of birth control lies beneath the visual rhetoric: birth control for the poor could interfere with this capitalistic war machine by enabling poor women to control their fertility, cutting off the supply of cheap labor. *The Blast* connects these threads in its February 26, 1916, edition when, in "A Menace to Profit," the writer argues that Sanger and Goldman were arrested because they are "a menace" to the manufacturer who "needs 'hands' for his factories. The State needs cannon fodder to protect the manufacturer, its partner" (5).

Illustrators who contributed to both *The Masses* and *Birth Control Review* explored the relationship between reproduction, production, and war. These illustrations reinforced the written message of surrounding pages, together forming a coherent and powerful argument. A drawing in the April/May 1917 *Review* by K. R. Chamberlain shows a woman surveying a graveyard, a sign reading "Breed! We Need Men" slipping out of her hand (fig. 2). This image appears above a brief piece by Olive Schreiner, the South African feminist, entitled "Breeding Men for Battle." The need for men to replace those who died in war was symbolized by the vast graveyard setting. Although the United States had just entered the war in April of 1917, reports of earlier casualties indicated that one of women's wartime roles would be the traditional one, maternal rather than martial.[10] To refuse to breed is a denial of patriotic as well as gendered duty. In her radical early writings, Sanger encouraged women not to become "a mere breeding machine grinding out a humanity, which fills insane asylums, almshouses, and sweatshops, and provides cannon fodder that tyrants may rise to power on the sacrifice of her offspring" (qtd. in Miriam Reed 101).

The figure of woman as an assembly-line breeder was prominent during wartime, but the birth control movement changed the focus slightly after peace was declared. In the December 1918 *Review*, after the close of World War I, a drawing by Lou Rogers gives a more hopeful outlook of "The New Vision" (fig. 3). A young woman, surveying a graveyard, sees shining from the heavens "quality not quantity," and ignores the glowering man behind her holding open a book reading "Traditional After-The-War Duties for Women: 1st Commandment—Breed." The second and third commandments are also to breed, the repetition emphasizing the inescapable duty of women, who, it seems, are good for little else. But the illustration denies this call to duty with a different message coming from the heavens. It extols not unthinking mass production but a call to quality control in reproductive labor. The woman standing in front of the man, her gaze fixed on a heavenly message, clearly overthrows male authority and encourages women to break with tradition. The visual rhetoric of these images articulates the intersection between war and women's role(s) in the economic machine. By opposing this message of female reproductive duty, the images represent the early location of birth control as implicitly feminist and socialist. Birth control is thus a way to stop the mindless breeding of materials for the war machine. It offers poor women a means to power over their bodies and lives.

By foregrounding the female body as a machine implicated in the economy, these narrative images critiqued the gendered and classed social system. Appealing to values that would trigger emotion, they sought a reader response similar to the rhetorical questions asked by Margaret Sanger in *Woman and the New Race* (1920): "What shall this woman say to a society that would make of her body a reproductive machine only to waste prodigally the fruit of her being? Does society value her offspring? Does it not let them die by the hundreds of thousands of want, hunger

---

10. In "Arms and the Woman: The Con[tra]ception of the War Text," Helen M. Cooper, Susan Merrill Squier, and Adrienne Auslander Munich offer a sweeping look at the intersection of war and contraception in texts from the *Aeneid* to Chinua Achebe.

FIGURE 2. K. R. Chamberlain, "Breed! We Need Men," *Birth Control Review*, April/May 1917: 5.

and preventable disease? Does it not drive them to the factories, the mills, the mines and the stores to be stunted physically and mentally? Does it not throw them into the labor market to be competitors with her and their father?" (90–91).

This trope of the breeding woman's body being used by evil capitalists also runs through later birth control literature. The poem "Breed, Women, Breed" by Lucia Trent, reprinted in the *Birth Control Review* in April 1930, reveals this strand of thinking's reappearance when economic issues again came to the fore during the Depression Era.[11] The poem describes poor women as breeding machines for a capitalist system, producing workers and soldiers:

Breed, little mothers,
With tired backs and tired hands,
Breed for the owners of mills and the owners of mines,
Breed a race of danger-haunted men,
A race of toiling, sweating, miserable men,
Breed, little mothers,

11. Chapter 6 will discuss how the birth control movement continued to focus on the economic disparities but, during the Depression years, shifted its rhetoric to appeal to the wealthy.

FIGURE 3. Lou Rogers, "The New Vision," *Birth Control Review*, December 1918: 8–9.

Breed for the owners of mills and the owners of mines,
Breed, breed, breed! (113)

This image envisions woman as an automaton, her body a reproductive factory without subjectivity, producing interchangeable commodities on the assembly line of her womb. Breeding is a word most often applied to animals, signaling an unthinking fecundity. The repetition of the word *breed* foregrounds the dual action of the woman, the internal reproduction mirroring the external action of the "tired backs and tired hands" that keep the factory running. Both labors are repetitive, numbing the mind and deadening the soul. The tropes of machine as feminine and woman as machine contrast with a cultural ideal of the sentimental "little mother," pitting greedy and faceless capitalists against frail female bodies. Women thus remained within a matrix of power such as described by Michel Foucault: "political investment of the body is bound up, in accordance with complex reciprocal relations, with its economic use; it is largely as a force of production that the body is invested with relations of power and domination; but, on the other hand, its constitution as labour power is possible only if it is caught up in a system of subjection" (25). Birth control offers the possibility of disrupting this system of subjection of the female body, although its actual effects have often served to reinscribe women in an oppressive system.

Birth Control as Social Revolution
"IF YOU'RE RICH, THE LAW DON'T COUNT"

While the First World War combined with the language of industrialization helped establish the rhetorical trope of breeding woman as a factory, a second and supporting strain ran through the radical rhetoric: the message of social injustice couched in the images of the pathetic poor. Radical activism for birth control grew stronger as the decade progressed: Dennett founded the first birth control organization in the United States, the National Birth Control League, in March 1915. (In 1919 it was renamed the Voluntary Parenthood League.) A year later, Sanger opened the first birth control clinic in the Brownsville section of New York City, and in 1917, the same year that Alice Paul's National Woman's Party began to picket the White House to pressure President Woodrow Wilson into supporting women's suffrage, Sanger began the *Birth Control Review* to spread her message. Although the rhetoric of the *Birth Control Review* was less radical than its predecessor, *The Woman Rebel*, the implicit message of birth control retained its revolutionary appeal, and the class divide became a rally call that brought together the increasingly mainstream Sanger and radical thinkers. To many radical thinkers, birth control was a logical part of the revolution and "destructive to the capitalist system," as a 1917 article in the *Birth Control Review* argued (W. Roberts 7). *The Blast*, anarchist Alexander Berkman's short-lived periodical (January 1916–June 1917), advocated for birth control and rallied its socialist readers to support the work of Goldman and Sanger, posting notices of their lectures and trials.[12] Although Sanger's rhetoric began to distance the movement from socialism, her arguments remained tied to class oppression. Indeed, her decision to open her clinic in Brownsville was an attempt to reach those most in need of contraception: poor immigrant women.

Although the American Medical Association did not formally accept birth control until 1937, ample statistical evidence shows that some American women were controlling their reproduction long before that

---

12. Sanger's article "Not Guilty" in the first edition of *The Blast* explained her indictment for *The Woman Rebel* (7); later issues updated readers and explained "The Meaning of Margaret Sanger's Stand."

FIGURE 4. Lydia Gibson, "The Boss's wife can buy information to limit her family," cover of *The Blast*, February 12, 1916.

year. But how was this information made available, and to whom? The decline in family size among the wealthy clearly indicates that the rich had access to information on birth control from sympathetic doctors.[13] The poor, however, often did not, creating a divide in resources and knowledge. The contradiction, of course, is that those who would most benefit from birth control were the poor. The ability to control family size would allow them to budget their meager resources rather than to fall further into debt. This contradiction is prevalent in the literature and in political cartoons. The cover of *The Blast* for February 12, 1916, features a drawing by Lydia Gibson in which an "M.D." hands "birth control information" to a well-dressed woman with a single child, while holding a warning hand up to a poor woman surrounded by children (fig. 4). A Lou Rogers drawing

13. See Dawson, Meny, and Ridley, "Fertility Control in the United States before the Contraceptive Revolution," and Riley and White, "The Use of Various Methods of Contraception."

FIGURE 5. Lou Rogers, "Mrs. Poor Patient,"
Birth Control Review, June 1918: 5.

in the June 1918 issue of the *Birth Control Review* sends a similar message (fig. 5). A man labeled "Medical Profession" whispers (contraceptive information?) to a well-dressed woman, while in the background a haggard woman holding a baby, with a small child tugging at her skirts, looks on. It is captioned, "Mrs. Poor Patient: — 'If you're rich, the law don't count.'" Class is a clear determinant to access, and the visual placement of the figures emphasizes the poor patient's marginality. The caption also stresses that the law is applied unevenly based on class. Wealthy women could often receive birth control from sympathetic private physicians who would prescribe a pessary, a device worn in the vagina to support a prolapsed uterus, which also acted as a contraceptive.

The economic implications of the law's enforcement were clear, especially when one considered the wealth of the judges and lawyers enforcing the law against poor women. The *Birth Control Review* made much of this disparity and the attendant hypocrisy. When activist Kitty Marion was arrested for selling the *Review* on the streets in 1918, an anonymous article addressed her judges with, "One wonders, Your Honors, why Kitty Marion is in jail and your families, to all appearance, have been the subject of a wise and judicious limitation?" ("Judges with small families jail Kitty Marion" 5). The legal system may have intended "blind justice," but the application of the law served only to oppress the poor. *The Blast*, in a "Reflection" entitled "Birth Control Fight," reiterates this rhetoric that "Law has ever been enemy of human welfare" (5).

This divide in knowledge and resources appears to have been common knowledge, judging from letters, fiction, and articles of the period.[14] Margaret Sanger received thousands of letters written to the *Review* each year begging for information. These letters reveal poor women asking for the information they are sure wealthier women had. For example, a series of letters in 1917 entitled "Raising Garbage Collectors for the Doctors" foregrounds the re-entrenchment of class difference in its title, while the contents implicate uncontrolled fertility as the mechanism of continued oppression. One letter reads, "Have you any literature on Birth Control? I have six children, and we are so poor and no work I feel as though there was any more children I should go crazy." A series of letters in the May 1928 *Review*, "The Mother's Question—Is Poverty Inevitable?" demonstrates that poor women were in the same straits eleven years later. These letters demonstrate how knowledge was a commodity that reinforced class divisions. As Dr. Alice Hamilton argued in the *Review*, "It is a question of offering to the poor who need it most, the knowledge and the power which has long been the possession of those who need it least" (228).

Pro-contraceptive fiction also discussed this knowledge divide. Humor and farce are the tone of Lawrence Langner's 1914 play, *Wedded: A Social Comedy*, published in the *Little Review*. Margaret Anderson's *Little Review*, a literary magazine devoted to publishing the works of avant-garde writers, attracted "a more upscale segment of the modern audience" than *The Masses* (Stansell 175). As Mark S. Morrisson argues, the *Little Review* marketed itself to an emerging youth culture by adopting images of youth from advertising and the advice column genre of

14. In the April 1927 *Birth Control Review*, John P. Troxell and James H. Maurer, in separate articles on facing pages, argue that the wealthy and middle class have access to birth control, but the poor needed it more. In "Women and U.S. Literary Radicalism," Paula Rabinowitz notes that the Communist Party USA Women's Commission journal, *Working Woman*, reprinted a letter to a birth control clinic and provided an editorial response acknowledging the class-based knowledge divide of contraception, calling for women to fight for more birth control clinics (6). In her 1934 study of women's labor, *Women Who Work*, Grace Hutchins quotes from several letters to the American Birth Control League to argue for more clinics and the dissemination of information to the working class (because, as she states, anyone who can afford a private physician already received this information "as a matter of course" [qtd in Rabinowitz, "Women" 336]).

commercial magazines. Thus, it gained a surprisingly diverse readership and a respectable circulation of 2,000 to 4,000 subscribers, selling to both political radicals and literary bohemians in thirty-six cities across the country by 1914. Like *The Masses* and *Birth Control Review*, the *Little Review* was based on the "bedrock assumption that art must have a public function" (Morrisson 6). And, like the other radical periodicals under discussion, the *Little Review* ran afoul of the Comstock Act for printing "lewd and lascivious" material, in this case installments of James Joyce's *Ulysses*.[15]

Wedded opens with an absurd tragicomic scene: The groom has died shortly before the wedding, leaving the bride pregnant and unmarried. Janet, the bride, and her mother attempt to persuade the priest to pretend that Bob died after, not before, the ceremony, thus allowing Janet the security of "marriage." Janet reveals that she and Bob had heard of birth control but had no access to it. The Minister argues that birth control is unnatural and therefore evil, saying, "let me tell you that there is nothing worse than trying to interfere with the workings of nature, or—if I may say so—of God." Janet replies, "Well, Bob said the rich people do it. He said they must know how to do it, because they never have more'n two or three children in a family; but you've only got to walk on the next block—where it's all tenements—to see ten and twelve in every family, because the workin' people don't know any better" (16). Family size, a physical sign of hidden knowledge, was apparent to the poor, leading to the supposition that the wealthy must know something that they didn't. The commodity of knowledge manifests, and is embodied by, family size. The play uses morbid humor to critique how the Comstock Act (and public morality) kept birth control a black-market commodity that only the rich could afford. Janet and Bob delayed their marriage for years because of their poverty, and Janet believes economics are again holding her back.

One of the few fictional pieces in Margaret Sanger's first publication, *The Woman Rebel*, appears in the April 1914 issue and demonstrates the effects of uncontrolled fertility on female health and marriage. "Man's Law" by Sonia Ureles reveals the short-lived *Woman Rebel*'s emotional tone and revolutionary combination of feminism and socialism. The tragic story demonstrates the "typical" course of married life for the poor, and the effects of poverty and ignorance on women and children: "The first

15. The 1918 *Little Review* containing a portion of *Ulysses* in which Gertie McDowell exposes herself to Leopold Bloom was seized; in 1920 Margaret Anderson and Jane Heap were found guilty of publishing obscene material. *Ulysses* contains references to several types of birth control, including condoms and the diaphragm.

three years of married life crowned them with two babies. The first, a son, was proudly cared for. The second brought no enthusiasm. The third made it harder for them" (Ureles 9). At last, broken in health and in despair, the mother "stumbled into the nurses room" at the local hospital and "gasped, in a broken whisper, 'that I'm pregnant again.'"

> "Tell me what to do," she pleaded, frantic with fear. "I can't," said the nurse, averting her eyes in misery, "the law won't allow it." [. . .] "I'm sick—my babies are dying," whispered the mother. "And now—another! Never!" She screamed, terror holding her rigid. "Never! I'll kill myself first." (9)

Later hearing that the woman has indeed drowned herself, the nurse weeps, "Man's law is bitter cruel!" (9). This melodramatic vignette asserts that the law against birth control is solely man's law, an artificial construction whose effect is to unjustly penalize the poor. The story employs tragic extremes—of broken health, poverty, and suicide—to evoke an emotional reaction against the Comstock Act. The heroine's broken body becomes the terrain on which the reader engages in political action.

Images of poverty and its destructive effects on love and family infiltrated political cartoons as well as stories and plays. *The Masses* contained many political cartoons directly supporting birth control by linking the issue of uncontrolled fertility to class struggle. In July 1915 Editor Max Eastman explained the connection between birth control and the larger struggle for the working class in "Revolutionary Birth Control." This article appears under a cartoon by K. R. Chamberlain entitled "The Jones Family Group (Mr. Jones believes that Family-Limitation is criminal)," which depicted a haggard-looking couple with eight children. Birth control, Eastman argued, was a needed part of the revolution for class equity, and he championed it along with a wide range of issues such as suffrage and sexual liberation. The image thus reinforces the written argument in support of birth control, making visual the economic imperative of contraception for the working class.

If the poor lacked the tool of birth control to gain power over their economic plights, what did they have? Official "solutions" to the problem of poverty, which took the form of "good works" rather than knowledge and empowerment, exacerbated class differences. Whereas birth control contained the possibility of transcending inherited class distinctions, the "philanthropy" given in its place reinscribed class boundaries. Charity differed by race, as white welfare activists advocated for government programs that were means and morals tested, while black activists focused on building private institutions by raising private funds.[16] However, many left-leaning thinkers were harshly critical of "charity" and "philanthropy," depicting it as simply another form of social control. This attitude can be seen in *The Masses*, a magazine that endorsed no single ideology but was, according to its masthead, "directed against Rigidity and Dogma wherever it is found."

Seymour Barnard's humorous "Philanthropy," published in the March 1915 *Masses*, is a satire of well-meaning uplift agencies and wealthy philanthropists. The characters debate in sing-song rhyme the "cure" for poverty, coming up with solutions like cash, prayer, and study, but in the end leaving Poverty "just where he stood" (16). Although this brief "Comic Opera" does not explicitly name birth control, the absence is certainly to the point. While theorists, social workers, and clergy study and argue over the problem, they do nothing at all to solve it. The true solutions are exactly what they do not consider; indeed, they cannot consider these solutions, because that plan would destroy their world and livelihood. As the Social Workers admit in an aside:

When we discover the
Reason of Poverty,
Minus our jobs are we,
Standing and stations. (15)

The act of philanthropy literally employs them, and thus their motives are selfish as much as charitable. Indeed, the deployment of charity reinforces the economic structure. Socialism would wipe out the distinctions that allow the wealthy to "give" alms to the poor. Reading this piece in conjunction with the editorial and cartoon described earlier reveals how birth control fits into any plan that addresses structural inequity. Knowledge is a resource of the wealthy, and contraceptives are more valuable than philanthropy.

While the sharpest tool of critique for *The Masses* was satire, they

---

16. See Linda Gordon, "Black and White Visions of Welfare." Gordon provides revealing statistics on the black and white women welfare activists from 1900 to 1920 and their use of contraception. Of black welfare activists, 85 percent were married, but 34 percent of those had no children (as compared to a rate of 28 percent in the general black population). Only 34 percent of white women activists were married, and of those only 28 percent had children (compared to 69 percent in the general white population). Gordon concludes from these statistics, "It thus seems likely that these women welfare activists used birth control, although long physical separations from their husbands may have contributed to their low fertility. In their contraceptive practices these women may have been as modern as contemporary white women in comparable class positions" (568).

also published pieces that deployed sentimental appeals more reminiscent of the *Birth Control Review*. The economic discourse of the birth control movement argued that poverty harmed children and families, thus appealing to emotional and moral sentiment. As Martha Banta notes, "the sentimental tradition was mainly the most effective weapon the woman journalist possessed to rake up the muck caused by an industrial process that left women's bodies at the mercies of men and machines. What mattered was that the seemingly sentimental (a soft, fantasy form) be revealed as the ultimate realism (strong, brutal, true)" (148). The struggle of poor women to provide for their children is the theme of "The Wash," a narrative poem by Wilton Agnew Barrett in the April 1916 issue of *The Masses*. Barrett describes a visit of the Church Relief Committee to the home of a washerwoman, Mrs. Driggs, who had requested "a little ready money" so that she can have more time to look after her four children (19). The churchwomen argue that if they give money rather than their (and the congregation's) laundry, Mrs. Driggs will give it to her alcoholic husband, or cease to work at all (one wonders then who would wash the committee's fine clothing?). This dehumanization of Mrs. Driggs as a woman incapable of good judgment is belied by the subtext of the story, which depicts her as reasonable, valiant, and motivated by maternal love. The committee women are compared to a "tribunal" of "the Fates," implacable in their judgment, holding supreme power over the life of the poor, but whose judgment is clearly clouded by class prejudice. The piece concludes without the resolution of the committee's decision, but with a plaintive vision of Mrs. Driggs staring out at the thin, dirty faces of the two youngest children hiding under the "dank lines of the wash" (20). This emotional vision emphasizes the effects of poverty on children and criticizes the "means and morals" testing approach of this charity.

As in the earlier "Philanthropy," the "good works" of the wealthy are more a salve to their conscience than an actual help to the poor. Mrs. Driggs's impassioned arguments present a view of fierce and sacrificial mother-love while supporting the birth control movement by dramatizing the problems of poor women and children. How can a woman who must work constantly to feed her children find the time to raise them properly, especially as the overwork, poverty, and repeated childbearing break her health? Birth control advocates used these arguments to demonstrate the need for contraception among the working class. Knowledge and means, not laundry, are what the poor needed. These stories, and the rhetorical discourse they accompanied, did not send an anti-motherhood message, but rather argued that the poor could not afford so many children, and that it was better to provide a good life to a few children than to recreate the cycle of poverty for many. A survey of the immediate context in which "The Wash" appears supports this reading: The page following contains a column entitled "Birth Control," which reports on the trials of Sanger and Goldman as well as two legislative bills put forth by the National Birth Control League. Thus, readers were to interpret the story in the framework of real political events and birth control's importance to socialist economic policy.

The fiction acting as contraceptive propaganda focused on the abject poverty of the noble-but-poor. These short stories, often thinly plotted, rely on descriptions of squalid settings, a despairing tone, and stereotypic characters for their persuasive value. The May 1916 issue of *The Masses* contains two stories demonstrating the economic need for birth control. In "The Hunky Woman" Helen Forbes depicts a poor Hungarian immigrant who works all day in a laundry to feed her two small children. When she is jailed overnight for her absent husband's crime, the children are left alone in the tenement. She returns home to find her baby dead and her daughter taken to Associated Charities. Hampered by her broken English, her boss does not believe her story because "things like that don't happen in this country" (13). The Hungarian woman is dehumanized by her poverty and her immigrant status. Indeed, one speaker in the story comments, "those Hunkies are just animals," a sentiment that corresponds with a growing public negativity toward immigrants during the middle of the decade (13). This story contrasts immigrant tragedy against naïve native wealth to argue that "things like that" do happen to the poor.

John Reed's "Broadway Night" comments on birth control more explicitly from an unusual first-person male perspective. Reed, a journalist and revolutionary who was involved in the splintering of the American Communist Party from the Socialists in 1919, is perhaps best known for his coverage of the Mexican Revolution, World War I, and the Bolshevik Revolution. In "Broadway Night," a man relates how his loving marriage was destroyed by the death of his wife and children. The first child died "largely because our means did not permit us to dwell in a neighborhood where there was sufficient light and air for a sickly baby," another died of a typhoid epidemic, a third died of scarlet fever, and his wife died giving birth to a fourth stillborn child. Soon after the death of one of her children "she was going to have another baby. We knew that her condition wouldn't permit it, and tried our best to find some means of prevention. I've heard there were things—but we did not know them, and the doctor would do nothing. The child was born dead. My wife did not survive it" (20). The male speaker makes the emotional case for contraception with his tale of how repeated pregnancy not only destroys a woman's health but drags a family into poverty and thus endangers the health of the children, all while doctors know of safe preventatives that they will not speak of. The use of a male narrator reminds readers that the issue affected men as well as women. It also depicts a descent into poverty, thus acknowledging the permeability of class boundaries.

The physically worn-out wife appears so frequently as to become a stock figure in the radical fiction of the 1910s and 1920s. While used in a critique of class inequity, this trope also appealed to a general public steeped in sentimental mother-love, as evidenced by the response to a 1916 *Pictorial Review* article on birth control that drew thousands of letters in support: "the reader letters quoted all argued for birth control, primarily on the grounds of preserving mother's strength and producing healthier children" (Zuckerman 88). The trope of the physically exhausted woman appeared in *The Masses* and other radical periodicals. In "Till Death—," a 1917 *Masses* story, Helen Hull tells another tragic tale of broken marriage and the trap of unwanted pregnancy. The characters, an alcoholic husband and a struggling mother, call up a mythic narrative of suffering. When her husband threatens to go find "some un as'll be glad to sleep with me," the woman replies, "The doctor said I needed to be let alone—" (Hull 5). This was the usual "birth control" recommended by physicians—abstinence.[17]

The wife is torn between saving her health and saving her marriage. Hull uses stark characterizations to ensure the reader's sympathy with the wife. She is working to save money for her children's education but needs "[a]nother year—I thought—if he'd let me alone! I get so scared, worrying—if he got me with child—what could I do! There's ways—but I don't know 'em" (6). With her unnamed heroine, Hull emphasizes the inevitability of the familiar female life-plot. The woman's ignorance of birth control methods leads to another pregnancy, and the doctor, while sympathetic, remarks, "There's nothing I can do now. It's too late" (6). The story's title makes the vow "till death do us part" tragic, as it implies both that the husband will soon break his vow with infidelity, and that repeated childbearing will hasten the wife's death. The story's simplistic didacticism relies upon a familiar narrative told about and through the female body—the traditional female plot of marriage and motherhood cast in the context of poverty. The story thus contributes to a wider cultural narrative that erased female difference through a focus on a generic female body, deploying sentimentality to "argue through embodiment

---

17. See James Reed, "Doctors, Birth Control, and Social Values: 1830–1970," for a comprehensive examination of medical attitudes toward birth control.

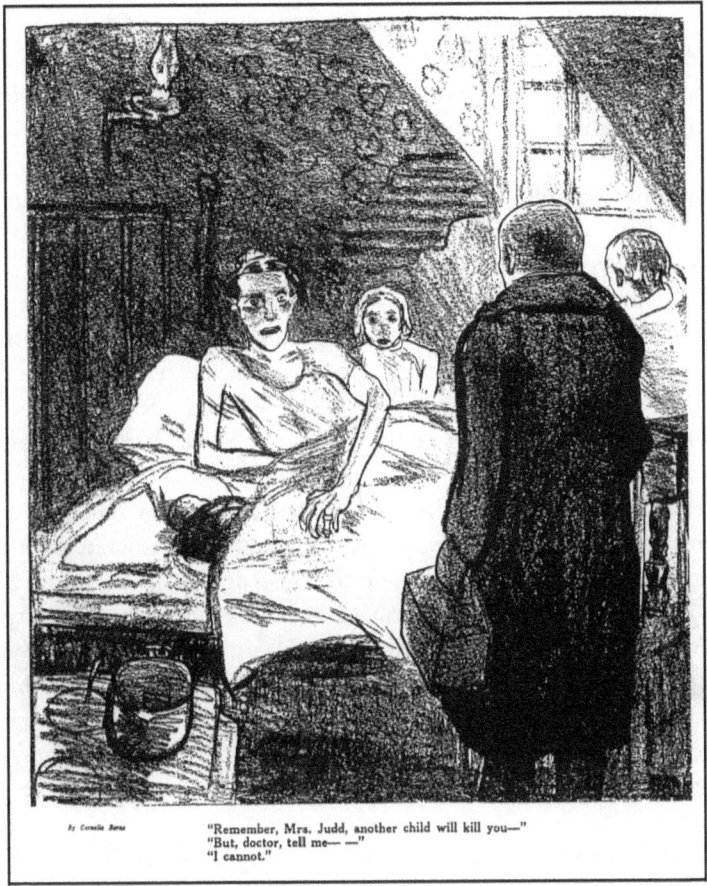

FIGURE 6. Cornelia Barns, "Remember, Mrs. Judd," *Birth Control Review*, August 1919: 9.

and an appeal to experience: the sentimental locates moral values in the (feminized) heart and denies the importance of external differences" (Clark 22). Hull's story gains rhetorical force through its use of extreme emotional appeals.

A drawing by Cornelia Barns, published in *The Masses*, graphically depicts the repeated narrative image of the dying mother unable to find help from a doctor and could have served as an illustration to these stories (fig. 6). The drawing shows a gaunt woman half-rising from bed in a one-room shack, newborn at her side and several smaller children gathered around. The doctor tells her, "another child will kill you," but then refuses to tell her how to prevent pregnancy with the brief denial, "I cannot." Through both satire and sentiment, image and word, *The Masses* used its editorial freedom to provide early support for birth control as part of an economic revolution. This pro-contraceptive method appeared consistently in articles, fiction, and artwork from 1915 until *The Masses* ended publication in 1917 (after several editors were charged under the Espionage Act).

This message of class-based oppression is also evident in some of the early fiction of the *Birth Control Review*. The polluted industrial setting of Rita Wellman's 1918 "On the Dump" mirrors the ugliness of life for Mrs. Robinson, who for ten years "had not had one year free from child-bearing" (7). The waste of the trash dump is both Mrs. Robinson's landscape—her only place to escape from the overcrowded tenement in which her family struggles for existence—and a symbol for her own life—she feels as discarded as the stained corset at her feet. Pregnant again, she remembers the shame of charity the last time her factory-worker husband was on strike. The insistent futility of repeated child-bearing and inescapable poverty lead her to consider suicide, and when her unwieldy pregnant body slips on the trash and slides down the dump heap into the "yellow and sluggish" river below, she ceases her struggle (7). Mrs. Robinson and her unborn child are simply more unwanted trash, expendable material goods. The characterization of Mrs. Robinson as a woman who loves beauty and feels shame counteracts stereotypes of the poor as coarse and unfeeling, a device that more accomplished writers such as Nella Larsen employ to complicate reader reactions to their characters.[18]

What was to blame for this tragic waste, this social injustice? The title of a 1918 *Birth Control Review* story by Jessie Ashley clearly attributes blame. In "The Law at Work" Ashley shows that ignorance of birth control harms all women, even those of the middle class. The husband, George, finds his pregnant wife, Helen, drowned in the bathtub with the note, "I cannot endure it so soon again. I will not go through it. Five babies in six years and another coming. No one would help me, so I must help myself" (3). The husband, confused, tries to resolve the suicide with his belief that "[i]f people loved and were married, wasn't it the woman's happiness to have children?" (3). He goes to his family physician, who reveals that every "sensible man" knows how to "prevent disease," there are simple ways for a woman to protect herself that "are not against the law, everyone who knows them uses them," and "it is only against the law to tell anyone what the methods are" (3). The husband's traditional view of women, not class barriers, stops him from practicing birth control.

---

18. See my discussion of Larsen's *Quicksand* in chapters 3 and 4.

The story highlights the tragic consequences of a law that censors needed information.

Ashley does not end her story by indicting the medical profession, but by showing the many institutions that contributed to Helen's death. George next visits his lawyer, only to find that Helen had been asking about her rights to get "some information she wanted" (4). But the lawyer had told her that only if she had grounds to separate from her husband did she have a right not to fulfill her "marital duties." When George returns home, he learns that the nurse he had engaged to care for the baby had been arrested for distributing birth control information. The nurse tells him that she would have given contraceptive information to his wife, as she does to all women in need. While the male professionals would deny a woman the knowledge to control her fertility, a birth controller is the potential heroine. Ashley reminds the reader that even wealthy women can be trapped by their conditions, thus transcending class by referring to a kinship of women created by shared experience. As the title indicates, "The Law at Work" is an instrument of death and despair to all women.

Birth control clinics and the medical profession itself acted as sites of institutionalized power, enforcing traditional morality and the class divide. Clinic policy was to serve only married women, and while clinics helped many indigent clients, private physicians were available only to the wealthy. Behind these political machinations, propagandistic stories indicted the medical profession for its class bias. Many stories in the *Birth Control Review* focused on families in abject poverty denied contraceptive information by the medical profession. Mary Burrill's "They That Sit in Darkness" typifies the terms of this discourse. The play portrays a large family in extreme poverty in the South. The subtitle, "A One-Act Play of Negro Life," indicates that the family is black, as does the dialect and the mention of Tuskegee, but the tragedy that occurs could be applied to any poor family. The play places particular emphasis on the material affects of poverty. The visiting nurse tells Mrs. Jasper, a week past the birth of her tenth child (eight live, although one is simpleminded and one has stunted legs), that the last pregnancy has left her with a bad heart and she must give up her laundry work. Mrs. Jasper, who cannot afford to stop taking in laundry, begs the nurse to tell her how to prevent conception, but the nurse can only reply, "I wish to God it were lawful for me to do so! My heart goes out to you poor people that sit in darkness, having, year after year, children that you are physically too weak to bring into the world—children that you are unable not only to educate but even to clothe and feed. Malinda, when I took my oath as nurse, I swore to abide by the laws of the State, and the law forbids my telling you what you have a right to know!" (7). The nurse embodies the moral conflict between current law and a woman's right not to be killed by repeated childbearing. The nurse obviously knows successful birth control methods but is bound by "man's cruel law." Soon after this exchange Mrs. Jasper dies, and her oldest daughter must give up a scholarship to attend Tuskegee, a chance to lead her family out of the "darkness" of ignorance and poverty. Uncontrolled fertility creates tragedy for this loving and honest family, sucking them deeper into poverty and ensuring that the next generation will continue the cycle.

Other fictional works effectively revealed with dramatic descriptions of poverty the complicity of enforced ignorance with class oppression. A forgotten "playlet" by Coralie Haman in the *Birth Control Review*, "Children" centers on a conversation by several tenement women. As a work of propaganda fiction it lacks narrative complexity, but this short piece provides an effective example of the use of sentiment to make a contraceptive argument. "Children" uses vivid description to evoke an emotional reaction. It is set outside a tenement house and specifies the setting as "a pile of rusty iron debris, paper litter, etc., can be seen in the yard" (230). "A mob of children of all ages, tattered, ragged, dirty" fight in the opening scene (230). Indeed, in its crowded, filthy setting, the play echoes Margaret Sanger's description of the Lower East Side tenements in which she worked as a visiting nurse.[19] The characters, Irish and Italian immigrant and black women, speak in heavy dialect about their large broods. Poverty and excessive childbearing defines these women: racial and ethnic differences are subsumed into a generic class and gender identification.[20] When Mrs. O'Flaherty complains that ten children are too many, Mrs. O'Roarke replies, "Why thin, don't yez do something about it? Somethin' to kape yerself from havin' so many? I've heard tell there's a way, but I don't rightly know just what it is at all" (230). Both women express a desire for information on contraception and link large families with poverty.

---

19. Sanger, "Impressions of the East Side," a multiple-part publication in the *New York Call* in 1911.

20. In much of the fiction under discussion, race is subsumed within the generic designation of class and gender, erasing differential experience based on race. Race and ethnicity were often ignored in Socialist Party propaganda as well, according to Sally M. Miller, who writes that "the Socialist Party in the Progressive Era failed, as did the country at large, to view the Negro as an individual, as a distinct human being in a unique dilemma. . . . The party did not reject Negro membership—it stood for Negro suffrage when the issue arose—yet with the exception of a vocal minority, it doubted Negro equality and undertook no meaningful struggles against second-class citizenship" (34).

Mrs. O'Rourke: 'Tis not the Lard's will, I do be thinkin'. 'Tis the ignorance av us poor human mortals. If we didn' have so manny children 'tis out av this muck we could be gittin'.

Mrs. O'Flaherty: God knows 'tis fair strangled we aire wid 'em.

Mrs. O'Rourke: An' takin'care o' the family, trying to find food for 'em at all. An' just as ye think ye can git away somewheres, along cooms anither wan, an' ties ye doon to this hell, an' while ye're havin' a new wan, wan av the ithers dies on ye. Oh, 'tis a dog's life, so it is. (231)

Their friend Mrs. Johnson, a black woman who takes in laundry for the wealthy, brings the knowledge divide into the conversation by talking about her employer, who "ain't got so many chillen" (232). Haman's use of dialect and descriptions of poverty make a narrative link between class and knowledge. These women recognize the enslaving links of poverty, ignorance, and reproduction.

The conversation of Jim and Annie, a young couple in the play, reinforces this message. When Jim proposes to Annie, she turns him down because she knows marriage means children: "'tis bitter hard, so it is, and that's God's room there is for so manny on 'em. For me, I'm think' I'd rather work in the factory" (236). The factory promises money and autonomy for Annie, but marriage would only bring children and hardship. Annie recognizes her limited choices, and she consciously chooses commercial production over reproduction. However, the text's larger message questions whether such a choice should be necessary. Annie recognizes that class and knowledge are intertwined, as the doctors tell the "up-town women" but not the poor "how we can kape our families small" (236). Jim presents a reason that is similar to Dreiser's hint of class conspiracy: "I suppose them rich fellahs wants us poor people to have a lot o' childher so as they kin have more av 'em in their factories. Childer come cheaper than grown folks" (236). The profit motive makes poor bodies—children and adults—expendable. While the play is comic in its exaggerated, broadly stereotypical characters and dialect, its message is serious. It concludes with a drunken Italian immigrant killing his young pregnant wife because if she is dead, "Den she can't have any more children" (237). The play thus falls into an undeveloped sentimental tragedy to underscore the serious need for birth control. Without contraception, the only way to end the reproductive capacities of the female body, to shut down the assembly line, is death or abstinence.

This fiction reveals how knowledge of birth control was a commodity in the social economy. Ironically, what the poor needed was exactly what they did not get in the fiction or articles of the *Birth Control Review* and

FIGURE 7. Lou Rogers, "Must She Always Plead in Vain?," cover of *Birth Control Review*, July 1919.

other radical journals: specific information on contraceptive methods. The fictional characters dramatized the plight of the poor to elicit sympathy, anger, and support for the movement. The stories of nurses and doctors unable to give needed information supported Sanger's advocacy of a "doctors only" bill that would allow medical professionals to give contraceptive information at their discretion. The cover of the July 1919 *Review* also makes this case, depicting a nurse and a poor woman, with the caption, "Must she always plead in Vain? You are a nurse—can't you tell me? For the children's sake—help me!" (fig. 7). The U.S. legal and medical systems operated under class constraints, and it was poor women and children who suffered the consequences.

While these stories and images use melodrama to give impact to their short sketches of working-class life, they serve to humanize the statistics underlying the argument for birth control. The frequent death of young children in these stories was no exaggeration: "300,000 babies, according to the baby welfare association, are sacrificed in the United States each year," Emma Goldman stated in her trial defense, reprinted in the June 1916 *Masses*. Birth controllers advocated limiting the number of children in proportion to the available income. The texts make a composite argument for contraception as a solution to poverty and as a tool in the emancipation of women. By focusing on depictions of abject hardship and the sense of despair it engenders, these works use emotional arguments for birth control while never explicitly discussing it.

Sanger and Goldman both believed that the fight for women's suffrage was too narrow, but they shared the radical notion that women such as Alice Paul embodied—that women must break the law to change it. Both women were breaking the law by speaking out on and providing information about birth control, and both were eventually arrested—Sanger in 1916 for distributing information at her clinic and Goldman in February and again in October 1916 for speaking publicly about specific birth control methods. These arrests made contraception "a topic of discussion and interest among strap hangers in subways and housewives at home. The significance of family planning was discussed openly and widely by many who some months earlier would have only broached the subject in hushed and secretive tones" (Baskin xvi). This discourse of rights extended from women to children, as a January 17, 1916, headline in the *New York Times* indicates: "Teddy Roosevelt Wrong, Says Anarchist—Emma Goldman Asserts Child Has A Right Not To Be Born."

But a strategic choice to court upper- and middle-class professionals and politicians quickly subsumed the radical possibilities of birth control, and conservative arguments in alignment with traditional morality tempered the movement's rhetoric by the 1920s. Historian Linda Gordon notes, "two separate factors pushed the birth control movement away from the organized Left: attacks on birth control by leftists and even some feminists and the independent decline of socialism and feminism" (*Moral Property of Women* 167). "Red" Emma Goldman, the earliest radical advocate for birth control in America, shifted to the topic of conscription and was deported in 1919 for opposing the draft. Margaret Sanger, who made the birth control movement her life, toned down the "red and flaming" rhetoric for a more conservative message meant to appeal to the mainstream. The radical rhetoric faded away, and, by 1917, the *Birth Control Review*, the movement's main outlet, adopted other tactics. The new publication changed audience as well, aiming its message at the middle and upper classes rather than at working women and anarchists/socialists. While much of the later fiction continued its sentimental depictions and served a vital role by adding dramatic narrative elements to the arguments, it ceased to imply that social and sexual revolution were imminent. The following chapters will discuss this approach and its appeals to the values of motherhood, marriage, eugenics, and economics.

3

"For Married Women Only"
Birth Control and Modern Marriage

> Why is Birth Control Necessary? . . . it will give to the home peace, harmony and love and it will, by encouraging early marriage, lessen prostitution and promote morality.
> —"The Birth Control Primer,"
> Birth Control Review, February 1926

ALTHOUGH THE March 1914 *Woman Rebel* claimed that "Rebel Women" have "The Right to be unmarried mothers," by the 1920s the birth control movement was operating within a cultural norm that assumed marriage (3). In the 1920s, new ideas regarding marriage and sexuality circulated in liberal circles such as Greenwich Village. Some couples engaged in companionate marriage, a more egalitarian union that rested on the emotional and physical compatibility of husband and wife.[1] The short skirts and bobbed hair of the 1920s symbolized changing rules and the loosening of sexuality from reproduction. Claude McKay's character Rose in his 1928 novel, *Home to Harlem*, exemplifies the extreme sexual freedom that horrified some and delighted others. McKay wrote, "Rose had her friends of both sexes and was quite free in her ways. At the Congo she sat and drank and flirted with many fellows. That was a part of her business. She got more tips that way, and the extra personal bargains that gave her the means to maintain her style of living. All her lovers had always accepted her living entirely free" (113).[2]

1. On "sex radicals" and changing conceptions of marriage, see Simmons, "Women's Power in Sex: Radical Challenges to Marriage in the Early-Twentieth-Century United States."
2. Some writers and critics criticized McKay's celebration of sexual freedom for add-

The New Woman enjoyed increased sexual freedom, and growing numbers engaged in premarital sex and looked down upon traditional marriage. In *Plum Bun*, Jessie Redmon Fauset depicts the protagonist's friend Paulette as a bohemian New Woman who has sexual affairs with no intention of marrying: "I see what I want; I use my wiles as a woman to get it," she tells Angela (105). Paulette views marriage as a burden and asks, "[W]hat's the use of tying yourself up now, while you're young?" (106). Although Paulette's attitude symbolized the sexual freedom of the Jazz Age, she did not represent the statistical norm. As marriage historian Stephanie Coontz notes, "there was no widespread rejection of marriage in the 1920s; indeed, rates of lifelong singlehood fell" (203). The institution of marriage sanctioned female desire, and this desire led, inevitably it seemed, to motherhood and children. The protagonist of Fauset's 1924 novel, *There Is Confusion*, articulates this link to her boyfriend, Peter, when she tells him, "You know perfectly well that for a woman love usually means a household of children" (95). Even the noted sexologist Havelock Ellis, a frequent contributor to the *Birth Control Review*, discussed female sexuality in terms of the "marital embrace" enjoyed by husband and wife ("The Love Rights of Women" 3). Conscious of marriage's social framework as a necessary condition for female sexuality, the birth control movement was inherently embroiled in debates about marriage and motherhood.

How did American advocates of birth control in the 1920s reconcile their arguments with traditional morality after the "red and flaming" years of radical rhetoric? What role did fiction play in changing popular perceptions of female sexuality and gender roles? The antithetical pairings of marriage and prostitution, motherhood and abortion reveal the birth control movement's attempts to gain legitimacy from a wider audience in the 1920s. The table of contents of several issues of the *Birth Control Review* highlights this close association between contraception and marriage. Titles of articles include "Education in Marriage," "Marriage and Birth Control," and the five-part series, "Marriage Today and in the Future," among many others.[3] Advertisements for marriage manuals such as *The*

---

ing to the popular notion of black sexuality as primitive. W. E. B. DuBois, for instance, wrote, "Reading it makes me want to take a bath" ("The Browsing Reader"). Other writers of the Harlem Renaissance, however, including Zora Neale Hurston and Langston Hughes, appreciated McKay's frankness.

3. "Marriage Today and in the Future" by John Haynes Holmes; "Marriage and Birth Control" by C. Gasquoine Hartley; "Education for Marriage" by Meyer E. Nimkoff. Other articles on marriage in the *Birth Control Review* included "Birth Control and Early Marriage" by William F. Ogburn, Ph.D. (December 1926); "Harmony in Marriage" by Hornell Hart (November 1927); and "A Research in Marriage" by Havelock Ellis (May 1929).

Sex Technique in Marriage by I. E. Hutton, M.D. and *The Hygiene of Marriage: A Detailed Consideration of Sex and Marriage* by Dr. Millard S. Everett appeared in the *Review*. Margaret Sanger contributed to the genre with *Happiness in Marriage* in 1926.[4] Even though the New Woman of the 1920s was engaging in more premarital sex than before (D'Emilio and Freedman 241), the birth control movement firmly set its discourse into the matrix of marriage and morality.

The argument that birth control was moral rebutted three basic premises: that birth control's purpose was to destroy motherhood and allow women sex without consequence; that contraception was the same as abortion; and that it would allow an explosion in licentiousness and prostitution. This tension is evident in V. F. Calverton's 1929 work, *The Bankruptcy of Marriage*. Calverton, who was generally pro-contraception, depicts birth control as antithetical to marriage. He writes, "an important factor in the growth of the new morality, and the decay of modern marriage, has been the advancing perfection of modern contraceptives.... Marriage thus is rapidly coming to lose sexual significance for women as well as men" (118, 121). Birth control was a potential threat to traditional morality because it made public the possibility of female sexuality outside of marriage (without pregnancy). But by the 1920s the birth control movement rhetorically grounded its arguments in traditional morality, strategically invoking a normative ideology of gender and class. These issues were implicated in and impacted by the possibility of birth control, as can be seen in an examination of fictional portrayals of marriage.

"New Woman," Old Institution

The New Woman corresponded with changing ideas about morality and sexuality. As early as 1913 the country was talking about the "sex hysteria and sex discussion" that had "invaded this country" ("Sex O'Clock in America" 113). Increased acceptance of female sexuality was a minor argument for contraception. In her earlier arguments Sanger attacked withdrawal and coitus interruptus on the grounds that they denied female sexual satisfaction and left a woman in a state of "high nervous tension" (qtd. in D'Emilio and Freedman 244). An editorial in a 1915 issue of *The New Republic*, a mainstream periodical, encapsulates this

---

4. Margaret Sanger divorced her first husband, William Sanger, in 1921 after a long separation and married millionaire Noah Slee in 1922.

tension between traditional morality (female chastity) and the growing arguments for birth control: "The question is whether earlier marriages, the reduction of illegitimacy and abortion, the prevention of too frequent pregnancy with its disastrous effect on the health of the wife and the morale of the husband, the lightening of economic burdens, the decrease in the birth of the unfit, are not reasons which far outweigh the importance attached to the personal chastity of a minority among women" ("The Control of Births" 115). Although perhaps conventional to twenty-first-century readers, the early birth control movement's critiques of conventional marriage and the double standard placed on female sexuality contributed to shifting ideas about marriage.

Growing out of various social movements, including Victoria Woodhull's nineteenth-century free love ideas and the ongoing movement for women's suffrage, some early birth controllers argued that controlling her body was a woman's right. In 1914 Goldman wrote, "Woman's development, her freedom, her independence, must come from and through herself. First by asserting herself as a personality, and not as a sex commodity. Second, by refusing the right to anyone over her body; by refusing to bear children, unless she wants them" ("Woman's Suffrage" 202). That same year Sanger wrote in *The Woman Rebel*, "A Woman's Body belongs to herself alone" ("Suppression" 25). As Sara Bard Field claimed in the December 15, 1916, issue of *The Blast*, "Birth control is a woman's declaration of right as to the use to which her body shall be put" (7). These ideas of female control removed sexuality, however briefly, from the context of marriage.

Fiction also revealed this shifting morality. In 1913 *Current Opinion* reported that "[a]t the present moment, novels and plays may be said fairly to reek with sex" ("Literary Censorship and the Novels of the Winter" 353). This section will examine a few fictional depictions from the 1910s before moving to works of the 1920s that subtly critique conventional marriage. These presentations function in terms set out by Joseph Allen Boone as tradition and countertradition: ideological structures of belief (such as the institution of marriage) "are translated into narrative structures that at once encode and perpetuate those beliefs" in some works supporting birth control, thus serving a conservative social function, while other works present a "counter narrative" by exploring the tensions and contradictions underlying the social marital contract (2).

While *The Masses* was only published from 1911 to 1917, it appealed to "a wide variety of readers . . . not limited by age or gender . . . [including] working class and immigrant readers" (Morrisson

178). This wide audience, combined with a liberal editorial policy, makes *The Masses* an interesting site to begin examining the New [Married] Woman. Although many of the bohemian Villagers contributing to *The Masses* advocated free love, their work often provided only a gentle critique of marriage or none at all. "A New Woman?" by Dorothy Weil dramatizes this ambivalence, portraying an unmarried mother and the negative public perceptions of her throughout the class structure. The question mark in the title of this 1916 story indicates the skeptical judgment of the New Woman's choices. The first-person narrator laments that her regular cleaning woman, Mrs. Knox, has to take a vacation to have another child. The narrator is surprised since "[h]er husband's a good-for-nothing that she's had to get away from; though she, being a Catholic, couldn't divorce him once and for all" (Weil 17). Mrs. Knox became pregnant when she exchanged sex for her alcoholic husband's financial help, an exchange that equates marriage with prostitution. She is trapped by her poverty, by her dependence on an alcoholic husband, and by her inability to control her fertility.

With the story of Mrs. Knox, Weil seemingly criticizes an institution that traps women in abusive situations, but the narrative focus on the replacement cleaning woman, "a pleasant young thing, but frail and consumptive looking," challenges this interpretation (17). This younger woman, Jennie, has a child out of wedlock. When Mrs. Knox returns to work she refuses to work with "that critter . . . a woman unmarried who has a child" (17). Mrs. Knox, herself the victim of an unhappy marriage, has nothing but contempt for unmarried mothers like Jennie. This traditional morality unites Mrs. Knox and her wealthy employer. Yet Weil does not provide easy judgments of the characters, complicating Mrs. Knox's virtue with the implication that she prostituted herself to her abusive husband and depicting in the "fallen" Jennie a representative working-class figure, a young woman who helped raise ten siblings and who had worked since the age of twelve. In the face of these virtues, Jennie's flaw is acting on her sexual desire: she admits to having "done it, ma'am—because I wanted to" (18). This desire was for sexual intimacy, not a child: "of course we didn't think of that, ma'am. How many people in their goings on do you suppose there is that do?" Jennie represents premarital sexuality and the commonplace ignorance of contraception. Although Jennie is a sterling character despite the blemish of her admitted sexuality and unwed pregnancy, Weil seems suspicious of free love. Jennie is ill and her prospects are very bleak, because no one will help her. The troubled narrator considers calling the authorities, but in the end, highly conflicted, she fires Jennie. While Jennie is portrayed sympathetically, the story does not provide an inspiring vision of the brave New Woman. Rather, it implies that no woman can be free, within or outside of marriage, when encumbered by unwanted children.

"Usury," by Helen R. Hull, another 1916 *Masses* story, offers a simultaneous reinforcement and reshaping of traditional views of marriage. Like "A New Woman?" "Usury" focuses on the relationship between an unmarried, pregnant servant and her middle-class employer, a narrative pattern that Margaret C. Jones has noted is both frequently and effectively employed by female contributors to *The Masses* (65). In Hull's story, the spinster Cora MacAllister advises her "fallen" maid Lizzie to marry the man who had fathered her dead baby, as "[m]arriage was the way in which such mistakes as Lizzie's were remedied" (5). But Lizzie is engaged to another man, a man who loves her. The idea that female sexuality outside of marriage must be punished remains in Cora's mind even as she agrees that Lizzie can marry the man she loves, as long as she marries. The act of marriage, its institutional ability to cleanse former sins by carefully guarding female actions, transcends the characters themselves. The story follows the traditional romantic plot structure equating marriage for women with a happy ending. However, the idea that unwed sexuality must be punished is somewhat negated by allowing the "fallen woman" to be happy within marriage, to have her marry for love rather than as redemption. Cora confirms marriage as woman's ultimate goal, and those women who did not marry were increasingly "objects of scorn and pity: spinsters were seen as neurotic and unfulfilled because they had not participated in the heterosexual experience now so highly valued by society" (Ware 64–65). By placing traditional views in the mouth of a spinster, Hull further questions their validity.

Writers also used humor to advocate for birth control and to critique marriage. *Wedded: A Social Comedy*, the 1914 play by Lawrence Langner, examines the role of marriage in sanctioning female desire and birth control's place in this matrix. Although the subtitle probably refers to the literary convention of ending a comedy in marriage (Gainor 170), *Wedded* offers an implicit critique of marriage as a social convention while making strong arguments for birth control. Indeed, this is no ideal escape story, despite its comic nature, because class is foregrounded in the setting ("a cheap district of Brooklyn") and the dialogue (a lower-class dialect).

As with countless other fictional and real-life couples, an unwanted pregnancy precipitates the wedding. Janet Ransome is no innocent virgin seduced by an unfeeling villain, but a modern woman with sexual feelings. Pregnant outside of wedlock, she will be socially ostracized, her sin physically written on her body. But Langner complicates social judgment. He does not present Janet as carelessly promiscuous but places his couple in a situation that would have been familiar to his audience, eliciting sympathy: Janet and Bob had been engaged for three years but were too poor to wed. As Mrs. Ransome explains to the minister, "My girl ain't naturally bad. It isn't as though she'd pick up any feller that happened to come along. Hundreds and thousands do it, sir, indeed they do" (13–14). When reprimanded by the minister for not waiting to engage in intercourse, Janet replies, "We did wait. Isn't three years long enough? D'ye think we was made of stone? How much longer d'ye think we could wait? We waited until we couldn't hold out no longer" (15).

The play reveals another common problem, lack of knowledge about birth control and about sexuality in general: Janet's mother asks her, "Are you sure? D'ye know how to tell fer certain?" (9). Prudery and strict morality have prevented frank conversations between mother and daughter, and any discussion of "how to tell" would have occurred after marriage. And the results extend beyond pregnancy. As Mrs. Ransome hysterically announces, Janet will get kicked out of the house and lose her job, which will inevitably lead to prostitution: "That's how they get started on the streets, sir," she cries to the minister (14). This impending tragedy is due to ignorance of birth control methods as much as illicit sexuality, as Janet makes clear: "D'ye think I wanted a baby? I didn't want one. I didn't know how to stop it. If you don't like it—it's a pity you don't preach sermons on how to stop havin' babies when they're not wanted. There'd be some sense in that. That'd be more sense than talkin' about waitin'—an' waitin'—an' waitin'. There's hundreds of women round here—starvin' and sufferin'—an' havin' one baby after another, and don't know the first thing about how to stop it. 'Tisn't my fault I'm going to have one. I didn't want it" (15). There is both humor and pathos in the image of the minister preaching a gospel of birth control. Unlike the grim despair of most radical narratives, Langner's play ends happily enough, with the minister signing the marriage register after being convinced of Janet's contrition. But this posthumous wedding reveals that the social institution of marriage can be a farce.

The controversy over the New Woman, birth control, and marriage continued into the 1920s in mainstream magazines such as *Harper's*, *The Nation*, and *Outlook*.[5] Magazines aimed at white middle-class women

5. For an overview of early birth control coverage in the mainstream press, specifically the *New York Times*, *Harper's Weekly*, and *The New Republic*, see Dolores Flamiano. Interestingly, Mary Alden Hopkins presented birth control neutrally in a *Harper's Weekly*

grew in popularity from the 1910s through the 1920s and played a significant role in shaping acceptable female behavior and attitudes. While circulation of the *Birth Control Review* fluctuated between 15,000 and 30,000 subscriptions, the *Ladies' Home Journal* and *Pictorial Review,* two of the "big six" women's magazines, reached over two million women each.[6] Unsurprisingly, the ideas they circulated were largely conservative, and the fiction memorialized traditional roles for women within marriage and the home. The *Ladies' Home Journal* established its stance quite early, printing on March 1, 1905, a speech by Theodore Roosevelt, "The American Woman as Mother," which attacked women and birth control for moral degeneracy and race suicide. The *Ladies' Home Journal* published only a few articles on birth control, such as "Alarming Decrease in American Babies" (July 1922), "College Women and Race Suicide" (April 1922), and "What of Birth Regulation?" (October 1931).

Stories in women's magazines differed in tone and purpose from those in politically oriented periodicals such as the *Birth Control Review.* The fiction in women's magazines focused on love, romance, fantasy, and escape, providing entertainment while reinforcing traditional values (Hoekstra 44). These magazines, due to the need for advertising revenue, competition for subscribers, and outside pressure, reinforced women's roles as housewife, mother, and wife. Birth control did not neatly fit into this equation. (The *Birth Control Review* contained minimal advertisements and relied heavily on funding from Sanger's second husband, the millionaire Noah Slee.) Editors of women's magazines looked for stories that promoted consumerism. As Katherine Fullerton Gerould noted in 1936, women's magazines "print a great many serials and short stories calculated to appeal to the same subscribers who cut out the receipts, send for the dress patterns, and write to the sub-editor" (3).[7] Readers tried to copy the fictional heroines, to "consume" the lifestyle, and therefore the stories are both sentimental and "realistic" in terms of object descriptions. The fiction of the *Ladies' Home Journal* focused on "middle class virtues" and a theme of "love" (Johns-Heine and Gerth 109, 111). In style and theme, these stories contrast with the more radical fiction, whose starkly negative melodrama deconstructed complacency and radi-

---

series in 1915–16: "*Harper's Weekly* feels that whatever the decision, full and accurate information about the controversy, with the arguments on both sides and the important facts in the case, is due to its readers"; however, the articles largely supported the arguments made in the *Birth Control Review* without ever mentioning birth control.

6. Peck provides the approximate figure for the *Birth Control Review* (38), while Zuckerman's excellent history of popular women's magazines provides circulation information for *Ladies' Home Journal* and *Pictorial Review* (105–14).

7. See also Scanlon.

calized readers: readers were not meant to identify with the poor, physically broken women, but instead meant to view them as representatives of a grave social ill.

While fiction in both genres of magazine focused on marriage, their depictions of the stability of love differed markedly. In part, the difference is one of timing and emphasis. In her study of women's magazines from 1900 to 1920, Hoekstra identifies six major plots, including "boy meets girl" (45). These stories "end in marriage; there is no hint of premarital sex, and the final marriage ceremony chastely suggests the physical consummation of love" (45). These narratives explicate emotional rather than physical courtship, ignoring the contemporary social increase in premarital "petting," which was aided by the introduction of the automobile as a private space for young couples. By 1938, a study by Dorothy Dunbar Bromley and Florence Britten revealed that one-quarter of college women had premarital sex with their fiancés. Many of these couples relied on condoms, available in gas stations, for contraception. This greater sexual freedom occurred within the bounds of expected marriage, since "an overwhelming majority of college women in the 1930s saw marriage as the main goal of their lives . . . love, and a clear commitment to matrimony, justified the intimacy" (Ware 66, 63).

This narrative pattern contrasts with stories where premarital sex initiated an unplanned marriage. A character such as Weil's New Woman would never appear in popular women's magazines because she is not the victim of an unscrupulous seducer but a woman with her own desires. The propaganda fiction of the *Birth Control Review* during the 1920s would also be unlikely to sympathetically depict women with sexual desire outside of marriage. Indeed, the stories used rhetorically by the birth control movement always begin *after* the inception of a relationship, whereas the romance stories of the popular magazines emphasize the romantic early days of love. In the women's magazines, marriage is the heroine's ultimate goal, and "[i]nterest in sexuality is forbidden; physical attraction can be expressed only in etherealized romantic love; the only other allowable love is maternal" (Hoekstra 54). Thus these stories ignore the ugly conditions that are central to the radical fiction. These fictional escapes reinforce the idea that marriage is woman's ultimate goal, wife and mother her predestined role, without examining the impending threats to the sanctity of marriage.

The tales of marriage in the radical press exhibit a narrative stability from the 1920s through the 1930s, as the birth control movement attempted to align itself with the moral majority. Fiction in women's magazines offered a more flexible depiction of marriage, shifting their message slightly to appeal to a growing number of career women. According to Maureen Honey, during the 1920s magazines such as *Ladies' Home Journal* began positively portraying heroines with careers who do not either marry or enter into a companionate marriage. However, these heroines often sacrifice their sexuality for their careers, rejecting both marriage and sexuality. In this way the women's magazines took a small step in opening discussion of women's roles: Marriage is not inevitable, but female sexuality cannot exist outside of marriage without threatening gender norms. Sexuality and the attendant need for birth control remain within marriage. These positive portrayals of fictional career women who sacrificed their sexuality were short-lived, lasting approximately two decades. During the 1940s, especially after the return of husbands from World War II, the fiction of women's magazines returned to glorifying wife and mother roles within the domestic sphere (Franzwa 43).

Mainstream, middle-class women's magazines unsurprisingly did not advocate for birth control, but what is interesting is how the contraceptive movement's situating of birth control within marriage aligned it ideologically with the women's magazines. Although the escape fiction of women's magazines ignored the reality of what can go wrong in marriage, and the subsequent need for birth control, the presence of advertisements for "female hygiene" products within their pages demonstrates a tacit acknowledgment that the subject was indeed on many readers' minds. By 1938, in a rare article on the subject, the *Ladies' Home Journal* acknowledged this fact in "What the Women of America Think about Birth Control," which revealed that 79 percent of the women surveyed supported birth control so that they could regulate the number of children they could care for (Pringle 14).

The stories published in the *Birth Control Review* and mainstream periodicals, by turns melodramatic and sentimental, have largely been lost to the critical gaze. Their broad characterizations, thin plots, and dated subject matter relegate them to virtual oblivion. Luckily, the relationship between marriage and birth control transcended their yellowed pages and attracted more canonical authors interested in the changing nuances of marriage and morality. Theodore Dreiser, an author firmly fixed in the literary canon, is one American author who integrated the issues of marriage, female sexuality, and birth control into his work. The public reception of several of Dreiser's novels demonstrates why the birth control movement itself needed to retain a conservative stance.

Theodore Dreiser supported the movement and contributed nonfiction to the *Birth Control Review*. In April 1921 he offered "A Word Concerning Birth Control," and he is quoted in the January 1934 issue as saying, "If it is necessary, and hence legitimate, for the government to control production and distribution, income and wages, why is it not equally necessary for it to control the number of the beneficiaries of all this? In other words, why is not birth control as necessary to the welfare of the state as any of these others?" (2). Scholars have noted the concordance of Dreiser's biography, beliefs, and fiction. Richard Lingeman argues that "because of the troubles in his own marriage, he shared the ideas on the family, sexual morality, and contraception proclaimed by Emma Goldman, Margaret Sanger, and the Swedish feminist Ellen Key" (292). These comments demonstrate Dreiser's public stance on the issue and illuminate the implicit message of his fiction.

Although Theodore Dreiser's novels don't explicitly give birth control the "unqualified endorsement" of his public statements, they do critique conventional sexuality sanctioned by marriage and imply knowledge of birth control methods (Dreiser, "A Word Concerning Birth Control" 13). Dreiser defied traditional social codes in his work by writing in a naturalistic style about sexuality. He chafed against the same censoring morality that restricted the public distribution of birth control information. Two of his novels, *An American Tragedy* and *The Genius*, were banned in some cities for obscenity. Dreiser and the birth control movement were linked by more than his contributions to the *Birth Control Review* and the restrictions they both labored under. When Boston tried to ban *An American Tragedy* in 1927, "In protest, an anticensorship rally was held, and Margaret Sanger appeared with her mouth taped shut in a gesture of opposition to the city's ban on birth control" (Gogol xiii, n1). Dreiser also spoke at this rally and was an official sponsor of the First American Birth Control Conference organized by Sanger in New York in 1921.

Ideologically Dreiser supported the birth control movement, and a brief examination of his fiction reveals arguments for birth control embedded in implicit critiques of marriage. Dreiser published *Sister Carrie* and *Jennie Gerhardt* prior to 1914, but they offer interesting insights into how Dreiser's fiction was in dialogue with the issues of the movement. Nancy Barrineau remarks, "Certainly Dreiser wrote *Sister Carrie* with an eye tipped toward the forces of Comstock; and in 1911, while he was finishing *Jennie Gerhardt*, the 1873 Comstock Act still prohibited honest discussion and dissemination of birth control information" (59). Thus, while Dreiser could be open within the pages of the *Birth Control Review*, he had to weave his views more subtly into his fiction. *Sister Carrie* appeared in 1900, a time when "[m]arriage was really the only plot women could enact in literature as well as life" (Fishkin 8). Dreiser rejected that plot, which is perhaps why the publisher Doubleday found the novel objectionable. The novel contains seduction, adultery, bigamy, sex out of wedlock, and, implicitly, birth control. Drouet and Carrie live together for an extended period, and sexual relations are assumed but not described. Drouet promises to marry Carrie but never does, demonstrating the link between marriage and sanctioned sexuality. Later, Carrie lives with and marries Hurstwood, again without becoming pregnant. The logical deduction is that they use birth control. The novel aroused controversy because Carrie's sins remain unpunished and she becomes a successful actress. Carrie is sexually active while remaining free from the burdens of marriage and motherhood. Although the novel lacks an explicit mention of birth control, it is a very definite subtext.

In his second novel, *Jennie Gerhardt* (originally entitled *The Transgressor* as though to emphasize the breaking of social norms), Dreiser attempted to be more realistic about the consequences of sexuality. Nancy Barrineau writes, "Even with the censorship, this novel reveals Dreiser's awareness that to women like Jennie—regardless of their wishes—pregnancy is the probable consequence of sex. Dreiser's ability to imagine and dramatize the full implications of a working woman's sexuality had advanced considerably since his first novel. Here Dreiser acknowledges that, in an age when unhampered access to birth control is still woefully inadequate, women must often pay a high price for their half of the sexual contract" (57–58). Indeed, Jennie is so fertile that she becomes pregnant after a single sexual encounter, symbolizing her innocence and natural fertility. To Jennie's German immigrant father, her unwanted pregnancy transforms her from virgin to "streetwalker" (85). *Jennie Gerhardt*, like *Sister Carrie* and *An American Tragedy*, was heavily edited by the publishers, who excised the only passage with a reference to birth control. Without even mentioning birth control, Lester's statement that a woman "doesn't have to have children unless she wants to" was too threatening. With this brief statement deleted, readers could only deduce, as in the earlier *Sister Carrie*, the infertility of young, healthy women was the result of birth control.[8]

Theodore Dreiser's 1925 novel, *An American Tragedy*, also explores themes relevant to the birth control movement, and indeed Ivan Bloch

8. We now have the restored edition based on the original manuscripts thanks to James L. W. West III. West writes of the extensive editing to the original novel at Harper Brothers: "Some 25,000 words had been cut, and the prose rewritten extensively. Profanity had been removed; slang spoken by characters had been corrected; virtually all mention of sex had been muted or cut.... The net effect had been to turn a powerful piece of social realism into a touching love story isolated from much of its context" (West, Introduction to *Jennie Gerhardt* xiv). See also Edward de Grazia, *Girls Lean Back Everywhere*, for a discussion of how Dreiser was affected by censorship.

reviewed it glowingly in the September 1926 *Birth Control Review*. The novel's protagonist, a simple factory worker named Roberta, is seduced and impregnated by Clyde. She attempts to procure an abortion, but when the attempt fails, she pressures Clyde into marriage. In response, Clyde murders Roberta. *An American Tragedy*, like the original text of *Jennie Gerhardt*, refers to birth control. This time, however, it treats ignorance of birth control as explicitly to blame for the evil that follows. Dreiser writes, "But there was this to be said in connection with the relationship between these two, that no time, owing to the inexperience of Clyde, as well as Roberta, had there been any adequate understanding or use of more than the simplest, and for the most part unsatisfactory, contraceptive devices" (368). Critics overlook this reference, but I argue that Clyde's ignorance of contraception is part of his larger moral cowardice. While the novel does depict one man's weakness and failure, when read in the context of the birth control movement Roberta's death and Clyde's downfall are clearly spurred by sexual ignorance.

Theodore Dreiser's depiction of premarital sex was controversial even though one-third to half "of women who came of age in the 1920s had had sex before marriage" (Coontz 200). He goes further in his fictional critique of marriage than the rhetoric of the birth control movement, which was courting widespread social acceptance to enact legal change. Dreiser celebrated "sexuality as the major driving force in life, holding it up as a force of progress endlessly engaged in battles against sexually repressive social conventions and institutions" (Gammel 32). By the 1920s, the birth control movement itself could not so openly forward the idea of sex and contraception outside of marriage without alienating the middle-class support it needed. Dreiser, however, tempered his radical depiction of marriage with a more traditional characterization of women. His heroines are sexually passive, which may be what redeems them finally in the public eye. They retain their innocence and are "good" and "natural" despite their sexual transgressions. Charles Glicksberg perhaps best explains the inherent tension in Dreiser's work between sexual daring and gender stereotype: "[I]t is not surprising that the treatment of the sexual motif in American literature is beset by a number of seemingly irreconcilable contradictions. Shall the writer defy the regnant social conventions and run the risk of not having his work accepted for publication? Then, too, since he belongs to American history and the tradition it has built up, he must reckon with the residual but still active force of Puritanism that has shaped his mind as well as the mind of his people" (6). Dreiser's struggle to push against traditional morality added to the public debate on birth control and marriage.

Two additional texts from the 1920s provide examples of the possibility for a new depiction of women and demonstrate how fiction can push artistic as well as ideological boundaries. In "The Probation in Literature," published in the January 1929 *Birth Control Review*, Edgar Wood Pangborn celebrates a new freedom in American fiction. Making a direct link between the aesthetic and political in literature, he notes, "Writing was invented to influence human minds; that purpose has not changed with the ages. Literature is the voice of life—but a mastering, urgent voice, not an echo" (14). For modern fiction to be vital and viable it must engage with the growing public discourse regarding sexuality, influencing rather than echoing public opinion.

Pangborn singles out Vina Delmar's *Bad Girl* (1928) for its "uncastrated language and expression of honest convictions" (14). He praises Delmar for her realization that "it is now possible, with one restriction, to say just about anything that needs to be said, and 'get away with it.' (The one restriction, of course, is the obscene legal Comstockery which prohibits any statements of contraceptive measures)" (14). In describing a sexual woman in modern courtship and marriage, *Bad Girl* provides an example of the New Woman who ultimately opts for the traditional female life narrative of marriage and motherhood.

Dot is a modern young woman rescued from a foray into unmarried sexuality by a marriage proposal. This traditional turn is bound up with the text's treatment of birth control. The novel's ambivalent stance on contraception corresponds to the inability of Dot and Delmar to consider other fulfilling roles for women. Vina Delmar provides several vague textual mentions of birth control, but it is something that her "bad girl" is too good to consider. When a friend mentions it, "Dot said nothing. She was not anxious to debate the pro and con of birth control" (Delmar 119). This lack of contraceptive practice leads inevitably to pregnancy. The novel devolves into a light comedy, depicting the miscommunication between Dot and her husband. They both want the child but discuss abortion when each believes the other is unhappy with the pregnancy. Birth control is equated with abortion, since the couple discusses it only after Dot is pregnant. This link between contraception and abortion and Dot's happiness with her prescribed role reinforce the plot of marriage and motherhood for modern women. While critics praised the novel for its honest discussion of sexuality, it hid a traditional message in a "progressive" wrapper.

Despite Delmar's conventional plotting for her modern "bad girl," American women were finding new opportunities through increased access to education and employment. At the same time as the "life plots" of women expanded, modernist writers were transforming the traditional forms of fiction. The modernist impulse to explore sexuality developed simultaneously with and from the same social conditions as the birth control movement. Indeed, calls for freer sexuality added impetus to demands for safe and effective means of contraception. The literary experiments of modernist writers such as Ernest Hemingway and William Faulkner often include the interruption of traditional female life narratives, such as the characterization of Charlotte in Faulkner's *If I Forget Thee, Jerusalem*. While these writers attempt to think beyond motherhood, they often write into another biological trap: death.[9]

A truly contraceptive text would imagine a new story for women, one that ends in neither motherhood nor death. The text would circulate new narrative possibilities for women in public discourse, much like birth control enabled biological control for women. However, since literature mirrors the age and ideologies in which it is produced, any contraceptive text would necessarily display the tensions and contradictions of working against inherited gender roles. One interesting example of such a text is Susan Glaspell's *Chains of Dew*, a play that both deploys birth control as its direct narrative impetus and enacts the textual contraception that I am proposing. Produced by the Provincetown Players at the end of the 1921–22 season, *Chains of Dew* was never published.[10] While Glaspell satirizes an overzealous birth controller in her depiction of Nora, she accurately depicts the inner workings of the movement, including the description of a birth control league office and its official rhetoric.[11] Glaspell does not use her drama as propaganda for the birth control movement, but rather uses the movement to explore new roles

9. This corresponds to the two traditional fictional narratives for women identified by Rachel Blau DuPlessis: motherhood and death.

10. The typescript is held by the Library of Congress; references are to this text. The play was not well received by critics, but rather dismissed as an underdeveloped sketch. Interestingly, the *New York Times* review by Alexander Woollcott does not mention birth control, focusing its brief plot summary on the male poet Seymore and his mother. Whether this odd omission indicates the reviewer's discomfort with the subject, or his gendered identification with the male lead, makes for interesting speculation.

11. Susan Glaspell had many social connections with members of the birth control movement. As a denizen of Greenwich Village and visitor to Mabel Dodge's salon, she would have discussed sexuality, free love, and birth control. She likely met Margaret Sanger at Dodge's salon or in Provincetown, a vacation spot frequented by the Sangers and by Glaspell and her husband, George Cram Cook. Glaspell was also a member of the Heterodoxy Club, a group of liberal Village women, along with birth control activists Mary Ware Dennett and Rose Pastor Stokes. See Gainor for a discussion of *Chains of Dew* and the birth control movement; see Schwarz on the Heterodoxy Club.

for women and the tensions inherent in their choices. As J. Ellen Gainor notes, "Although the movement is certainly important to the play, it is not exclusively a politically or socially motivated work" (186). However, *Chains of Dew* can be read as an artistic response to birth control that integrates a contraceptive ideology into its own narrative plotting.

Set during the birth control campaign, the main character, Nora Powers, is an unmarried birth control activist, a professional young woman who takes her identity not from marriage but from her commitment to the movement. Her maiden name indicates her independently "power"ful position. Nora is representative of the Greenwich Village "free lover," as multiple mentions of her short hair indicate. Her office, complete with posters comparing a mother of nine children to a mother with two, serves as the meeting place for her literary friends, including Leon, the editor of the *New Nation*, and Seymore Standish, a poet. These men are squeamish about birth control, arguing that it should be a private matter, and set up art (rather than politics) as man(kind)'s highest calling. When the two men tease Nora about her dedication to birth control, she responds with typical birth control rhetoric: "Do you wish to give birth to seven children you cannot feed? Have you no respect for children? A child has a right to be wanted. You bring into this world an impoverished, defective, degenerate—but here. I will give you our literature" (*Chains of Dew* 1.9). Thus, Glaspell invokes common birth control arguments to establish her character's values. Nora's work with birth control and her involvement with the married Seymore mark her as outside the realm of traditional values.

In contrast to the vibrant political and artistic life of Nora and the city, Seymore is from Bluff City, a small town where "they never even heard of birth control" (1.17). This lack of knowledge serves as shorthand for a backward, conventional and stifling way of life. In a move that mirrors the birth control movement's spread from urban to rural areas, Nora decides to be a "missionary," carrying the gospel to the wilderness of Bluff City. Here Seymore lives a comfortable life and exhibits conventional attitudes towards women, including his wife, Dotty. Into this world of tea and gossip comes Nora, who promptly convinces Dotty to start a local birth control headquarters. Although upper-class women in Bluff City have been quietly practicing fertility control, they join the public movement because, in their own words, "Birth control is the smart thing in New York this season. . . . The really exclusive people turned to birth control" (2.26). The shallow vanity of the Bluff City social set mocks the superficial lives that these women lead. Dotty, however, finds political purpose in the movement, and Glaspell's explicit stage directions visually mark

Dotty's turn to modern ideas: Dotty has her hair bobbed and replaces a Sistine Madonna image in the living room with Nora's family planning exhibit.

But even as Dotty begins to break out of the traditional wife-and-mother role, her husband's traditional gender expectations restrain her. Although she finds personal satisfaction with her new purpose in life, Dotty gives it up for Seymore so that things can be "just as it was before" (3.39). While this may seem to undermine the idea that *Chains of Dew* enacts the contraceptive textuality I have discussed, Glaspell clearly depicts Dotty as making a conscious decision. While Gainor argues that "[i]ronically, although women of their class may have learned how to control their fertility, they have yet to gain real control over the trajectory of their lives," Dotty cannot be understood as simply resuming her old role (Gainor 190). Rather, her decision to return to the traditional marks the difficulties that new roles bring to individual women and foregrounds the consideration of choice. The birth control movement provides the means for Dotty to come to full subjectivity and raises her consciousness such that her decision to succumb to Seymore's wishes, while deplored by current feminist readers, is in fact a rational one. Although Dotty returns to her traditional role, Glaspell leaves no doubt that the relationship will not be "as it was before." Dotty has begun a process of self-discovery that has altered the power dynamics of her marriage. And through Nora, who leaves Bluff City to continue her contraceptive crusade, Glaspell provides an alternative to the biological plot. Rather than a sacrificial spinster, Nora represents a single career woman who is young, attractive, and vital. Thus, her character presents a potentially viable alternative role, outside of marriage and motherhood, for female fulfillment. Birth control, as a political movement and as a method of biological control, offers a latent choice to women's lives, at least to women not constrained by race and class.

"A HUSBAND . . . A WIFE . . . ANd hER FEARS"
IGNORANCE AND FEAR

Rather than offering a radical feminist message about women's reproductive freedom, by the 1920s contraceptive advocates argued that birth control was necessary to a successful modern marriage. They downplayed what could have been threatening to social norms and presented birth control in the plain brown wrapper of traditional morality: birth control would only be used by married couples and would scientifically improve marriage and the lives of children. Thus, allowing women control over their reproductive lives was offset by the assurance that reproduction would remain within the institution of marriage and therefore within the frame of male control. This was a change from the earlier radical rhetoric of a woman's right to control her own body. When Margaret Sanger opened her first clinic in the Brownsville section of New York City, she advertised directly to mothers and served only married women. Indeed, not until 1972 did the Supreme Court overturn a law that prohibited the distribution of contraceptives to unmarried people in *Eisenstadt v. Baird*.

By the 1920s official birth control rhetoric presented ignorance of contraceptive techniques as injurious to marriage. This embracing of traditional values was largely in response to claims by opponents that birth control was immoral. Advocates sought to dissipate past public perceptions of birth control as linked to "loose living," especially prostitution and venereal disease (McLaren 232–33). Margaret Sanger herself "was painted as a dangerous radical bent on destroying the American family in order to achieve a subversive feminist agenda" and "blamed for everything from divorce, infidelity, and promiscuity to a lack of work ethic among oversexed men" ("Family Values in Margaret Sanger's Time"). Through careful self-presentation as a wife and mother, and by emphasizing the benefits to married women and children, Margaret Sanger placed birth control within traditional values.

This strategy of alignment with conservative values is much like that used by the movement among African American clubwomen seeking to change public perception of black women.[12] The women of the "New Negro" movement wanted to overcome the stereotype of uncontrolled black female sexuality by emphasizing the importance of respectable black women who followed the "natural" course of marriage and motherhood.[13] Much like their white counterparts, many middle-class African Americans supported the ideal of companionate marriage and saw birth control as a necessary component. Writers such as Angelina Grimke and Jessie Redmon Fauset depicted black middle-class families in their fiction to counter conceptions of black women as sexually licentious. For

---

12. See Morton on the negative depictions that African American clubwomen were attempting to disprove.
13. Not all African American women agreed on the benefits of birth control. See Berg on the connections between race and motherhood during the Progressive Era; see also Rodrique, "The Black Community and the Birth-Control Movement," and Simmons, "'Modern Marriage' for African Americans, 1920–1940."

instance, Fauset's 1928 novel, *Plum Bun*, describes the protagonist's middle-class black family as "[f]ather, mother and children, well-dressed, well-fed, united, going to church on a beautiful Sunday morning" (22). The white characters in this novel are more sexualized than the blacks, counteracting the portrayal of African Americans as primitive and hypersexualized that writers such as Carl Van Vechten were creating.

Much like their white counterparts, African American women writers sought a balance between repudiating sexualized stereotypes and embracing the benefits of birth control. Many African American women supported the birth control movement for its potential benefit to marriage. According to Johanna Schoen, "African American women were even more dependent on home remedies and abortion than white women were. Until the mid-1940s, the black press printed copious mail-order advertisements for douche powders, suppositories, preventive antiseptics, and vaginal jellies" (45). Viewing contraception as an aid against poverty and abuse, the Harlem Women's Political Association ran an educational lecture series in 1918. "Racial uplift" would occur through education, marriage, and scientific reproduction. But birth control could also be a tool of the modern woman, freeing her from overlarge families. In Fauset's *The Chinaberry Tree*, Melissa, who "had the modern girl's own clear ideas on birth control," rejects her fiancé's dream that they have eight children (132). Melissa wants to adapt the traditional plot for women, marrying but controlling the size of her family.

The goal of the birth control movement was to make information about contraception legal and widespread. Most young women entering marriage during the 1910s and 1920s were ignorant of effective birth control methods (and many of sex in general). This ignorance was a threat to marriage, as was the fear and disinformation that accompanied it. Mary Austin's 1912 novel *A Woman of Genius* provides an interesting look at this ignorance before the birth control movement began. Austin, a novelist, essayist, and feminist, reviewed several books on marriage in the *Birth Control Review* in 1927. In *A Woman of Genius* she describes married life in a small town as suffocating for intelligent women. The novel reproduces the cultural narrative of marital fear fed by ignorance: "nothing that pertained to the mystery of marriage reached us through all the suppression and evasions of the social conspiracy, except the obviousness of maternity" (90). This silence creates "a world all of the care and expectancy of children overshadowed by the recurrent monthly dread, crept about by whispers, heretical but persistent, of methods of circumventing it, of a secret practice of things openly condemned" (219). Taboo knowledge of birth control circulated in whispers to married women who feared more children, pregnancy signaled by the "monthly dread" of a missed period. The heroine's personal terror is of living a life like her mother: "in the country phrase, so appalling in its easy acceptance, my mother had 'never seen a well day'; and what was meant to be the joy of loving was utterly swamped for her in its accompanying dread" (19). For Austin's narrator, the whispered knowledge of birth control reaches her in time to protect her from her mother's fate. The subtext implies that fear of unwanted pregnancy is detrimental to a healthy marriage. Austin's friendship with Margaret Sanger, Emma Goldman, and H. G. Wells (another frequent contributor to the *Birth Control Review*) reinforces the pro-contraceptive stance of the novel, and Austin contributed articles on marriage and motherhood to the *Birth Control Review* in the late 1920s.

A concrete threat for married women, especially for the poor, was the physical danger of pregnancy. A common narrative thread in these texts is the toll of repeated childbearing on female health and the subsequent damage to marriage. The trope of the physically endangered mother recirculated social values such as a reverence of motherhood and played on the knowledge that pregnancy and childbirth were dangerous health risks. According to Wertz and Wertz, "after World War I women came to recognize that maternity was the second highest killer of women aged fifteen to forty-five, after tuberculosis," and maternal mortality did not improve significantly until after 1930 (155). Many of the propagandistic stories supporting birth control focused on the brave but fragile woman struggling against murderous maternity. These works played on women's fears to argue for lifting the veil of ignorance.

Other genres contributed to the public discussion on marriage and contraception. A rare film on birth control, *The Hand That Rocks the Cradle* by Lois Weber (1917), depicted three married couples (Stamp 286). Dr. Broome and his wife use birth control to limit their family size for the sake of the wife's health, and Mrs. Broome is charged under the Comstock Act with distributing birth control information. A sequence of flashbacks reveals the story of Sarah, a former servant, whose health and marriage had "disintegrated" after too many children. Only Mrs. Broome's contraceptive information saves them from poverty. A third couple are against "artificial" birth control and practice abstinence instead, but their marriage collapses under this method. The film carefully explores sexuality and birth control within marriages across a class spectrum. Ultimately, Mrs. Broome is arrested, tried, and imprisoned but pardoned after a heroic hunger strike (Stamp 286). The Film Board of Review deemed the film "impartial" and educational, but reviewers found its overt message "too preachy" (Stamp 287–89). The same message and tone, however, abounded in fiction.

While the birth control movement lost its radical rhetoric, it retained the strategic use of pathos in its fiction. These stories, often thinly plotted, complement the rhetorical work accomplished by the factual debate also found in the pages of periodicals such as the *Birth Control Review*. Rather than fully developing plot and character, these stories rely on melodrama to persuade readers that birth control is necessary. Remembering the period, Inez Haynes Irwin, a fiction editor for *The Masses*, stated, "A profound horror of the woman's life filled me. Nothing terrified me so much as the thought of marriage and child-bearing. Marriages seemed to me, at least so far as women were concerned, as the cruelest of traps" (39).

Most of the stories in the *Review* emphasize the destructive effects of uncontrolled reproduction on marriage, including several in which the desperate woman commits suicide rather than bear another child. "A Matter of Life and Death," a 1920 "playlet" by L. L. Pruette, depicts a woman driven to suicide by the despair of poverty and repeated childbirth. The nameless character would "sooner die than have another baby" and threatens to take "the bitter apple," a neighbor's abortifacient, unless the visiting social worker can tell her how to end her current pregnancy (13). The woman already has seven living children, one in jail and another "running wild," and five dead children. As the frantic nurse tries to wake the alcoholic husband, passed out in the corner, the woman drains the bottle of poison and dies. The medical profession and social workers cannot help to assuage the poverty and despair. In "A Holiday" (1921) by Ethel Watts Mumford, a pregnant woman contemplates her troubles—husband newly dead, two children at home, bills unpaid, and the loss of her cleaning job when her condition is noted—as those around her enjoy a patriotic orator in a sweltering city park. With no one to turn to, and the fear that her children would be taken from her if she cannot "scratch and paw the money of a scant wage," Mary is incensed by the public speaker's message of how lucky people are to have freedom. Driven by rage and despair, she drowns herself in the park reservoir (6). The author highlights the disjunction between the patriotic rhetoric of American good fortune and poor widow's reality, rendering the title of "A Holiday" a poignant irony. Both stories demonstrate the conditions that conspire to create situations in which suicide appears the best alternative to bearing another child in a broken marriage. Knowledge of birth control would alleviate these conditions, and thus implicitly save marriages and lives.

Although usually the female character commits suicide, several stories twist the plot by emphasizing marital love and having the husband commit suicide. In "The Magnet," a 1921 story by Mary Heaton Vorse set in an urban tenement, even the children know that pregnancy is not a joy to be celebrated. They play while listening to a woman's anguished cries: "Don't you know what for she cries—she *cries for why she's going to have another baby!*" Reba hissed the last words at Rosie. 'Babies is awful any time, but in lockouts, Jeze! they's fierce.' Reba made this self evident statement without emphasis. Everybody in the tenement knows it's fierce to have babies. Rosie had known that as long as she had known anything. Whenever her mother heard of a new baby, 'Poor thing!' she would sigh" (8). In the mouths of children the stark reality takes on additional pathos. Children grow up fast in the tenement: they know that marriage means babies, and babies mean physical pain and poverty.

Repeated pregnancy, even within a loving marriage, is a "terrible thing to do to a woman." The "anguished breathing of inhuman effort" and tortured screams of a woman in labor create a horrific scene in which to examine the consequences of uncontrolled fertility—broken health, increased poverty, and marital strain. In this story, Vorse depicts a husband who loves his wife and is frantic because "[t]he midwife won't come out unless I pay her—I—fifteen dollars—where should I get fifteen dollars—not a penny—a month too soon—on the street—the landlord—six more days—he won't wait—Oh God" (8). The next day, after the birth of his son, unable to find work or any sympathy from the landlord, the father comes up with his only solution: "There are asylums for orphans—widows with week-old babies—are taken care of," he says, before shooting himself in the backyard (16). An honest man, unable to find work, cannot support his growing family, and the only answer is state charity. The story demonstrates that the working poor deserve (rather than just need) birth control knowledge to sustain a loving marriage.

While location could determine important economic differences, the birth control movement sought to apply its message across geographic boundaries. Genevieve Taggard's sketch "Legend," in the July 1925 *Birth Control Review*, deconstructs in a single page the myth of the hardy, happy rural farm wife.[14] Using a party telephone line and first-person narrative, Taggard revises "the literary legend, started by Glaspell and Frost and O'Neil," by describing a thirty-year-old farm woman who decided

---

14. Genevieve Taggard was also a contributor to *The Liberator*, successor to *The Masses*. Many of the authors and artists discussed contributed to both *The Masses* and *Birth Control Review*, including Vorse, Floyd Dell, and Cornelia Barns, who joined *The Masses* in 1914 and became art editor and associate editor of the *Review* in 1921.

"[o]ne baby a year. Better die" (199). Her daughter "has vowed never to marry," as she equates marriage with endless childbirth. While this brief sketch does not describe conditions of poverty, it establishes that rural isolation and uncontrolled fertility lead to the same despair. In 1927 a montage of letters and poetry entitled "Four Farmers' Wives" reinforced Taggard's message of rural poverty, isolation, and despondency on married women.

A wife's fear of pregnancy's damage to relationships was one plank in the birth control movement's argument for widespread acceptance. The February 1926 *Birth Control Review*, for example, argued that "Birth Control will increase the happiness of the wife and mother by freeing her from the haunting fear month by month of a pregnancy that is undesired and unprepared for" ("Birth Control Primer"). A story published the same year in the *Review* reinforced this argument. In "The Nation's Backbone" by Louis Adamic, Minnie and Joe were economically successful and in love when they married, but seven years of marriage brought them seven children. Minnie, "her young-oldish face haggard and yellow, her dark eyes large, liquid and sunk deep into the sockets," finds herself with an infant of thirteen months, her newborn twins, and four older children (Adamic 252). Her health is so broken that she can't get out of bed and care for her children. This story is a vivid example of birth controller Frederick Blossom's argument for contraception to protect the health of mother and child: "Unregulated childbearing means a progressive decline in the mother's health accompanied by progressive debility in her offspring" (12). Bereft, Joe determines "that he and Minnie would bring no more children into the world. He knew that there was a method of preventing the birth of unwanted children, though he was unfamiliar with the technique. He had come sufficiently in contact with the sinful world to know that there was a safe and sure way of doing that" (Adamic 253). But abstinence is impossible for the young couple, and nine months later they have "another blessing, their eighth descendant" (289). What is "sinful" and what is a "blessing" take on opposite meanings from the way Joe innocently employs them. Adamic does not need to write the story's ultimate ending, as the reader can complete for themselves the inevitable tragedy of Minnie's death and the family's ruin.

This ignorance and fear affected women of all ethnicities. In her 1928 novel, *Quicksand*, Nella Larsen depicts a mixed-race protagonist coming to sexual awakening while searching for her identity. Helga Crane, whom Hazel Carby has called the "first truly sexual black female protagonist" in African American literature (174), answers a question about her marital status by responding, "Marriage—that means children, to me" (Larsen

103). Helga turned down the marriage offer of Danish artist Axel Olsen, equating marriage with ownership: "I'm not for sale. Not to you. Not to any white man. I don't care at all to be owned" (87). But later, tormented by unnamed sexual desires that cannot be expressed outside of marriage, Helga marries an unlikely man: the Reverend Mr. Pleasant Green, a "rattish yellow man" who takes her to a tiny Alabama town (118). As Allison Berg convincingly argues, "by consigning her rebellious heroine to marriage and motherhood, Larsen disavows Helga's illicit sexuality, mitigating its implications" (104). Marriage is again the expected avenue of female progress, and the only sanctioned outlet for female desire.

Even though Helga's sexuality is contained within marriage, the results are clear. As Ann duCille notes, through Helga's plight Larsen addresses "what having children can mean to a woman's physical and mental health, as well as to her independence" (87). Ignorance of contraception means that, for Helga, marriage is quickly followed by motherhood, which entails pain, resignation, and death. Death in childbirth is not unique to this novel. "The Gentle Lena" of Gertrude Stein's earlier *Three Lives* becomes "more and more lifeless" and dies in her fourth childbirth (Stein 241). Jennifer Fleissner argues that killing the protagonists in childbirth resists that normative maternity narrative (265). However, in reiterating the dangers of childbirth these narratives support an argument for contraception within marriage.

Letters from real women published in the *Birth Control Review* revealed that "husband and wife can be put asunder by the coming of too many children" ("A Menace to Marriage" 144). A series of letters entitled "Breaking Up the Home" contains "Mothers' Letters which show that the lack of Birth Control frequently causes disaster to the home" (208). These letters condemn abstinence, the only recognized form of "natural" birth control, as inadequate and unnatural for married adults. Sexual intercourse was a marital privilege, but if it led to repeated pregnancies in quick succession, it could kill the wife. Solving that problem through "self control" could damage intimacy and lead men to prostitutes and venereal disease. Knowledge of safe contraception, advocates argued, would strengthen marriage and the family on multiple levels. This argument gained force in the accumulation of pleading letters, tragic stories, and logical articles published. Advocates constructed a coherent narrative surrounding marriage and female health from multiple discourses, including articles such as "Family Limitation and Family Health," which argued that the health of the mother and existing children was a strong medical indication for birth control (H. Stone).

Knowledge often circulated in veiled and illicit avenues that fed women's fears. Although the Comstock Act forbade contraceptive advertisements, some products hid beneath a "plain brown wrapper" of euphemism. Advertisements for "feminine hygiene" products invoked an unnamed stress on young married couples. A series of full-page advertisements by the manufacturers of Lysol, appearing in the popular women's magazine *McCall's* in July 1933, reads:

The most frequent eternal triangle:

A HUSBAND . . . A WIFE . . . and her FEARS
Fewer marriages would flounder around in a maze of misunderstanding and unhappiness if more wives knew and practiced regular marriage hygiene. Without it, some minor physical irregularity plants in a woman's mind the fear of a major crisis. Let so devastating a fear recur again and again, and the most gracious wife turns into a nerve-ridden, irritable travesty of herself.

Using Lysol for feminine hygiene would ensure "health and harmony . . . throughout her married life." The restrictions of the Comstock Act and of "public decency" forced contraceptives to masquerade under the aliases of "female hygiene" or "marriage hygiene."[15] Advertisements for these products were widespread: a 1938 article in *Fortune* magazine reported 636 products sold under the euphemism of "feminine hygiene" ("Accident of Birth" 112). Female readers, to whom "irregularity" signals pregnancy, decoded the underlying meaning of "hygiene." Lysol advertised its function as a douche for "vaginal cleanliness," a cleanliness that included flushing the womb of sperm after intercourse.[16] Although the birth control movement carefully distanced itself from these companies, they both "sold" their products "for married women only." The headlines for these products, such as "Can a Married Woman Ever Feel Safe?" and "Young Wives Are Often Secretly Terrified," reveal the concurrent themes of marriage, ignorance, and fear that continued throughout the 1920s (Tone, *Controlling Reproduction* 494).

Both Mary Ware Dennett and Margaret Sanger "publicly condemned contraceptive advertising" (Sarch 38) to align birth control with science

15. See Tone (1996, 2001) and Sarch for a more detailed analysis of the marketing of feminine hygiene products and their relationship to the birth control movement.
16. Ironically, the douching products could also harm female health. As both Sarch and Tone (2002) note, the veiled advertisements for "female hygiene" did not include specific instructions for how to mix a douching solution, and the wrong mixture could be toxic.

and gain the medical establishment's support. Indeed, no advertisements for "female hygiene" products ever appeared in the *Birth Control Review* (which offered the women who bought it no practical advice as to contraceptive methods). Likewise, the fiction it published does not mention or condone feminine hygiene as a form of birth control. The *Review*'s attempts to distance itself from marital hygiene products represent its struggle to gain scientific credibility. This alliance grew in strength during the 1920s and 1930s, as Margaret Sanger focused on convincing the medical establishment to support a "doctors only" bill.

The Threats of Prostitution and Abuse

Even threats from outside of marriage, such as the illicit sexuality of prostitution, could affect women's health within marriage via the spread of venereal disease from an unfaithful husband to his wife. The U.S. government addressed prostitution and venereal disease as threats to public health during World War I, initiating a campaign to educate soldiers about prophylactics.[17] As Jake, the protagonist of Claude McKay's *Home to Harlem*, remembers, "When I was in the army, chappie, they useter give us all sorts o' lechers about canshankerous nights and prophet-lactic days" (206). While critics of the birth control movement argued that contraception would promote prostitution and harm the sacred bonds of marriage, advocates inverted this logic. For example, implying that opponents were dirty minded, Sidney Goldstein argued in 1922 for the natural purity of women, writing, "Women are virtuous not because they fear the consequences of sin, but because they reverence the right. No knowledge that we can place in their hands will shake the foundation upon which their ethical life is built" (196). Contraceptive advocates continued to place themselves on the moral high ground, arguing that birth control would eradicate prostitution by enabling husband and wife to engage in sanctioned sexual intercourse without the constant fear of pregnancy.

The discourse of prostitution as a marital threat also appeared in fiction. In "A Way Out," published in 1922, May Pierce Guest depicts the struggle of a young man who is caught between love for his fragile wife and his own sexual desire. After the birth of their first son nearly kills his wife, Ben is wracked by guilt and sleeps on the sofa, tormented by sexual desire. The passion of the young couple is plagued by the constant worry

---

17. See Solinger, *Pregnancy and Power* 98, and J. Carter, especially 219–20.

of "What if—What if? Oh no, there must be no chances taken!" (Guest 85). In part 2 of the story, Ben is tempted by prostitutes, but his "moral nature" prevents his sin. In the third installment, Ben is returning home when he meets a young woman selling the *Birth Control Review* on the street corner. He begs her to tell him "how to be happy, though married." "Can you tell me a way out? Can you?" (132). The final installment defies the predominant narrative script of tragedy, ending happily due to Ben's newfound knowledge. Guest paces her story from physical despair to moral temptation to the marital salvation of contraceptive knowledge. The longest, and by far happiest, story to deal with this issue, Guest allows her young married couple to avoid tragedy through the intervention of birth control.

Desperate wives seized upon contraceptive knowledge as a powerful life editor, erasing prostitution as a threat to marriage, just as it was by Guest's young husband. The voices revealed in a series of letters entitled "Family Problems," published in the March 1926 *Birth Control Review*, demonstrate how real women were searching for alternatives to the trajectory of marriage—motherhood—ill health—abstinence—prostitution. One woman's experience poignantly represents this script. Married young, she and her husband had two children in quick succession and now "are so afraid of having more that we have had no intercourse since before the birth of the second child, three and one-half years ago tomorrow" ("Family Problems" 88). This prolonged abstinence has harmed her marriage. "Although my husband says he is still faithful to me (and I have seen no indication that he isn't)," the woman writes, "naturally we are not very happy; we have a good many quarrels and he has told me a good many times that he could divorce me because of my refusing him" (88). Worried about losing her husband, the woman asks for help; she needs contraceptive information so that she and her husband can resume marital relations without the "dread" of more children.

Guest's rewriting of marital tragedy is exceptional and utopian, standing out amidst the despair that characterizes the genre. The majority of texts contribute to the argument for birth control by appealing to tragedy, ending with the continued ignorance of the characters to emphasize the goal of the birth control movement. Angela Oakes's "Nature," published in the *Review* in 1926, exemplifies this plot structure. Marriage for "pure genuine love" was followed by three living children and "those others, those children that couldn't live, those children who never were children at all, only illness and distress and trouble" (Oakes 10, 11). Told that they can't have any more children but not how to prevent them, the couple practices abstinence. After four years of sleeping in separate rooms and watching her husband grow distant, the wife confronts him only to learn that it is too late—his encounters with prostitutes have rendered him blind from venereal disease. While the story recycles stock characters and highly charged emotion, it adds to the popular discourse by showing that birth control, practiced within marriage, opposes prostitution and prevents venereal disease. The story also reflects a larger social concern with the spread of disease into "respectable" homes. D'Emilio and Freedman note that "prostitutes served as transmitting agents that spread the scourge of venereal infection from red-light districts to respectable households. As long as middle-class men patronized prostitutes, their wives and fiancées would harbor anxieties about the safety of conjugal relations" (183).

Oakes also writes within and against popular conceptions of what is natural. The "Nature" of the title is a natural sex drive, one that can't and shouldn't be repressed within marriage. John is powerless to resist: "I couldn't stand it, so I made believe those other women were you," sobs John. "I couldn't go against Nature" (12). Marriage and sexual desire are both natural occurrences. Why, then, is tragedy inevitable? The story asks, "Is it man's fault or Nature's?" (12). This question aligns birth control with nature and morality, counterpoised against the law and prostitution. When man and wife can enjoy married sex without the constant fear of more children, lustful husbands won't turn to prostitutes. Indeed, the eleventh reason for birth control given in the monthly "Birth Control Primer" (a regular feature of the *Review*) is "The Promotion of Morality," specifically that "Birth Control will attack the institution of prostitution and increase the stability of the family" ("More Reasons for Birth Control" 35).

In addition to prostitution and failing female health, alcohol and abuse also threatened marriage. Birth control advocates argued that the emotional and financial stress put on marriage by unwanted children led to abusive situations. Not only would birth control help husband and wife control the size of their family, but in doing so it would also allow women an easier escape from abusive situations. In a letter from the November 1926 *Review* a woman describes the physical and mental abuse she suffers: "I am 28 years old and the mother to be very soon of my sixth child. I am a farmer's wife. My husband is a drunkard and so very abusive. He tries to kill me and beats at my door. I have to hide the butcher and paring knives and the guns" ("Are These Fit Fathers?" 338). Such letters share the despair of women who are equally trapped by abuse and by their own uncontrollable bodies.[18]

The *Birth Control Review* set stories of abusive marriages in the context of articles and letters advocating the dissemination of contraceptive techniques. Percy Norwood Stone's 1922 story, "Consummation—The Story of a Woman's Soul," vividly describes an abusive relationship. A woman with "no spirit" sits surrounded by the filth of poverty as her youngest child wails. Her husband shows no interest in her besides a carnal lust. They have been quarreling because "[j]ust like I told you last night, we can't have any more kids." The man responds, "Aw, for Christ's sake, lay off that. You make me sick. You married me didn't you? And you knew what it meant, too, didn't you?" (202, 203). Stone emphasizes the degradation and brutality of the titular "consummation," marital rape on the wife's unresisting body as her four children, told gruffly to "turn over," sleep on the floor beside the bed (203).

The story's grim setting and tone argue that poverty and despair can bleed a marriage of love, making it little more than a prison. Stone transgresses the cultural assumption of mother love to emphasize the extremity of the situation. By linking the death of mother love to the ravages of repeated childbirth, Stone implies that birth control could have prevented the tragedy: "There was no conscious thought of the children already born. Gone was whatever maternal instinct she might have had in the struggle following her marriage six years before. There had been seven children born. Three had died" (203). In an attempt to gain power over her own body, the woman contemplates suicide. How would this marriage have been different if the couple had practiced birth control? When read alongside the letters written by real women, the liberating promise of birth control becomes clear.

Love and Marriage

Do these depictions of unhappy marriages, or marriages threatened by uncontrolled fertility, critique marriage? Perhaps, if only by acknowledging the prevalence of unhappy unions. But any critique is muted by the

18. Sanger received thousands of letters each year requesting information on birth control. In *Motherhood in Bondage* she compiled a representative sampling, broken down into chapters according to themes such as "Girl Mothers," "The Trap of Maternity," "The Struggle of the Unfit," "Marital Relations," "Methods That Fail," and "The Doctor Warns—But Does Not Tell." The January 1933 edition of the *Review* also provides an analysis of the letters received by the American Birth Control League from 1931 to 1932 in "What 7309 Mothers Want" (Boughton).

alignment of birth control with traditional views on the proper place for sexuality, a strategic position that strengthened throughout the 1920s. Examining the fiction that became part of this public discourse reveals the inherent contradictions in this mode of argument, the strain hidden beneath marriage's apparent ability to sanction sexuality. These works not only examined marriage but also implicated birth control as an aid across class and race. This cultural belief in marriage as the road to happiness surfaced in contemporary surveys:

> Presented with three alternatives, three-fourths of young women polled in 1943 preferred marriage and domesticity. Eighteen percent wished to combine marriage with a career, but less than one in ten considered a successful career as a single woman to be a desirable alternative. That most Americans sought marriage is not surprising, but that only 9 percent believed a single person could be happy indicated the power of the marital imperative. Women who failed to conform lived under a social stigma greater than that which had marked their forbearers. (Hartmann 179)

But the fiction of the birth control movement reveals the tension inherent in upholding marriage while changing conceptions of female sexuality, the incipient contradiction between the revolutionary potential of contraception and its strategic location within conservative morality. The fiction discussed in this chapter exhibits many of the contradictions in the logic of the birth control movement itself. The sentimental style of these plots makes birth control less threatening by using accepted and conservative modes. Cover graphics for the *Birth Control Review* reinforced these associations, often featuring classic family or mother and child images, such as December 1931's drawing entitled "Mother and Child" by Warren Wheelock (fig. 8). This tactic allowed the birth control movement to invade the sensibility expressed by many small-town Americans that "God punishes people who deliberately try not to have children" (Lynd and Lynd 124). By presenting birth control as a marital aid, the movement gained momentum and support.

Threats to marriage included the destruction of the mother's health, prostitution, and abuse. Birth control advocates argued that contraception was the cure to these problems, implicitly reinforcing the cultural plot of women's lives (marriage—sex—motherhood). However, in its claims that abstinence and coitus interruptus were "unnatural" and both physically and emotionally harmful, the movement also contributed to the growing acceptance that women also had natural desires. By allowing women

FIGURE 8. Warren Wheelock, "Mother and Child," Cover of *Birth Control Review*, December 1931. Reprinted with permission of Alexander Sanger.

to engage in sex without the risk of pregnancy, birth control implicitly validated female sexuality, even as the movement's rhetoric restricted its expression. While literary critics often consider the fiction discussed in this chapter sentimental and conventional, this mode of presentation was a rhetorical strategy, introducing potentially radical ideas in a plain brown wrapper for public consumption (much as mail-order prophylactics were disguised as innocuous packages).

The critiques offered were not of marriage itself but of problems within marriage. Birth control was not so that women could enjoy promiscuous sex, but to ensure that they were better able to fulfill traditional roles within the home. Although conceptions of marriage were reshaped by greater acceptance of sexuality as integral to normal development, the rhetoric of the movement remained conservative. This is rather ironic, since "[s]exual expression was moving beyond the confines of marriage, not as the deviant behavior of prostitutes and their customers, but as the normative behavior of many Americans," at least in part due to the growing availability of contraceptives (D'Emilio and Freedman 241). While the efforts of the birth control movement fostered this social trend, and no doubt benefited from the more open discussion, the movement kept itself rhetorically situated within conventional morality.

By depicting the psychological, physical, and economic consequences of involuntary reproduction, these authors both challenged and reinforced sentimental views of marriage. Their decidedly unglamorous depictions made implicit arguments for the necessity of birth control in improving marriage for women of all races and classes. While the fiction depicted the possible damage too-frequent childbearing inflicted on marriage, it did little to ameliorate the confusion over intercourse. Birth control contributed to the movement for freer discussion of sexuality and the growth of "sexual science," but depictions of fictional sex remained largely absent from mainstream fiction.

4

"Conscious Makers of People"

Achieving a Free Motherhood

> The most important force in the remaking of the world is a free motherhood.
>
> —Sanger, *Woman and the New Race*, 1

THE BIRTH CONTROL movement built a conservative position throughout the 1920s by arguing that, just as birth control would strengthen marriage, contraception was beneficial and indeed necessary to motherhood. The movement extolled motherhood in articles, illustrations, and fiction, reinforcing the mother figure in U.S. popular culture.[1] The ideal of motherhood that became prominent at the end of the nineteenth century continued to influence social policy and artistic production. Dana Seitler argues, "The figure of the mother emerged with new meaning and significance at the *fin de siècle* as a fantasy of moral idealism, a symbol of quintessential American identity, and moreover, as a privileged site of material and biological value" (62). For instance, in the 1908 *Muller v. State of Oregon* case, the Supreme Court upheld a state law prohibiting women from working more than ten hours a day, basing its judgment on social conceptions of women's role as mothers. As Justice Louis D. Brandeis stated in his brief, women needed protection for the "[p]roper discharge of her maternal function." Other protective legislation followed, making reproduction a public social interest rather than an individual woman's decision to become a mother. How did the birth control movement co-opt the figure of the mother to advocate for its cause?

---

1. While popular culture praised motherhood, more women in the 1920s were "refusing" motherhood by remaining childless, according to Cott.

Assessing whether birth controllers believed in motherhood as woman's natural role or if this approach was a conscious strategy to veil a more radical agenda is difficult. The growing notion that scientific control was a more ethical choice than "natural" motherhood influenced visions of motherhood. As demographers Paul David and Warren Sanderson have demonstrated, birth controllers adopted a two-child norm, revealing their own use of fertility control while maintaining the marriage/motherhood system. Just as birth control advocates did not suggest that contraceptives were for use by the unmarried, by the 1920s the mainstream movement would have denied that the purpose of marriage was anything other than to reproduce.[2]

As with the invocation of sexuality within marriage, the movement's supporters depicted contraception nostalgically, as a protector against the threats of modernity. If this seems counterintuitive, it was: birth controllers extolled traditional motherhood while arguing that contraceptive technology improved motherhood. In 1920 Margaret Sanger attacked modern motherhood, linking birth control to a nostalgic and utopian mother love: "How narrow, how pitifully puny has become motherhood in its chains! The modern motherhood enfolds one or two adoring children of its own blood, and cherishes, protects, and loves them. It does not reach out to all children. When motherhood is a high privilege, not a sordid, slavish requirement, it will encircle all" (*Woman and the New Race* 232). This appeal resonated with both women and men because it simultaneously revealed the practical dangers of maternity and upheld a sense of the mother as long-suffering and pure.

The ideological link between contraception and health led to a campaign among public health officials to include birth control in a comprehensive infant and maternal health program. Women's groups such as the Children's Bureau supported the passage of the Sheppard-Towner Maternity and Infancy Protection Act in 1921 to provide maternal and well-baby care.[3] Much of the period's pro-contraceptive fiction corre-

---

2. Stories and articles about single pregnancy began to appear in mass-circulation confession magazines in the 1920s, according to Kunzel. While single pregnancy was socially taboo, these magazine stories "rendered unmarried motherhood at once more public and more private: by making information about maternity homes widely accessible for the first time, these stories could relieve women and girls of having to confide in parents or doctors" (Kunzel 1466). Kunzel focuses her argument on stories after World War II. See Solinger, *Wake Up Little Susie*, for a discussion of race and single motherhood after World War II.

3. Many activists worked to improve conditions for women and children, but these groups, including birth controllers, did not agree on methods. Sanger's American Birth Control League argued that, without the ability to control family size, the Sheppard-Towner Act wasted resources. But the common belief that motherhood was an assumed

sponded with public opinion on the importance of mother/child health. Indeed, a wide range of fiction added to the discourse of motherhood and birth control, from simplistic poems reiterating the trope of mother-goddess, to experimental writers who assessed the reproduction of mothering and female control.

Fiction often includes a vision of the "natural" or ideal mother, and many critics have analyzed how depictions of the mother figure reflect social values.[4] When the trope of the mother is read in the context of birth control, however, these analyses place motherhood and birth control too easily in opposition.[5] Charlotte Perkins Gilman, an advocate of voluntary motherhood, or the right of a woman to deny intercourse to her husband unless she wanted a child, is one earlier writer whose views on motherhood appear in her fiction. Her 1915 utopian novel, *Herland*, reflects Gilman's belief that "the desire for motherhood, though not the ability to be a good mother, is inherent in the female condition" (Lane xiii). But while Gilman believed that all women desired motherhood, she created in her novel a form of female-centered telepathic birth control. The all-female society of *Herland* reproduces via parthenogenesis, and women control their fertility with a thought—the *desire* for children impregnates them.[6] One of the male interlopers in the novel remarks

---

practice for all women and that the conditions surrounding it needed to be improved as official public health policy linked these groups. See Ladd-Taylor, *Mother-Work*; Meckel; and McCann on the Sheppard-Towner Act; see Schoen on the fight for birth control in the public health system of North Carolina; see Rosen for an examination of "the political circumstances that led to deep divisions among women activists who shared a commitment to improving the conditions under which women mothered" ("Federal" 53).

4. Many feminist literary scholars discuss fictional representations of motherhood and childbirth. Burstein examines motherhood in texts by Jewish women writers, Daly and Reddy examine the position of the maternal subject as narrator, and Kloepfer looks at the mother figure in selected works of H. D. and Jean Rhys. Homans examines nineteenth-century women writers, while Hirsch takes a psychoanalytic approach. Brown-Guillory examines motherhood in twentieth-century African American texts. Hansen, Adams, and Cosslett discuss contemporary fiction. Poston argues that childbirth is ignored in literature and, when written about, is characterized by a male point of view and male language even if the writer is female. See Berg, Doyle, and Irving on race and motherhood.

5. Hansen, whose work focuses on fictional nontraditional mothers separated from their children, links second-wave feminism and "stories about mothers who give up or lose their children. Most obviously, in its critique of motherhood as a site of female oppression, feminism, *like birth control*, seems to threaten to take women away from the children they bear, or ought to bear" (19; emphasis added). This comment implies that birth control acts as a force separating women from their duty ("children they bear") or fate ("or ought to bear"). This negative view of birth control characterizes much of the work that focuses on literary representations of motherhood and childbirth. These works focus on women's attempts to write about childbirth, or on the mother/child relationship, thus offering more scholarship on maternal subjectivity.

6. Originally serialized in 1915 in Gilman's monthly magazine, *The Forerunner*, *Her-*

on the difference between this method and his own society's: "You see, they were Mothers, not in our sense of helpless involuntary fecundity, forced to fill and overfill the land, every land, and then see their children suffer, sin, and die, fighting horribly with one another; but in the sense of Conscious Makers of People. Mother-love with them was not a brute passion, a mere 'instinct,' a wholly personal feeling; it was—a religion" (Gilman, *Herland* 68). Gilman creates a utopian vision of true voluntary motherhood in a society where childcare is communal and all children are precious, in the process critiquing the inability of American women to exercise reproductive control. This utopian vision reinforced the role of woman as mother while inserting an inherent argument for female fertility control into public discourse.

Other authors, like Gilman, recognized the central role of motherhood in women's lives and in the larger society. They envisioned what having control of this process, being "conscious makers of people" rather than victims of biology, could mean. The ideal of motherhood was important in the birth control movement's rhetoric, and fiction offered the grounds upon which to experiment. How did the fiction forward the argument that motherhood was more sacred if it was limited? How did the "feminine" value of selflessness become a major battle in this war of words, encoded in arguments over economics and female bodily control? Was it more selfish to limit births, or to overproduce? How was birth control differentiated from infanticide and abortion? These questions build in complexity, and this chapter will follow that progression to analyze how birth control propaganda reinforced images of motherhood as part of its campaign to gain mainstream acceptance, particularly during the 1920s. This fiction adds to our understanding of the social discourse of motherhood shaping the terms of the debate that mediated female experience.

"Do women want children?"

"Do women want children?" asked the title of a March 1929 *Birth Control Review* article. The answer: "The experience of the Clinical Research Bureau Proves that They Do" (80). This evidence, taken from former patients of birth control clinics and gathered by the Clinical Research Bureau (founded in 1923 as a research center in New York City), reaffirmed that women naturally desire children. The cases cited emphasize the "blessing of contraception" in enabling women to plan

---

land was published as a novel in 1979.

FIGURE 9. "Dedicated to Voluntary Motherhood," cover of *Birth Control Review*, February 1921.

their pregnancies. Thus, in answer to their critics, advocates responded that birth control is for women who want to create a better home for their families through scientific planning. This logic was consistent throughout the run of the *Birth Control Review*, and indeed is still a strong undercurrent in modern-day thought.[7]

Images of strong, healthy, loving mothers are central to birth control literature. Mother and child images commonly graced the cover of the *Review*, often in iconography invoking a biblical Madonna. Photographs reinforced this visual rhetoric, modernizing the mother and child trope by combining the idea of scientific birth control with the natural course

---

7. Signs abound that motherhood is still the assumed female destiny. One strand of current birth control advertising feeds this belief. An advertisement for Depo-Provera contraceptive injection reads, "Sure I'd like to have kids. Eventually. Until then it's Depo-Provera." In my own experience, gynecologists encourage women in their 20s and 30s to drink milk and take a multivitamin with folic acid to help future embryo development even if the purpose of the visit is a prescription for birth control. And many states give women applying for a marriage license a brochure with similar advice.

of marriage and motherhood. This visual association of motherhood with contraception was reinforced by the subtitles, which changed regularly but often emphasized the well-being of children: among others, "Fewer Babies Better Born" (December 1927), "We Want Children of Choice Rather Than Children of Chance" (September 1927), "Dedicated to the Cause of Voluntary Motherhood" (October 1927), and "Fewer but Healthier Children" (February 1928) (fig. 9). Both the visual and written rhetoric reinforced the belief that women naturally want children. By repeatedly associating birth control with this image, the movement aligned itself with an ideology of sacred motherhood.

How, then, to reconcile birth control, which prevents pregnancy, and the constant romanticization of pregnancy and motherhood? Advocates argued that children must be wanted, that "the most important force in the remaking of the world is a free motherhood" (Sanger, *Woman and the New Race* 1). Thus, they criticized the conditions of motherhood, not the institution itself. In addition, while many of the stories and poems of the *Review* valorized the figure of woman as mother, other works complicated this simplistic association by distinguishing between glorious motherhood freely chosen and the bonds of unwanted pregnancy.[8] In Kate Mullen's short story "The Pregnant Woman" (1925), the protagonist enjoys a wanted pregnancy. The woman views her pregnant body as glorious and not "a dark thing to be hid" (170). Enraptured by her pregnancy, the title character feels that "[s]he was the great mother now, brooding, epic—god-like, as though from her warm breasts should soon flow milk to nourish man in the continuity of eternity" (190). Clifford Gessler's 1930 poem "Pregnancy" provides a brief example of a simplistic ode to motherhood. He extols the round, ripe body of a pregnant woman:

> You are the Race, you are the seeded Earth,
> you are the Torch that carries on the flame,
> and you are God made woman for a space.
> Now, as that inward glory lights your face,
> I, man, abase myself before your name
> and envy you the power of giving birth. (352)

The pregnant woman's creative powers should be worshipped by men. Healthy women experiencing voluntary motherhood are mythic mother-goddess figures, but uncontrolled fertility destroys women's health and

8. Other poetry and short fiction in the *Review* portrayed the mother ideal, including Katherine Mansfield's 1925 poem "The Mother," reprinted from the *New Republic*, which describes the feelings of a young mother holding her newborn son (317).

their ability to care for their excessively large broods; only birth control can restrain the excesses of nature and uphold the figure of the mother as goddess.

While many of the poems and stories in the *Review* valorizing motherhood were interchangeable with those found in popular women's magazines, others offer a more complex understanding of the pregnant body. Genevieve Taggard's 1925 poem "With Child" takes the perspective of the pregnant woman, awed and a little frightened by her condition.[9] Describing herself as "slow and placid. . . . Torpid, mellow, stupid as stone," the speaker enters a state of deep communion with her unborn child, an unthinking fecundity waiting for labor. This description is similar to Gessler's and Mullen's pregnant woman as ripe and natural. However, the poem, taken from Taggard's collection *For Eager Lovers*, reveals an ambivalence that was usually absent. Taggard's pregnant woman experiences the fetus as a stranger and an invader: "Defiant even now, it tugs and moans / To be untangled from these mother's bones" (344). The woman refers to the child as an "it" and herself as "big with loneliness." Engaged with the changes occurring in her body, the woman's experience is one not of unquestioned bliss but of fear and invasion. While the focus on the pregnant woman figure is consistent with other pieces in the *Review*, Taggard's poem does not participate in the simplistic idolization of motherhood but hints at the more complex analysis of the pregnant body made by modernist authors and published elsewhere.

Many of the propagandistic texts in the *Review* shifted the focus from mother to child while retaining strong sentimental appeals. These works adopt the consciousness of the unborn child, an effective trope often found in antiabortion works. In "Hymn of the Unborn Babe," the anonymous author writes:

Out of the Land of Children's Souls,
Comes forth this cry unceasingly:
"Mother of mine, mother-to-be,
Oh, bear me not unwillingly!" ("A Friend," 16)

Putting these words in the mouth of the unborn argues, in effect, that unwanted children would prefer never to be born. This powerful change in perspective shifts the ground of argument from the mother to the child.

9. Genevieve Taggard was also a contributor to *The Liberator*, the Socialist successor to *The Masses*.

This rhetoric established a discourse of rights—the child's rights, not the mother's. In the March 1929 *Birth Control Review* we find "Still Another Reason for Birth Control—The Right of the Child to Be Welcome" (67). Quoting from Sanger's "Woman, Morality, and Birth Control," the author argues that children are often harmed unintentionally when they are not planned for and wanted. Citing the "evil prenatal effect the emotional condition of the mother may have upon it," Sanger implies that unwanted children are often timid, fretful, feeble, and feebleminded.[10] She also critiques the unthinking "sentimentality about unfailing mother love," citing the strain and stress among poor women under which "the strongest mother love may turn bitter and cruel" (qtd. in "Still Another Reason for Birth Control"). The argument that bringing children into a world where they may suffer is wrong also circulated in poetry and fiction. This argument recalls the earlier socialist emphasis on economic injustice. George Lysander's 1918 poem, reprinted in the *Review* from the *New York Call*, addressed an unborn child. The poem transitions from a sense of wonder at the infinite variety and mystery of children, to a sad plea:

> O my beautiful babes! do not rush into this snare!
> You besiege the rotting doorways of infested tenements;
> You risk birth into dirt, disease, degradation;
> You must toil until you lose all sense of beauty;
> You will ache and agonize in body and spirit.
> You may be born on Fifth avenue and be unwelcome.
> Or on Canal street, where your brothers fight for food. (Lysander 4)

Entitled "Birth Control," the poem enacts many of the tactics used by the movement. The sentimental first half establishes a love for children, setting up the melodrama of the poem's later half, the direct appeal to the unborn not to seek entrance into the harsh world. The title clearly indicates that birth control is the solution. Advocates aligned themselves as sentimental lovers of mothers and children but insisted that it was their duty, for the sake of the children, to remind others that the world was not an ideal place.

The context of racial hatred in the 1920s and 1930s complicated images of mother love. The birth control relationship to better motherhood was reinforced by black leaders such as W. E. B. DuBois, who

---

10. The belief that a mother could "imprint" a physical or mental deformity on her unborn fetus was common in eighteenth-century medical debate. See Julia Epstein.

praised black female sacrifice and equated femininity with motherhood while arguing that a woman "must have the right of motherhood at her own discretion" (*Darkwater* 165). Motherhood is both the black woman's natural feminine and racial duty, yet, unlike during slavery, women should have discretion over their reproductive bodies.[11] Black clubwomen founded the "Little Mothers' League" for young girls, and *The Crisis*, much like the *Review*, featured pictures of mothers and children (Stavney 540). Anne Stavney notes "the defining characteristic of ideal womanhood became motherhood, and on this point many white and black men agreed" (538). Women as well saw motherhood as an ideology that could bridge racial divides. Writer Angelina Weld Grimke wrote, "If anything can make all women sisters underneath their skins, it is motherhood" ("*Rachel*: The Reason and Synopsis by the Author" 51). While black male political leadership and female activists praised motherhood, black women authors told a more complicated story. In a poem reprinted from DuBois's *The Crisis*, Georgia Douglas Johnson writes from the perspective of a mother who begs her spiritual children not to impregnate her body because the world is "cruel" and full of "monster men" ("Motherhood" 229). She writes in the poem "Motherhood,"

> Don't knock at my door, little child,
>   I cannot let you in,
> You know not what a world this is
>   Of cruelty and sin. (229)

The mother is protecting even her unborn children by ensuring that they are not born into a hostile society.

In their works of the 1920s, African American authors Angelina Grimke, Georgia Douglas Johnson, Mary Burrill, and Nella Larsen enter the debate over racism, motherhood, and fertility control. A loving mother would decide not to bear children, or would even kill her existing infants to protect them.[12] Stories and plays by Grimke, Burrill, and Johnson can be read as anti-lynching dramas, or "allegories of domestic and political

---

11. See D. Roberts 1997 on the relationship of race and reproduction; see Collins on how "issues of survival, power, and identity" are implicated in African American women's 'motherwork" (61).

12. See Dawkins on the trope of infanticide during the Harlem Renaissance. Dorothy Roberts notes that slave women might have committed infanticide "in desperation to protect their children" (*Killing the Black Body* 49). The legacy of slavery and the role of infanticide in black reproductive control, explored more recently by Toni Morrison in her award-winning novel *Beloved*, reveal how the greatest sign of maternal love can be murder.

protest" (English, *Unnatural Selections* 119). The stereotype that black men raped white women gained prevalence in the 1880s and continued to justify racial violence in the 1920s, when over 300 blacks were lynched (Bederman 47).[13] Daylanne English powerfully demonstrates how this violence inspired plays and stories that link lynching and infanticide. However, read more fully within the historical context of the birth control movement, we can further recognize the contraceptive argument in these fictions.

Two stories published in the *Birth Control Review* by Angelina Grimke sent the message that intelligent black people should reconsider having children when social racism is so strong. Published in 1919, "The Closing Door" is the tragedy of Agnes and Jim Milton, a happy young African American couple whose only sorrow is their childlessness. News that her brother has just been lynched in Mississippi mars the joyous occasion of Agnes's pregnancy. Stricken by the cruelty of the world, Agnes begins to see herself as "[a]n instrument of reproduction!—another of the many!—a colored woman—doomed!—cursed!—put here!—willing or unwilling! For what?—to bring children here—men children—for the sport—the lust—of possible orderly mobs" (October 1919, 10). She smothers the infant with a pillow shortly after its birth. By depicting the grim social reality of racism and brutality, Grimke's story argues for female control of the "instrument of reproduction" and leaves little doubt that birth control is preferable to insanity and murder. Birth control allows the woman to institute her own reproductive policy rather than following the dictates of racial betterment. Some critics, including Jennifer Fleissner and Gloria Hull, have been troubled by Grimke's choice to publish in the *Review*. Hull writes, "It seems somehow wrong that this tale of madness and infanticide would appear in such a journal and even more peculiar that the killing social reasons for Agnes's misfortune should be used as an argument for birth control among black people" (129). However, Grimke would have found a receptive audience in the *Review*, an audience familiar with many social ills. The birth control issue was complex, perhaps especially within the black community, where leaders like DuBois urged the survival of the race and black women's freedom to choose motherhood.

Impressed with "The Closing Door," the *Birth Control Review* solicited a story written specifically for its pages. In her 1920 "Goldie," Grimke returns to her earlier themes. Victor Forrest revisits the South to see his pregnant sister who had written that her husband had found out

---

13. See www.law.umkc.edu/faculty/projects/ftrials/shipp/lynchingyear.html.

about a white man "bothering" her. But Victor arrives too late and finds both his sister and her husband lynched: "Underneath those two terribly mutilated swinging bodies, lay a tiny unborn child, its head crushed in by a deliberate heel" (13). As Grimke makes clear, infants are no safer in this merciless society. The cycle of racial violence continues as Victor kills the man who had hurt his sister, only to then be lynched himself by the white townsfolk. These themes of racism and violence merge with an overall tone of futility, with the main characters isolated and withdrawn from the world. While Grimke presents motherhood as sacred, she also clearly implies that the world is too full of racial violence to bring black children into it. Although these stories do not explicitly mention birth control, they clearly do not advocate the birth of more black children and add fuel to the birth control movement. "All Art is propaganda and ever must be," DuBois wrote in his 1926 "Criteria of Negro Art," and he could have had Grimke's work in mind (*Writings* 1000).

The tension between the aesthetic and didactic functions of literature is evident in the critical response to another Grimke work dealing with lynching: *Rachel*.[14] According to Nellie McKay, some critics "objected to the propaganda aspects of the plot because they held firmly to the belief that black drama, as well as other forms of Afro-American creative writing, should focus strictly on artistic concerns and not become involved in political issues" (134). Grimke was accused of advocating genocide, her works interpreted as repeatedly arguing against black reproduction (Hull 121). But this criticism ignored Grimke's true audience: white women. Her play *Rachel*, staged in 1916 (but performed only three times) and published in 1920, used heavy-handed sympathy to convince a white, female audience of the tragedy of racism. An early title, *Blessed are the Barren*, reveals the play's message. Grimke characterized Rachel Loving as the perfect mother: set descriptions specify a prominent Madonna image, and the dialogue emphasizes Rachel's love of children and that she "is a graduate in Domestic science" (Grimke, *Rachel: A Play in Three Acts* 41). A close-knit, clean, and literally "loving" family, the Loving children are educated but cannot find professional work because of their race. Their father and half-brother had been lynched in the South when Rachel was very young, and even in the North they are snubbed and called "nigger." Confronted with racial hatred, Rachel decides that infanticide is preferable to raising children. She claims, "Why—it would be more merciful—to strangle the little things at birth" (28). Rachel struggles between her own love of children and the mounting evidence

14. *The Closing Door* was originally an early draft of *Rachel* (Hull 128).

that racism is cruelly destroying the children she encounters. She decides not to marry or to have children yet is haunted by dreams and visions of them. This is the tragedy: a woman so fit for motherhood will never have any and will indeed deny herself a loving marriage to ensure her barrenness. Indeed, the possibility of birth control within marriage is ignored, intensifying the tragedy.

According to Anne Balay, Grimke "rewrites birth control as the modern version of the protective infanticide whose appearance in Harriet Beecher Stowe's *Uncle Tom's Cabin* registers the pervasiveness of the practice in American cultural lore" (491). Like Stowe, Grimke writes to a white audience to influence their thinking on racial issues. Georgia Douglas Johnson also used the trope of lynching to present melodrama in which infanticide protects children from a violent world. In the 1929 play "Safe," the mother, traumatized by a lynching in her southern town, kills her newborn son. The Doctor's words end the play, reporting the tragedy that has just occurred offstage: "When I looked around again she had her hands about the baby's throat choking it. I tried to stop her, but its little tongue was already hanging from its mouth. It was dead! Then she began, she kept muttering over and over again: "Now he's safe—safe from the lynchers! Safe!" (384) The contradictory duties of black motherhood in a racist world is a theme in much of Johnson's work. In "Maternity," from her 1922 collection *Bronze*, the speaker fears that her child is doomed by the "mezzotint" of his skin, and wonders if she dare "[r]ecall the pulsing life I gave, / And fold him in the kindly grave!" (42). Infanticide as an act of love supports the argument that birth control was necessary to African American women in the 1920s, at least while lynching and other racist acts threaten children with violence and oppression.

Competing Mothers in *Mother*, *Weeds*, *Quicksand*, and *Ryder*

As pro– and anti–birth control forces wrestled over the definition of good motherhood, one field upon which they struggled was the issue of selflessness. Earlier in the century Theodore Roosevelt encouraged women to have children and stop the decline in family size. In a speech to the National Council of Mothers in 1905, reprinted in the *Ladies' Home Journal* as "The American Woman as a Mother," Roosevelt blames women for many of the nation's problems, including the looming specter of "race suicide":[15] "Unless the average woman is a good wife, a good mother, able and willing to perform the first and greatest duty of womanhood, able and willing to bear, and to bring up as they should be brought up, healthy children, sound in body, mind and character, and numerous enough so that the race shall increase and not decrease" (Roosevelt 3). The patriotic woman's duty was to marry and have a large family, and popular fiction reinforced this view, including Kathleen Norris's best-selling 1911 novel, Mother.[16] The text, praised by Roosevelt himself, reveals the romanticization of motherhood as a selfless act in the popular psyche. The novella, Norris's first (but not last) best seller, falls a few years before the focus of this study but provides insight into the context in which the birth control movement was operating, and the ideologies in which advocates were enmeshed.

Mother's title character is Mrs. Paget, a mother of seven who is romanticized as selfless and caring, serene and fulfilled. Her daughter, Margaret, is discontented with the genteel poverty and constant chaos of their household and dreams of a better life for herself than her mother's constant domesticity. Margaret states, "I've come to the conclusion that while there may have been a time when a woman could keep a house, tend a garden, sew and spin and raise twelve children, things are different now; life is more complicated" (12). Margaret's assertion that times have changed, that "you owe yourself something" other than domestic servitude, represents the modern ideas of the younger characters. But the novel presented these ideas as immature nonsense in the mouth of the selfish Margaret, and later replaced them with her womanly desire for home and family. After years of travel as the private secretary to a wealthy woman, Margaret falls in love with a man who idealizes Mrs. Paget, and succumbs to a romanticization of that role. The novel's title foregrounds its subject: Mother as role model and ideal of female fulfillment. As Anne Balay argues, this nostalgia creates an argument against birth control by enacting "a deliberate and effective intervention in the early twentieth-century debate about motherhood and reproduction" (472–73). That is,

15. Roosevelt is referring to the native, white, Anglo-Saxon Protestant "race." Black nationalist leader Marcus Garvey made arguments similar to Roosevelt's, encouraging black women to reproduce in order to ensure that the race would survive.

16. Kathleen Norris published over 80 novels as well as "hundreds of short stories, articles, newspaper columns, radio scripts, film scripts, and reviews" (Davison, "Sinclair Lewis, Charles G. Norris, and Kathleen Norris" 504). She was married to Charles G. Norris, author of Seed: A Novel of Birth Control, which is discussed in the next chapter. They were part of a literary circle including Sinclair Lewis, Theodore Dreiser, and F. Scott Fitzgerald.

Norris presents a simplistic view of motherhood as an alternative to birth control.

Kathleen Norris also plays upon class stereotypes in her argument for selfless maternity. The serene existence of Mother in her comfortable poverty contrasts against the wealth and beauty of Margaret's employer, Mrs. Carr-Boldt. Mrs. Carr-Boldt has only two daughters, indicating some knowledge of contraception. The size of Margaret's family is deemed "early Victorian" by Mrs. Carr-Boldt's wealthy friends, who discuss the benefits of a small family in this "complicated" world (111). Surrounded by luxury, Margaret at first adopts the wisdom of family limitation. But, as the "happy ending" demonstrates, this scene conveys an anti–birth control message. Norris depicts the indolent leisure of the wealthy gossips negatively, and Margaret realizes later that this life is selfish. Dr. Tennison, Margaret's love interest, waxes rhapsodically about Mrs. Paget, convincing Margaret that motherhood is woman's highest calling. "You know," Dr. Tennison muses, "in these days, when women just serenely ignore the question of children, or at most, as a special concession, bring up one or two—just the one or two whose expenses can be comfortably met!—there's something magnificent in a woman like your mother, who begins eight destinies instead of one!" (179–80). Only women who are frightened of responsibility would limit childbearing, he states. Deeply in love, Margaret sees marriage as her destiny and forgets traveling, a career, and "the idle ambitions of her girlhood," and dreams now only of the "miracle of a child" (185). The poverty of her childhood is forgotten in a wave of warmth toward her mother: "And suddenly theories and speculation ended, and she *knew*. She knew that faithful, self-forgetting service, and the love that spends itself over and over, only to be renewed again and again, are the secret of happiness" (189).

Mother reinforced Roosevelt's premise that "as for the mother, her very name stands for loving unselfishness and self-abnegation, and, in any society fit to exist, is fraught with associations which render it holy" (Roosevelt 3–4). Female happiness is found in selflessness, and through the daily drudgery of childbirth, childcare, and housekeeping she achieves sainthood. The female readers of *Mother* would have found its premise familiar, since this lauding of motherhood also was a common theme in magazine fiction. Ellen Hoekstra has shown that "[m]otherhood in the magazine fiction is considered a sacred office, for which a woman's superior intuitions particularly fit her. To a woman, motherhood is the ultimate fulfillment" (49). The extreme of this ideology led to the anti-contraceptive idea that any interference with fertility is murder. Margaret herself comes to this realization during her rapturous awakening to true womanhood: "Good God! That was what women did, then, when they denied the right of life to the distant, unwanted, possible little person! Calmly, constantly, in all placid philosophy and self-justification, they kept from the world—not only the troublesome new baby, with his tears and his illnesses, his merciless exactions, his endless claim on mind and body and spirit—but perhaps the glowing beauty of a Rebecca, the buoyant indomitable spirit of a Ted, the sturdy charm of a small Robert" (K. Norris 194–95). This encapsulates Margaret's final stand on motherhood and birth control at the novella's end, and readers who sympathized with her youthful emotions throughout are brought to this conclusion with her. (Perhaps a few wiser readers realized that her mind may continue to change as she experiences the demands of childbirth and a large family.) It is easy to see why this novella "served as anti-birth-control propaganda, and was often given as a gift to engaged couples" (Balay 481). Following the classic romance plot that scripts women's lives from childhood to love, marriage to motherhood, *Mother* exemplifies fiction that perpetuated the ideology of natural and noble maternity.

While Kathleen Norris sent a message for all women to breed without efforts to control their fertility, her depiction of motherhood was surprisingly similar to that of the birth control movement's official propaganda in the 1920s. The movement aligned itself with idealized depictions of motherhood to attract supporters with conservative values. Thus, Norris's Mother is much like the serene mother figures in many pro-contraception texts. However, while grounded in the familiar mother-goddess, many pro-contraceptive texts complicated this message by focusing on conditions that improve motherhood. For instance, rather than the genteel, shabby poverty of Mrs. Paget, birth control fiction would depict the suffering of real poverty.

Mrs. Paget is selfless, and Margaret decides that it is selfish for a woman to "interfere" with nature. But advocates of contraception argued that the true selfishness was to bring children into the world who couldn't be properly cared for. Many American writers investigated the material conditions under which women mother, shifting the focus from the reproduction of a healthy state apparatus to the individual experience of women. These texts, by authors such as Edith Summers Kelley, Nella Larsen, and Djuna Barnes, present pro-contraceptive narratives of motherhood.[17] These authors reject the romantic vision of Kathleen

17. See chapter 5 for a discussion of the eugenic implications of Ellen Glasgow's *Barren Ground*, Edith Summers Kelley's *Weeds*, and Nella Larsen's *Quicksand*. Allison Berg notes that Kelley may have taken the title of her novel from the 1922 short story "Weeds" by Richard Connell, published in the *Birth Control Review* (and discussed in the next chapter.)

Norris's self-sacrificing Mother, focusing instead on how class shapes the maternal experience.

Women did not experience marriage and motherhood in any universal way due to class, race, and other variables. Edith Summers Kelley's 1923 novel, *Weeds*, powerfully indicts popular conceptions of women's marital and maternal fulfillment.[18] Kelley focuses on the material conditions that affect female experiences of motherhood, depicting the toll this self-sacrifice takes on women's physical and mental health. Kelley narrates her protagonist Judith's journey from youthful hope to total exhaustion from her daily struggle as a tenant farmer and mother. Judith begins to view her children as parasites: "In such moments she hated them both, the born and the unborn, two little greedy vampires working on her incessantly, the one from without, the other from within . . . bent upon drinking her last drop of blood" (208). Motherhood is a competition for scarce resources and literal existence between woman and offspring. This physical struggle, with its life and death implications, is also present in childbirth. A chapter depicting Judith's first childbirth experience, cut from the original novel by an editor but included in the 1996 Feminist Press edition, graphically describes the violence of childbirth. Judith's body is out of her control, "driving, driving, driving, with the force and regularity of some great steel and iron monster" (345). She is dehumanized, an automaton, her body invaded and monstrous, and in other passages animalistic. Kelley wrote nearly seventeen pages depicting the graphic physical violence of childbirth in the original manuscript.

In *Why Women Are So* (1912), Mary Coolidge blamed women's fiction for perpetuating the silence surrounding sex and reproduction: In these romantic tales, she writes, "there were no puzzling and inevitable facts of nature—the lover was always pure and brave and considerate; the heroine beautiful and adored. There was no baby even, as in real life, to precipitate difficulties, except on the last page" (16). Kelley writes beyond the event of marriage, which ends the "roseate fiction" that Judith and her sisters read, romances that "allus ends when they git married. . . . They never tell what happened after. All they say is that they lived happy ever after" (120). This narrative trajectory allows *Weeds* to explore women's experiences within marriage and motherhood, including unwanted pregnancy. Judith's third child is unwanted, and she attempts to abort her fourth pregnancy, using the folk remedies of a wild horseback ride, a knitting needle, and "[p]ennyroyal and tansy and other

---

18. In *Mothering the Race*, Allison Berg presents a carefully developed reading of mothering in *Weeds* and *Quicksand*. See chapters 4 and 5.

noxious herbs" (285–86). This combination, and a failed suicide attempt, brings on the desired miscarriage, after which Judith sleeps apart from her husband. But when he begins sleeping with another woman to fulfill his "natural desires," Judith becomes resigned to her biological fate: "Henceforth she would accept what her life had to offer, carrying her burden with what patience and fortitude she could summon. She would go on for her allotted time bearing and nursing babies and rearing them as best she could" (331). The dehumanized language of the first childbirth scene is repeated, as Judith feels "like a dog tied by a strong chain" (330). Marriage may be the romantic goal of young girls who read romance novels, but once those vows are given motherhood seems inevitable. In the process, Judith becomes alienated from her previous identity as an artist and from her husband and children. Without birth control, Judith is doomed to reproduce the fate of her own mother, who died after three miscarriages and five live births.

Kelley supports an argument for birth control in her rejection of sentimental images of marriage and motherhood. A longhand revision of a draft of *Weeds* that was not included in the published version makes this point explicitly. Kelley writes, "Mrs. Sanger should send an apostle into these wilds," implying that birth control would ease Judith's hardships (qtd. in Berg 159). Although this reference was cut from the published text, *Weeds* contains many allusions to contraception, such as Judith's neighbor Hat's childlessness. Contemporary critics, such as Lawrence Stallings of the *New York World*, read the novel within the context of the birth control movement. Stallings wrote, "One may not accuse Miss Kelley of having written a pamphlet in a circuitous way to avoid those of the clergy who refuse the women of the poor the knowledge of birth control. She does not even suggest that a benign Government might issue pamphlets on the scientific breeding of the human race along with its gratuitous information as to the scientific breeding of hogs. She is too good a novelist for that, and she has a story to tell. The reader may draw his own conclusion as he witnesses the gradual disintegration of a woman's soul" (qtd. in Berg 185). Kelley's focus on the material conditions of motherhood challenge the predominant image of the selfless mother, inserting into popular discourse a more complicated exploration of female reproductive destiny.

Harlem Renaissance author Nella Larsen also offers a novel of the effects of motherhood on female identity that implicates selfishness and selflessness. To Helga Crane, the protagonist of Larsen's *Quicksand* (1928), physical reproduction leads to the loss of artistic and creative production. The novel does not focus on maternity but equates Helga's marriage and pregnancies with quicksand, sucking her inexorably toward death. "The children used her up," Larsen writes, leaving Helga "sinking into chairs" or "clinging desperately to some convenient fence or tree, waiting for the horrible nausea and hateful faintness to pass" (123). Larsen rejects marriage and motherhood as a happy ending, depicting instead the destructive impact of maternity on a woman who is not physically or mentally suited for it. Helga married to fulfill her sexual desires, a "selfish" motivation. Larsen glosses over Helga's early years as a mother, showing her later torn between wanting "to escape from the oppression, the degradation, that her life had become" and the knowledge that to leave her children "would be a tearing agony, a rending of deepest fibers" (135). Larsen ends the novel with Helga trapped in a cycle of endless childbearing that will surely end in death.

Nella Larsen's literary exploration of female sexuality is indicative of the growing willingness to explore sexuality in the 1920s. Other modernist writers, such as Djuna Barnes, experimented with fictional techniques, including shifting narrative perspective and altered chronology, to write about the taboo themes of abortion, unmarried sexuality, polygamy, homosexuality, and birth control. Published in 1928, *Ryder* was Barnes's first novel and was briefly a best seller. It provides a very untraditional portrayal of marriage and motherhood, as Wendell Ryder condemns monogamy and marries two wives. These female characters experience motherhood as "biological entrapment," to use the phrase of another modernist author, Ernest Hemingway, in *A Farewell to Arms* (1929). In its depiction of multiple generations, *Ryder* demonstrates what Nancy Chodorow named the "reproduction of mothering," or the socialization of women into mothers. However, in *Ryder* this education emphasizes the suffering of repeated childbirth. In the novel's second chapter a woman in labor is described as "a terrible suffering centre without extremities" (8). She dies shortly after the birth of her fourteenth child, leaving the newborn in the arms of her oldest daughter. Thus, while pregnancy kills one woman, it reproduces the mother role in her daughter. Chapter 13, "Midwives' Lament," is a short poem about a woman who

> died as women die, unequally
> Impaled upon a death that crawls within;
> For men die otherwise, of man unsheathed
> But women on a sword they scabbard to. (93)

This brief but graphic poem shows women threatened by the life they contain while punning on the penis as sword. The greatest threat to the woman warrior, then, is her own uncontrolled fecundity. Throughout *Ryder*, Barnes emphasizes the physical dangers of motherhood, undermining the image of motherhood as natural, uncomplicated, and fulfilling.[19]

In *Ryder*, mothers advise daughters not to marry or have children, a discursive attempt to end the reproduction of mothering. Ryder's wife Amelia tells her daughter, "don't let a man touch you, for their touching never ends, and screaming oneself into a mother is no pleasure at all" (117). Giving birth is a painful transformative process from "woman" to "wife" to "mother," with man's touch as catalyst. Kate, Ryder's other wife, feels trapped by motherhood and declares, "I'll kill it the minute it's born, but I'll bear it! . . . I'll stand over it like a distempered bitch before a wailing litter, and I'll stamp it into the ground, and be done with your filth! . . . I'll have my children, one, two, three, a dozen! until the mould breaks, and I'll stamp on them" (224). This passage disturbingly shows the psychological effects of uncontrolled fertility and depicts not the idyllic Madonna image but woman as violent animal, "a distempered bitch" dropping a litter, a body out of control.

Although Kate refers to a dozen children, family size declines through the generations of the Ryder family. As Sheryl Stevenson notes, this decline correlates with historical patterns, such that early generations have large numbers of children while later generations have only three or four. Although Barnes does not explicitly discuss birth control in *Ryder*, the text implies its presence through the decline in family size. As Stevenson notes, that Wendell's mother "probably benefited from some birth-control method (if only the currently most popular method, withdrawal) is suggested not only by the fact that she stopped having children so quickly, but also by hints that she continued to have many lovers" (100). Thus *Ryder* integrates historical trends in declining family size and infant mortality into its critique of motherhood.

Reading Djuna Barnes's experimental novel, *Ryder*, in the context of the birth control movement reveals how the cultural image of the selfless wife and mother became a contested issue within public discourse and served as one site for the acceptance of contraception. The novel contains many of the messages found within birth control arguments, such

---

19. According to Richard and Dorothy Wertz, maternal mortality peaked in 1920 at 90 deaths per 10,000 live births. It dropped steadily afterwards, due in part to increased use of hospitals for delivery, use of penicillin and antibiotics to fight puerperal fever, and advances in blood transfusion techniques (see especially 162). Maternal mortality rates for non-white women were up to three times higher than for white women. See also Hartmann 174–76.

as the evils of large families to women's health. Indeed, the stories of the female characters in *Ryder* correlate with the letters published in the *Birth Control Review* and collected in Sanger's *Motherhood in Bondage*. Many of these letters depict a state of "enslaved maternity," women trapped by their own bodies into repeated childbearing, broken health, and poverty. These voices merge with the voice of Barnes's characters, creating a space where women learn to articulate their ambivalence over morality and scientific control of the natural. Amelia Ryder tells her daughter, "Once I was safe enough and I could not let well enough alone, but must get myself in the way of doom and damnation by being natural" (95). Perhaps with birth control, the real letters to Sanger and the *Review* suggest, a woman could "be natural" without getting "in the way of doom and damnation" (95).

While Barnes employs arguments for birth control, she explicitly fought the same censorship law that so impeded the birth control movement. Even though she did not discuss contraceptive method, Barnes's descriptions of sexual intercourse caused her novel to be censored. Rather than rewrite her work, as Theodore Dreiser had earlier, Barnes published *Ryder* with stars to mark where text had been deleted by censors. In the preface she criticized the damage censors inflicted upon the "sense, continuity, and beauty" of her text (xi).

"Birth Control as a Prevention of Abortion"

The birth control movement established itself firmly against abortion as a way of aligning with traditional values such as motherhood. This section's heading is the title of an article by Benjamin T. Tilton, M.D., printed in the March 1925 *Birth Control Review*. Although illegal during the period of the American birth control movement, abortions could be procured from some sympathetic doctors, and "many women induced their own abortions at home. At drugstores, women could buy abortifacients and instruments, such as rubber catheters, to induce abortions" (Reagan 1245).[20] The public largely viewed both birth control and abortion as

20. According to Beisel, "Abortion, which during the first half of pregnancy had been legal in virtually all of the states until the 1850s, and which by 1870 was, according to physicians, moralists, and historians, still commonly practiced, if illegal, had become symbolic of the collapse of civilization" (25). Beisel notes, "During the early-nineteenth century abortion had been practiced primarily by desperate and unmarried women, but by midcentury married women increasingly used abortion to control the size of their families. Abortions were accomplished either through ingesting medicines that would end 'blocked menses,' poisoning the fetus without, hopefully, fatally poisoning the mother, or by resort

illicit practices, and the movement worked hard to remove the associative taint by consciously and vehemently arguing the difference between the two. Indeed, reason ten of the "Birth Control Primer," a regular feature of the *Review*, is "The Abolition of Abortion and Infanticide." "Year by year, in spite of prohibitory legislation, the murder of unborn children goes on, has gone on until it constitutes the scandal and tragedy of both Europe and America," continues the "Primer." The *Review* quotes from birth control advocates who abhorred "The Curse of Abortion" to overcome the common linkage in the minds of the general public. As Tilton argued, "Not only has Birth Control nothing in common with Abortion but it is a weapon of the greatest value in fighting this evil" (71).

By establishing abortion as an evil, the movement could set up contraception as a preventive of evil, and therefore as a good. Birth control would help to "eradicate this criminal practice" and save the "thousands of women who die annually from the effects of these illegal operations and other thousands become chronic invalids or permanently sterile" (Tilton 71). Tilton and other birth control advocates, such as Frederick Blossom, were careful not to blame the women who find themselves pregnant for the tragedy of abortion; rather, the blame rested "upon those forces of church and state which insist that these women be kept in ignorance of how to prevent pregnancy and thereby forestall any need of abortion" (Blossom 12).

Letters from readers of the *Review* supported the argument that contraception would eliminate abortion. Letters in the July 1923 issue, collectively entitled "Prevention or Abortion—Which?" set up a choice between two crimes: abortion or bringing an unwanted child into the world. One woman writes, "Since my last little girl was born, I can safely say I have been pregnant 15 times, most of the time doing things myself to get out of it and no one knows how I have suffered from the effect of it, but I would rather die than bring as many children into the world as my mother did and have nothing to offer them" (181–82). Other letters echo this woman's words and the painful choice they must make. These women have had abortions but found it "repugnant" and "sinful." They want reliable contraception to end the need for abortion and allow them to be better mothers to their existing children.

Although the fiction in the *Review* praised voluntary motherhood, it by no means advocated abortion for the woman who found herself pregnant when she didn't wish to be. Rather, writers made the argument for

---

to mechanical means of abortion, such as injecting water into the uterus or rupturing the placental membranes with instruments" (26). For a discussion of how the state enforced criminal abortion laws, see Reagan.

planned prevention. This allowed birth controllers to present their cause as a moral fight against the "great evil" of abortion. The *Review's* fiction never depicts women having abortions or receiving information about them. Indeed, the stories reference abortion only occasionally as an unnamed but understood evil that kills the woman who was driven to it. The authors condemn abortion while demonstrating the lengths to which a woman faced with unwanted pregnancy will go. Thus birth control, the moral alternative, would save the life of the mother and lead to future wanted children.

While the prevention of abortion was often the subtext of the *Review's* fiction, other writers made abortion an explicit topic in their works. While literary scholars have studied the role of abortion in fiction, especially women's fiction, they have not looked at the relationship between abortion and arguments for birth control.[21] These works implicitly assert the value of contraceptive knowledge by depicting the desperation of unwanted pregnancy. Authors provide insight into social perceptions of the "great evil" of abortion and the changing sexual reality. Not bound by an expressly political purpose of changing the laws regarding contraception and abortion, Theodore Dreiser, Ernest Hemingway, and others could explore the issues through their writings of the 1920s.[22]

Most abortions were performed on married women who already had several children, demonstrating yet again how marriage could sanction some otherwise illicit practices if the woman's motherhood was already established. In T. S. Eliot's *The Waste Land* (1922), the section "A Game of Chess" is based on the link between marriage and motherhood. One middle-class woman recounts a conversation to another woman in a British pub. The question "What you get married for if you don't want children?" succinctly summarizes a common logic used by anti-contraceptive rhetoric: the purpose of marriage is to have children, so why get married if you don't want any? But the question is facetious, as the conversation in which it is asked clearly shows. The woman who is being asked is the mother of five already. It is not a question of not wanting any children, then, but of wanting to control how many and when. The conversation demonstrates the pressures on women within marriage, as discussed in the previous chapter, and the need for birth control to end

21. See Barbara Johnson and Judith Wilt on abortion in fiction. Many critics have examined the trope of abortion in works by specific authors of this period. For example, see Parry on Sinclair Lewis; Hollenberg on H. D. and Kay Boyle; Henninger, Urgo, and Eldred on Faulkner; Koloze on Lorraine Hansberry; and Renner on Hemingway's "Hills Like White Elephants."

22. Abortion became more accepted during the Depression, as will be discussed in chapter 6.

abortion. The woman feels she can't ask her husband for abstinence, as her friend warns, "he wants a good time, / And if you don't give it him, there's others will" (1416). She has already attempted to control her fertility with the last unwanted pregnancy, buying pills from a druggist in the hopes she'll miscarry: "It's them pills I took, to bring it off, she said. / (She'd had five already, and nearly died of young George.) / The chemist said it would be all right, but I've never been the same" (1417). Her health broken, and afraid to refuse her husband, the woman is caught in a conundrum that could be solved with reliable birth control. As Eliot realizes, even within marriage women need birth control or they will resort to abortion.

Other American authors of the 1920s depicted women seeking abortions to end an unwed pregnancy, including Theodore Dreiser in *An American Tragedy*.[23] The text supports the argument of Sanger and others that birth control would prevent abortion. When Roberta finds herself pregnant, and her lover, Clyde, unwilling to marry her, she feels trapped. At Clyde's suggestion she visits a doctor and, posing as a married woman who can't afford more children, asks for an abortion.[24] As the letters to the *Review* discussed above suggest, married women most often sought and could find abortions, even though most doctors were not sympathetic and were wary of legal repercussions. The doctor Roberta approaches replies, "There are those who feel it quite all right if they can shirk the normal responsibilities in such cases as to perform these operations, but it's very dangerous, Mrs. Howard, very dangerous legally and ethically as well as medically very wrong. Many women who seek to escape childbirth die in this way. Besides it is a prison offense for any doctor to assist them, whether there are bad consequences or not" (403). Roberta also tries "preventatives" that Clyde procures from a druggist to bring on a miscarriage. In the end she dies not from an illegal abortion but from her inability to get one: that is, Clyde murders her because he feels trapped by Roberta and her pregnancy. Dreiser's references to Clyde's ignorance of birth control and his conviction after Roberta's unwanted pregnancy

23. The rate of illegitimate births rose throughout the eighteenth and nineteenth centuries, according to sexual historians John D'Emilio and Estelle Freedman (41, 42, 52). This trend generally continued during the first half of the twentieth century as strictures on premarital relationships relaxed somewhat. Hartmann notes that "during the Forties women demonstrated an increasing tendency to have children outside of marriage, as the rate of births to single women doubled during the decade. In 1940, single women bore children at the rate of 7.1 per 1,000 women aged fifteen to forty-four; by 1950 the rate had reached 14.1" (179).

24. According to Reagan, husbands involved in helping wives obtain an abortion were rarely arrested, but lovers were—revealing the importance of marriage in the eyes of the state (1260–61).

that "never again, without knowing a lot more than he did now, would he let himself drift into any such predicament as this" indicate that birth control could have prevented the tragedy of Roberta's death and Clyde's execution (376).

Authors treated abortion as an escape from enforced maternity (and paternity) in tones from tragedy to satire. Dorothy Parker's 1924 short story "Mr. Durant" takes on extramarital sex and illegal abortion as the topic of its satire. The blustery, self-satisfied businessman Mr. Durant has an affair with Rose, an office worker. When he finds out she is pregnant, Mr. Durant decides, "Cases like this could be what people of the world called 'fixed up'—New York society women, he understood, thought virtually nothing of it" (Parker, "Mr. Durant" 27). But he finds that he really knows nothing about how to get it done or whom to ask. While rumors float about the availability of abortion, especially among the wealthy, specific information was hard to find. Although respectable Mr. Durant is ignorant, one of Rose's friends knows of "a woman," and Mr. Durant provides the $25 fee. Parker sketches an emotionally distraught Rose and a callously shallow Mr. Durant, an exploitative sexual dynamic. Ignoring Rose's distress, Mr. Durant "chuckled" about his close call and immediately begins eyeing other young women. Parker satirizes Mr. Durant's middle-class values, his self-satisfied life, and his misogyny. While the story's overall message is neither pro- nor anti-abortion, its focus on sexual exploitation raises questions pertinent to the issue of contraception.

While the birth control movement positioned itself against the great evil of abortion, fiction demonstrates a more ambivalent exploration of the issue of reproductive control. Writers not associated with the political movement used their works to explore the complexity of the issue, including the relationships among economics, marriage, personal fulfillment, and creative expression with a woman's ability to be sexually active without pregnancy. Their texts joined a changing conversation that defined contraception within the parameters of social practice.

The birth control movement aligned itself with traditional values of motherhood and defined itself against abortion to persuade conservative politicians to change the law. There is an inherent contradiction here: the movement downplayed the radical possibilities to gain acceptance, so its rhetoric reinscribed motherhood even as the reality of access to birth control changed the paradigm of female reproductive destiny. While the mother figure was idealized, the movement distinguished between the conditions that allowed for ideal motherhood and sensationalized the death, illness, and poverty that could result. Motherhood should be voluntary, a "conscious" decision to be an active "maker" of people. Some writers consciously saw their work as propaganda to advance the cause even as others engaged with the debate from a more artistic and exploratory stance. While the tension over the control of female bodies continued throughout the period, the terms of the debate shifted. The issue circulated through the fiction just as it did in political discourse. These genres engaged in conversation, providing a place for birth control and abortion in public discourse.

5

Reading the Body, Controlling the Race
Birth Control and the Eugenic Impetus of the 1920s and 1930s

> [E]ugenics without birth control seemed to me a house built upon sands. It could not stand against the furious winds of economic pressure which had buffeted into partial or total helplessness a tremendous proportion of the human race. The eugenists wanted to shift the birth-control emphasis from less children for the poor to more children for the rich. We went back of that and sought first to stop the multiplication of the unfit.
>
> —Sanger, An Autobiography, 374–75

"How did you know?" Claude asks the doctor who advises him not to have children in the 1927 eugenic film, *Are You Fit to Marry?* Claude is referring to his family secret, an illicit affair through which his grandfather tainted the family blood.[1] Doctor Dickey responds, "I

---

1. The *Black Stork* played in public theatres from 1916 until 1918 and from 1918 until 1942 under the title *Are You Fit to Marry?* The movie was revised and re-released in 1927. The revised silent film put a new frame around the old narrative: Professor Worth, an authority on heredity, talks to Jack, his daughter's fiancé, about undergoing an exam to test for disease. When Jack refuses, the Professor tells the story of Claude, whose blood was "tainted by an indiscrete ancestor," and Dr. Dickey, a crusader for race betterment. Claude and Anne's defective baby is born, and Anne has a vision of his miserable life, shunned by others and falling from wealth into poverty, despair, mental illness, and finally breeding a large family of defectives. She asks Dr. Dickey not to save the baby's life, and soon after his spirit floats into the arms of Jesus. After this frightful tale, Jack agrees to the exam. Throughout the film there are many shots of animals (emphasizing that laws covered livestock but not human breeding) and deformed, insane, and retarded people. Other films added to the debate over birth control and eugenics, such as the positive eugenic *Race*

am a doctor—it is written on you. I can read." This metaphor of literacy explains the doctor's ability to interpret Claude as a palimpsest: he does not translate a physical defect on Claude's body but an inherited taint emanating from his blood. Thus, the (white, male) doctor is privileged with the ability to read both the past and the future through an apparently unmarked body and to make eugenic decisions based upon that reading. Between 1900 and 1930, when the American eugenics movement was at its strongest, the body was viewed scientifically as an objective material text to be (mis)read from genetic code to physical form to moral right to reproduce.[2] Belief in eugenics guided social policy, and by 1940 many states outlawed marriages between "genetic defectives" and interracial couples (D. Roberts, *Killing the Black Body* 65, 71). This eugenic paradigm of the material body as a text, where heredity writes the future of the individual and the nation, also shaped the rhetorical appeals for birth control in the 1920s and 1930s. Women's reproductive fitness, their assumed heterosexuality and race, took on new importance because of eugenic discourse.[3]

Eugenics was not a new idea in America. In 1898 Eugene Talbot had published *Degeneracy: Its Causes, Signs, and Results*, linking alcoholism, prostitution, poverty, insanity, and sexual perversion to racial characteristics, and in 1907 Indiana became the first state to involuntarily sterilize the "unfit." By the 1920s anxiety over increased immigration and a declining birth rate among the elite led to a growing cultural consensus, with politicians, birth controllers, eugenicists, and authors echoing eugenic theory in the public sphere.[4] Modernity was characterized by

---

Suicide (1916), the pro–birth control *Where Are My Children?* (1916), *The Hand That Rocks the Cradle* (1917), *The Law of Population, or Birth Control* (1917), and Sanger's semi-autobiographical *Birth Control* (1917). See Pernick 1996; 1997.

2. The Image Archive on the American Eugenics Movement, sponsored by the Dolan DNA Learning Center at Cold Spring Harbor Laboratory, offers a fascinating and comprehensive Web site detailing eugenic research, how it was popularized, and its effects on American society. See http://www.eugenicsarchive.org/eugenics/. For comprehensive histories of American eugenics, see Kevles and Haller. See Paul on eugenics and socialist scientists.

3. In his study of nineteenth-century white supremacist fiction, Mason Stokes argues that "whiteness and heterosexuality can usefully be seen as analogous structures" (191); this statement largely holds true for eugenic discourse. See also Doyle on "the hierarchies of race and gender" as forms of oppression operating in modern fiction (21).

4. The eugenics movement was responding to modern conditions, including the immigration of almost 28 million people to the United States from 1880 to 1920 and the migration of over 1.2 million African Americans to the North from 1890 to 1920. See Morawska and Model. According to Ludmerer, the Immigration Restriction Act of 1924 "was the greatest triumph of the American eugenics movement in national affairs" and was an example of the growing influence of eugenics on public policy (61). Anti-immigration arguments appeared in the popular press, from *Good Housekeeping* to the *Birth Control*

this turn toward rationality, science, management, and order, and eliminating "defectives" was part of a larger program that "permeated modern society and remained arguably the most salient feature of its collective spirit" (Bauman 36).[5]

Eugenicists combined a program encouraging the physically, racially, and economically "fit" to reproduce (positive eugenics) with discouraging or preventing the "unfit" from reproducing (negative eugenics). Categories of fitness intersected in a scheme for the scientific improvement of civilization, based on a misplaced logic of biology and the authorizing discourse of science. A faulty understanding of genetic principles, combined with strong social preferences, supported the belief that alcoholism, poverty, shiftlessness, promiscuity, and crime were inheritable traits along with mental illness and disease.

As Margaret Sanger notes in her autobiography, quoted in the chapter's epigraph, the birth control movement found natural alliances with the eugenics movement, and employed eugenic language for its veneer of scientific validity.[6] Birth control rhetoric shifted from the socialist feminist stance of the 1910s to contraception as the tool of eugenic population control by 1930.[7] In *Woman and the New Race* (1920), Sanger redefined the purpose of birth control as "nothing more or less than the facilitation of the process of weeding out the unfit, or preventing the birth of defectives or of those who will become defectives" (229). Her *Pivot of Civilization* (1922) reinforced this eugenic message. In 1928 Sanger considered combining the *Birth Control Review* with a eugenics magazine, and by 1930 the *Review* had aligned itself with the eugenics movement

---

Review. In a 1923 editorial the *Review* endorsed immigration restriction because of "the injury to our national life through the admission each year of hordes of immigrants whom we were not able to assimilate" ("Editorial" 219).

5. See also Banta and Biggs for fascinating studies of the rise of scientific management and its effects on narrative.

6. In *The Pivot of Civilization*, Sanger details in a chapter entitled "Science the Ally" the natural confluence of birth control and eugenics. For detailed discussion of the relationship between the birth control and eugenics movements, see Gordon, especially "The Politics of Population: Birth Control and the Eugenics Movement" and *The Moral Property of Women*. See also McCann and McLaren. While many historians view Sanger as firmly within the eugenics camp, McLaren argues that Sanger played on rather than mirrored eugenics-inspired fears. Linda Gordon, Dorothy Roberts, and Miriam Reed also argue that Sanger was not racist.

7. A content study of the *Birth Control Review* found that from 1921 to 1929 only 4.9 percent of articles were about women's freedom or independence (Gordon, *Woman's Body* 283.) While many of the proponents of eugenics were male, and their involvement in the birth control movement was symptomatic of a growing (white, professional) male presence in the movement, many women were active in eugenics. See Larson on the role of state women's organizations in the passage of eugenics legislation.

and featured articles by leading eugenicists.[8] Whereas their aims of the "improvement of the race, elimination of the unfit, and the propagation of the fit" were the same, the birth control leagues were more concerned with the practical problems of establishing clinics and removing legal restrictions ("Answer Box"). Sanger and eugenicists argued that women had a critical role to play in improving the population. This appeal to women emphasized their biological role as mothers. As Scott and Nellie Nearing wrote, "Woman is the race. . . . She is less specialized, hence nearer to race type, more typical of the race, and therefore prepared to transmit to future generations the characteristics of the race to which she belongs. To woman primarily the race must look for its biologic progress" (17).

Support for eugenics was widespread in popular culture, including film, sermons, and articles in magazines such as *Ladies' Home Journal*. Fiction and film shaped public debate on the moral implications of eugenic birth control and sterilization. In his study of *Black Stork*, a movie written by Chicago surgeon Harry Haiselden, who made news for allowing six "defective" infants to die between 1915 and 1918, Martin Pernick argues for the "crucial though little-recognized role played by mass culture in constructing both the meanings and memory of the early-twentieth-century movement for hereditary improvement known as eugenics" ("Defining the Defective" 89).[9] By examining fiction in the context of eugenic discourse, this chapter extends Pernick's examination of the mutual development of mass culture and social thought. Birth control fiction further supports the claim that "[m]ass culture did not 'diffuse' scientific definitions to a passive public, nor did it simply dilute once-precise technical terms as it filtered them down to the masses" (Pernick, *Black Stork* 14). Fiction such as *Tobacco Road* and *Torrents of Spring* did not introduce eugenic language to the public, but rather engaged with issues of positive and negative eugenics, including physical, mental, and social fitness. Reading these literary texts constituted a dialectical act of learning to read the eugenic code of the body. Almost a

---

8. The *Birth Control Review* became a forum for the eugenics debate, publishing articles such as Norman Haire, "Sterilization of the Unfit"; C. C. Little, "Unnatural Selection and Its Resulting Obligations"; F. H. Hankins, "Eugenics and Birth Control"; and Norman Himes, "Crime, Mental Deficiency, and Birth Control." The *Review* also sported various eugenic subtitles, such as, "In the creation of new life there should be full scientific knowledge of deliberate planning" (1926), "For those who believe in the great future of our race" (1927), and "Fewer but fitter children" (1928).

9. While birth control activists such as Margaret Sanger and Emma Goldman stayed silent on Haiselden's actions, William J. Robinson, Mary Ware Dennett, and Charles Davenport offered public support and saw his cause as congruent with efforts to legalize birth control (Pernick, *Black Stork* 33).

century later, readers can agree with Anne Balsamo's premise that "[a]ny given text within a discursive system is a symbolic enactment of the cultural preoccupations of a particular historical conjunction" (4).

Traces of eugenic concern occur in earlier American texts. Louisa May Alcott's 1873 novel, *Work*, explores the possibilities of labor for women, including the role of domestic companion to an invalid. Alcott presents readers with a chapter of eugenic tragedy in which the beautiful young invalid suffers from "the curse of insanity" (86). "We come of a mad race," she despairs, "and for years we have gone recklessly on bequeathing this awful inheritance to our descendants. It should end with us, we are the last; none of us should marry" (86). The clear eugenic message that the heroine and the reader learn—reproducing such defects is a sin—gained force and complexity in later literature. In Charlotte Perkins Gilman's 1911 novel, *The Crux*, readers learn with the heroine Vivian that "marriage is a woman's duty" and "[m]arriage is for motherhood," so she "must not marry Morton Elder," who has a venereal disease (30, 128, 129).[10] The Doctor asks her, "Will you tell that to your crippled children? Will they understand if they are idiots? Will they see it if they are blind? Will it satisfy you when they are dead? They may be deformed and twisted, have all manner of terrible and loathsome afflictions, they and their children after them, if they have any. And many do! Dear girl, don't you see that's wicked? Beware of biological sin, my dear, for it here is no forgiveness" (225–26). Some authors took the trope of eugenics to humorous extremes, as Anita Loos does in a 1915 story in *Vanity Fair*, "The Force of Heredity, and Nella: A Modern Fable with a Telling Moral for Eugenists." The protagonist ignores her mother's advice to "always be eugenic" and marries a wealthy man with a wooden leg; years later she has eleven children: "They had all been born with a wooden leg!" (42).

These literary texts often appeared alongside popular "family studies" such as Henry H. Goddard's 1912 *The Kallikak Family*, Richard Dugdale's *The Jukes: A Study in Crime, Pauperism, and Heredity* (first published 1875, reprinted many times), and Arthur H. Estabrook's *The Jukes* in 1915.[11] These studies, claiming to prove the hereditary nature of traits such as alcoholism and shiftlessness, were followed by tracts

---

10. Seitler argues that "Gilman fuses eugenics and feminism to constitute a new narrative form; in particular, a literary subgenre of feminist 'uplift' that I call 'regeneration narratives'" (65).

11. Nicole Hahn Rafter collected and edited eleven of these "family studies" in *White Trash: The Eugenic Family Studies 1877–1919*. Rafter notes, "Mythic in message, mildly salacious in detail, and Progressive in promise, the family studies attracted an enthusiastic audience among welfare workers and the general public" and "influenced social policy" (1).

arguing against immigration and for the genetic purity of American blood, such as Madison Grant's *The Passing of the Great Race* (1916) and Lothrop Stoddard's *The Rising Tide of Color Against White World-Supremacy* (1920). These "scientific" studies of racial heredity used the term *character* to describe inherited conditions. As with the metaphor of literacy and body reading, eugenic science shared the term *character* with literature. A general agreement that there were a limited number of human types, or characters, enabled the cognitive act of interpretation. As Cathy Boeckmann notes, "when literary debates are placed next to scientific ones, a shared vocabulary of character emerges" (5).[12] Hereditary background and physical traits acted as markers to guide reader expectations, be they readers of Erskine Caldwell's *Tobacco Road* (a novel), Dugdale's *The Jukes* (a eugenic family study), or their neighbor (a physical body). For instance, Dorothy Parker invokes mental degeneration in her 1934 story "Mrs. Hofstadter on Josephine Street" when a character jokingly refers to herself as "the former Miss Kallikak" (155). This shared vocabulary of literature and science also reflects shared actions.[13] Just as authors used stereotypic markers of race and class to signal the eugenic worth of a character, eugenicists read value on or through the body via the shorthand of stock characters. The depravity of literary characters reinforced and justified eugenic practices on actual people.

In this way, fictional texts portraying eugenic themes reinforced social anxiety and shaped public understanding.[14] In her 1925 novel, *Barren Ground*, Ellen Glasgow argues that "character is fate" and peppers the novel with reminders of the overwhelming dictates of blood (vi). The protagonist, Dorinda, "sprung from the finer strain" of her mother's family, with "Presbyterian in her blood," overcomes hardship and poverty with a character fated by heredity (36, 156). African American authors also spoke the language of blood as determining character. Jessie Redmon

---

12. Boeckmann's work focuses on novels of passing from 1891 to 1912 to demonstrate how characterization signaled race. Especially in the nineteenth century, the word *character* "referred to a quantifiable set of inherited behaviors and tendencies that were almost always racial" (3).

13. The other metaphoric language in eugenics is that of livestock breeding. Terms such as "pure stock" and "germ plasm" equated humans with animals and humans with their genes. For example, in *Are You Fit to Marry?* the image of a bull is superimposed over a beggar's face as Professor Worth argues that "[o]ur statute books contain many laws covering the breeding of livestock—but in the highest form of life—most precious of all living matter, almost no attention is paid to breeding." In *The Pivot of Civilization* Margaret Sanger suggests applying stock-breeding techniques to humans.

14. Haller notes that notions of criminal heredity were spread in the works of Jack London, Frank Norris, and other authors, who used a corrupt lineage to explain character (41).

Fauset's mulatto protagonist in *Plum Bun* (1928) muses, "Perhaps this selfishness was what the possession of white blood meant; the ultimate definition of Nordic Supremacy" (275).

Because of the congruence between birth control and eugenics, authors like Glasgow offer implicit commentary on contraception as a eugenic instrument. Glasgow's novel creates a scenario of possible "race suicide" that could be used to support a program of positive eugenics. After a miscarriage, Dorinda is "finished with all that," her body the titular barren ground (409). While her admirable character is not reproduced, so-called white trash like Almira Pryde had "children so numerous that their father could not be trusted to remember their names" (72). The Prydes reproduce the stereotype of underclass fertility and feed cultural anxiety that the degenerate and shiftless will overrun the population like rabbits.

While critics have examined the eugenics movement's influence on various authors, the extent to which fiction contributed to eugenic and birth control discourse has gone unappreciated.[15] For example, Glasgow's *Barren Ground* can be read in conjunction with Edith Summers Kelley's novel *Weeds* (1923) to explicate how stereotypes of character resonate with arguments for birth control within eugenic discourse. Like Glasgow, Kelley uses geographic location and economic conditions to establish reader expectations of character. Kelley writes, "In backwoods corners of America, where the people have been poor and benighted for several generations and where for as many generations no new blood has entered, where everybody is cousin, first, second, or third, to everybody else for miles around, the children are mostly dull of mind and scrawny of body" (13). Both authors use stereotypic ancestry and setting to emphasize the odds their exceptional heroines fight against. Reproductive control is the operative subtext allowing the possibility of escape. In *Barren Ground*, Dorinda's miscarriage and subsequent resolve to control her reproduction give her the chance to succeed. In contrast, Kelley's protagonist, Judith, is trapped by her body into reproducing familial poverty. Although the young Judith "[s]omehow, in spite of her ancestry . . . had escaped the curse of the soil," the demands of pregnancy extinguish her exceptional spark (88). These two novels reveal how fiction served as a mode of mass cultural conversation insisting on the importance of birth control.

This chapter examines depictions of eugenics in relation to the intersecting discourse of race, birth control, and human social value. As

---

15. See Keely, Fontana, Leon (1988), English (1997; 2004), and Nies on eugenics and modernist authors; for a fuller discussion of the period 1880–1940, see Cuddy and Roche.

Soloway notes, eugenics and birth control shared a "close, often uncomfortable relationship" (637). The two movements shared both contiguous time and many theoretical tenets and members. The fiction discussed in this chapter presents arguments on varying sides of the birth control and eugenic debates. Stories in the *Birth Control Review* and texts such as Charles Norris's *Seed* have not found a place in the literary canon and are usually ignored as propaganda, thin on substance and devoid of literary merit. Works by William Faulkner, Ernest Hemingway, Jack London, and Kay Boyle have been taken up by scholars, and indeed the "canonical" texts do offer a more complex investigation of eugenic issues. Taken together, these texts demonstrate the infiltration of eugenic issues into American fiction at all levels, and the often uneasy alliance of aesthetics and politics that evolved.

"Race Responsibility" and Positive Eugenics

Positive eugenics stemmed from fears that immigrants and the lower classes were outbreeding the "pure" American stock. Women and reproduction were at the center of the issue. According to Katrina Irving, "Nativists constructed an image of the nation as the besieged 'broodland' of the Anglo-Saxon race and presented the reproductive front as the critical arena of battle. They stressed the immigrants' sexual threat and underscored the link between aliens' putative fertility and Anglo-Saxon race suicide" (37). These arguments portrayed contraception as an instrument of "race suicide," and thus these texts espoused eugenic but not contraceptive arguments. While wealthy (white) women had smaller families, the poor continued to have large families. Early in the twentieth century President Theodore Roosevelt warned of "race suicide" in women's magazines and, recognizing the power of fiction to influence public behavior, endorsed *Mother* (1911) by Kathleen Norris "as an effective tract in his campaign against 'race suicide'" (Mott 221). This novel depicts wealthy women with small families as vain and selfish and encourages readers to seek fulfillment through motherhood. Norris's literary theme of eugenic motherhood is echoed in Albert Edward Wiggam's 1922 nonfiction best seller, *Fruit of the Family Tree*, which describes women as "the natural conservator of the race, guardian of its blood" (280). Appeals to the crucial role of middle- and upper-class mothers supported positive eugenics, balancing the population scales by increasing "good stock."

The implicit message of Norris's *Mother*, that the patriotic and moral duty of women of "good stock" is to reproduce, was made explicitly by authors such as British writer Mina Loy. While positive eugenics was less controversial than negative eugenics, since it encouraged large families among the fit, some modernist authors took up the flag in more radical ways by expressing these sentiments in experimental forms. Perhaps best known for her poetry, which greatly influenced her American contemporaries, Loy's unpublished "Feminist Manifesto" (1914) advocates positive eugenics by stating, "Every woman of superior intelligence should realize her race-responsibility by producing children in adequate proportion to the unfit or degenerate members of her sex" (155). Loy uses the revolutionary manifesto form, then popular in avant-garde circles, to reproduce a "logics of biology" without questioning woman's role as mother (Lyon 155).[16] Knowledge of Margaret Sanger and the American birth control movement, which she kept informed of through Mabel Dodge, influenced Loy's eugenic ideology. While seemingly an advocate of the birth control movement, in her "Manifesto" Loy exhorted women "of superior intelligence" to reproduce to offset the "degenerate" population. This manifesto reiterates the eugenic basis of human value, assuming the hereditary nature of "fitness."

Ernest Hemingway's *The Torrents of Spring* (1926) views positive eugenics and racial hierarchies more critically. The novella was a satiric response to Sherwood Anderson's *Dark Laughter* (1925), a best-selling novel written in an experimental style and exploring racial themes.[17] Hemingway found Anderson's novel poorly written and sentimental (as did F. Scott Fitzgerald), and in a week dashed off *Torrents* in response. In particular, Hemingway disliked Anderson's characters, which followed tracts such as Harry Laughlin's *Analysis of America's Modern Melting Pot* (1922) and cast immigrants as socially degenerate.

But *Torrents of Spring* also should be read in context of Madison Grant's *The Passing of the Great Race* (1916), as Walter Benn Michaels argues and Hemingway's subtitle, *A Romantic Novel in Honor of the Passing of a Great Race*, makes clear (95). In its depiction of Scripps O'Neil and Yogi Johnson, the novel attacks Grant's veneration of the Nordic race as the pinnacle of eugenic hierarchies.[18] Grant depicted the

16. For a fuller discussion of Loy's views on feminism and maternity, see DuPlessis, "'Seismic Orgasm.'" Carolyn Burke details the relationship between Loy, Dodge, and Sanger and reads Loy's poetry in the context of this new sexual freedom and debates of the "new woman" and "woman rebel" in *Becoming Modern*. Critics viewed Loy's *Love Songs* as "lewd and lascivious writing, in the same class as the pamphlets of Margaret Sanger or the lectures of Emma Goldman" (Burke, "The New Poetry and the New Woman" 45).

17. See Ray L. White's "Hemingway's Private Explanation of *The Torrents of Spring*."

18. Nies notes, however, that even as Hemingway critiqued Grant in *Torrents of*

Nordic male body as both culturally hegemonic and almost transcendentally pure. Immigrants, in contrast, were monstrous and degenerate. Such anti-immigrant sentiment led to the 1921 National Origins Quota System and subsequent legislation regulating immigration.[19] Hemingway deconstructs this hierarchy of race, creating in Scripps and Yogi two Nordic male bodies that are comical and grotesque. Yogi's impotence renders him unable to fulfill his racial duty. His brief commentary on the whole notion of race suicide parodies the fevered seriousness with which eugenicists wrote. Walking down the street beside a Native American man, "the only real Americans" (63), Yogi considers, "He was a white man, but he knew when he had enough. After all, the white race might not always be supreme. This Moslem revolt. Unrest in the East. Trouble in the West. Things looked black in the South. Now this condition of things in the North. Where was it taking him? Where did it all lead? Would it help him to want a woman? Would spring ever come? Was it worth while after all? He wondered" (74). To Yogi, the future of the race takes a back seat to his inability to desire a woman.

Scripps O'Neil, a drifting drinker whose first wife has left him, feels the effects of spring desire. He marries an elderly English waitress, a "Strange Nordic" (19), within a day of meeting her but quickly leaves her for a younger woman. Scripps and Yogi fail to fulfill the promise of the Nordic American male. They are not physically, mentally, or morally superior. Thus, *Torrents* satirizes not only the simplistic racialization and experimental style of *Dark Laughter*, but it also intervenes in the cultural debate of eugenics, discrediting the racial hierarchies upon which positive eugenics in general and Madison Grant in particular based their claims. Hemingway undermines the argument of the Nordic superman by offering a competing discourse of comedic characters ruled by desire but ultimately impotent.

Other authors wrote fiction that engaged explicitly with eugenic tracts, including F. Scott Fitzgerald, who argued against positive eugenics in *The Great Gatsby*.[20] Published in 1925, *Gatsby* responds to Lothrop Stoddard's *Revolt Against Civilization: The Menace of the*

Spring, he recreated eugenic racial values in *The Sun Also Rises* (1926). Daylanne English (2004) chides both Nies and Michaels for taking "the novel far too seriously" (208–9, n68).

19. The year 1921 was also when the ABCL was founded.

20. According to Bert Bender, Fitzgerald became acquainted with eugenic theory while at Princeton, and the "social consequences" are "reflected in much of his work" ("'His Mind Aglow'" 401). In *The Descent of Love: Darwin and the Theory of Sexual Selection in American Fiction, 1871–1926* (1996), Bender relates Darwinian Theory, especially sexual selection, to American texts by Henry James, Edith Wharton, Hemingway, and others.

Under Man (1920). Fitzgerald references Stoddard when the character Tom Buchanan recommends "The Rise of the Coloured Empires" by "Goddard" (17). The name change may also reference another eugenicist, Henry H. Goddard, whose 1912 *The Kallikak Family: A Study in the Heredity of Feeble-Mindedness* charted the genetic basis of feeblemindedness, crime, poverty, and sexual degeneracy.[21] Like Goddard, Fitzgerald provides descriptions of Gatsby's and Nick's ancestry. These brief pedigrees help explain character traits such as Gatsby's ambition and Nick's Midwestern honesty.

In *Revolt Against Civilization*, Stoddard argues that mental, physical, and racial "inferiors" are "enemies of civilization" because they "are more or less uncivilizable" (21). Fitzgerald alludes to the text's popularity among the educated classes by portraying Tom Buchanan as having read it. Tom summarizes the book with "Well, it's a fine book and everybody ought to read it. The idea is if we don't look out the white race will be—will be utterly submerged. It's all scientific stuff; it's been proved" (17). Fitzgerald implicitly critiques the eugenic argument in making Tom the character who mouths those beliefs (English, *Unnatural Selections* 75). Tom is a hypocrite and prig who carries on an extramarital affair while claiming, "Nowadays people begin by sneering at family life and family institutions and next they'll throw everything overboard and have intermarriage between black and white" (137). By putting eugenic beliefs in the mouth of an unsympathetic character, Fitzgerald undermines the validity of Stoddard's claims.

F. Scott Fitzgerald also defies eugenic hierarchies by attempting to disconnect class from value; by providing the pedigree of characters from different economic classes and depicting crime, insanity, and alcoholism as widespread among the elite (all traits early studies such as Goddard's "proved" to be hereditary), Fitzgerald undermines the notion that the wealthy are inherently less defective. However, Fitzgerald does not completely escape sanctioning eugenic theory: *The Great Gatsby* offers a subtle reinscription of class hidden beneath its mockery. The novel's tragic ending upholds notions linking genetic fitness to class. By killing off Myrtle and Gatsby, who had risen into the upper class, Fitzgerald allows the "careless" but wealthy Tom and Daisy to win the survival of the fittest. As Bert Bender notes, "Gatsby fails in his romantic quest and remains a 'poor son-of-a-bitch' because he denies his genetic identity and ignores the laws of sexual selection" ("'His Mind Aglow'" 411). Death, the

---

21. Goddard's study was last reprinted in 1973 and, according to Rafter, "has proved the most popular of all the family studies" (3).

ultimate birth control, will prevent Gatsby from reproducing, while Tom and Daisy live to potentially reproduce and fulfill the destiny of positive eugenics. From *Mother* to *The Great Gatsby*, an ideology of positive eugenics pervaded fiction and social thought, traveling from the printed page to the tip of every tongue, from "scientific" theory to social policy.

NEGATIVE EUGENICS

The "Menace of the Feebleminded"

While eugenics and birth control shared a belief in sex education and freer discourse on sexual issues, many positive eugenicists opposed contraception, distrusting its radical roots. They believed it would be "misused" by women who should breed, lead to illicit sex, and allow women out of the domestic sphere.[22] But negative eugenics, or preventing the reproduction of "bad stock," depended upon birth control or sterilization. In the 1920s many powerful eugenicists including Lothrop Stoddard, Paul Popenoe, and Guy Irving Burch joined the American Birth Control League (ABCL) and contributed articles to the *Birth Control Review*. The relationship benefited both movements: Stoddard and Clarence Little added prestige to the ABCL Board of Directors, while Havelock Ellis favorably reviewed Stoddard's *The Rising Tide Of Color* in the *Review*. In addition to publishing articles linking birth control with eugenics, the *Review* published fiction about ending the transmission of "defective" genes that led to epilepsy, mental illness, "degeneracy," and idiocy. The remainder of this chapter examines how fiction implicitly advocated birth control by presenting contraception and sterilization as a means to prevent the reproduction of the unfit.

The rise of statistics and demography and the introduction of IQ tests brought the number of the "mentally deficient" to public attention. Eugenicists used this new "science" to "prove" both a "differential birthrate" and differential "racial" intelligence (Doyle 13). Margaret Sanger also adopted the rhetoric of science to further her cause, and in 1923 opened the Birth Control Clinical Research Bureau to begin clinical studies while dispensing contraception under a physician's supervision. The media painted immigrant, poor, and "defective" populations as a dangerous specter, a "menace" to civilization. Eugenicists and birth controllers joined together to argue that society would soon "be faced with

---

22. See Gordon, "The Politics of Birth Control, 1920–1949."

the ever-increasing problem of feeble-mindedness, that fertile parent of degeneracy, crime, and pauperism" (Sanger, *The Pivot of Civilization* 81). Linking unsavory characteristics was a common rhetorical device, helping to build public anxiety over a threat that must be controlled. The accumulation of traits was also a fictional device that allowed authors to persuade readers to eugenic conclusions. Beulah Poynter's three-act play *The Unborn*, produced by the *Medical Review of Reviews* in 1915, used this trope convincingly to "arouse discussion of the subject of birth control" while demonstrating "the evils of reproduction without regard to heredity and circumstance" ("Plea for Birth Control on the Stage" 199). The mother's hereditary taint manifests in her son through a variety of degeneracies, including epilepsy, dissipation, and nervous weakness. His final acts of murder (of the fiancée who refuses to marry him when she discovers his epilepsy) and suicide underlined his reproductive unfitness.

Such rhetoric fed eugenic hierarchies of the social worth of various populations, defining reproductive fitness and enabling a state determination of that fitness. In the 1927 *Buck v. Bell* case, which legalized the involuntary sterilization of asylum inmates, U.S. Supreme Court Justice Oliver Wendell Holmes articulated this belief:

> We have seen more than once that the public welfare may call upon the best citizens for their lives. It would be strange if it could not call upon those who already sap the strength of the state for these lesser sacrifices, often not felt to be such by those concerned, in order to prevent our being swamped with incompetence. It is better for all the world, if instead of waiting to execute degenerate offspring for crime, or to let them starve for their imbecility, society can prevent those who are manifestly unfit from continuing their kind. The principle that sustains compulsory vaccination is broad enough to cover cutting the Fallopian tubes. . . . Three generations of imbeciles are enough. (qtd. in J. Trent 64)

Birth controllers and eugenicists united in the 1920s to find a contraceptive easy enough for the ignorant and undesirable to use.[23] In the meantime, sex segregation in institutions or involuntary sterilization was

23. Soloway notes that birth controllers were concerned that the contraceptive method recommended in clinics, the diaphragm, would be too complicated for many women. Birth control clinic data revealed that women provided with instruction and fitted for diaphragms "stopped using the appliance within two years" (645). The fuss of the diaphragm combined with a lack of privacy and input from their husbands were cited as reasons. The search for a simple fool-proof contraceptive eventually led to the development of the hormonal birth control pill.

the preferred method of reproductive control.[24] The moral imperative to cleanse the race of insanity and imbecility justified the extreme act of sterilization. Indeed, authors such as Eugene O'Neill suggested that even the taboo acts of abortion and adultery were defensible. In his 1928 play, *Strange Interlude,* Nina discovers that her husband Sam's family is "cursed" with hereditary insanity, and to reproduce that eugenic trait would be "a crime worse than murder" (107). Encouraged by her mother-in-law, she aborts her first pregnancy and becomes pregnant by another man, "a healthy man to breed by, same's we do with stock," without telling her husband (108). Sam remains ignorant of his hereditary taint and acts as a model father to the son he believes to be his. O'Neill thus submitted to public discourse abortion and adultery as possible alternatives to childlessness, while reinforcing the belief that insanity and feeblemindedness must not be reproduced.

The birth control movement, comfortably situated within conservative morality, did not argue for adultery as a eugenic solution. Rather, the ABCL advocated involuntary sterilization of the insane and feebleminded and encouraged sterilization for those with transmissible diseases. The March 1928 and April 1933 issues of the *Birth Control Review* focused on the relation of birth control and sterilization. This advocacy of sterilization reveals how much the movement's goal had shifted from one of giving women the means to control their own reproduction to one of giving society the right to judge and to control who should reproduce. Eugenic ideology thus offered the movement another way to downplay the potential threat to patriarchy that contraception offered: reproductive control belonged not directly to women but to a wise and fatherly society who would oversee its implementation for the good of "all." As Dorothy Roberts notes, "The language of eugenics did more than legitimate birth control. It defined the purpose of birth control, shaping the meaning of reproductive freedom. Birth control became a means of controlling a population rather than a means of increasing women's reproductive autonomy" (*Killing the Black Body* 80). As we saw with the tropes of marriage and motherhood, the movement rhetorically aligned itself with ideologies that supported a gendered status quo.

Much of the eugenic push was against the propagation of "men-

---

24. Lerner points out that sterilization was used for therapeutic as well as eugenic purposes for women with chronic diseases such as tuberculosis. But therapeutic and eugenic motives were not always distinct, and many sterilizations were medically unnecessary, caused by an exaggerated sense of the risk to pregnant women and the incorporation of non-medical factors, such as a belief in the hereditary transfer of disease and a desire for population control.

tal defectives." The *Review* ran articles such as "The Menace of the Feebleminded" (Hanna) and letters of "Family Trees Which Should Not Bear Fruit" to show how birth control would benefit the human race. As Goldstein wrote in his 1922 article, "Control of Parenthood as a Moral Problem," "We can prevent the defectives from bringing forth abundantly and peopling the earth after their own kind. We can agree that the birthrate of the defective now living, the feeble-minded, the epileptic, many of the insane and the criminal whose criminality is due to a deep-seated and transmissible cause, shall be controlled and cut off" (195). This "menace" was fueled by a belief that "the feebleminded are notoriously prolific in reproduction" (Sanger, *Woman and the New Race* 41), thus adding moral sin to genetic flaw.

Even the early fiction of the *Review* presents a message supporting a eugenics program. In "The Scrub Woman" (1919), told by a first-person office worker who becomes friendly with the cleaning woman, witness a typical woman's plight: a twenty-eight-year-old cleaning woman with four children and a husband in prison who was struggling to earn enough money to feed her children. "The children were often sick," and the woman herself appeared "half-starving" (Gray 13). The woman was too poor to take her children to where her husband couldn't find them when he got out of prison, and "I can't keep him away from me. I've tried before. It's the law he can come to me because I'm his wedded wife, but the law won't feed the baby he'll give me" (13). Predictably, the woman becomes pregnant after his most recent release. When the cleaning woman returns a year later, she reveals that the infant is "an idiot . . . the worst kind of an idiot" (13). But the cleaning woman doesn't understand the narrator's sympathy: she herself is happy, as the idiocy is an answer to her prayers—now the state will take care of the baby, and the woman can use her meager wages to feed her other children (13). The eugenic argument is clear: birth control would have prevented the birth of an unwanted child into poverty, and also the birth of an idiot that the state now has to support with public assistance. Ten years later, the character Jason Compson in William Faulkner's *The Sound and the Fury* (1929) makes a similar economic argument when he suggests sending his brother Benjy to the institution in Jackson: "why not send him there and get that much benefit out of the taxes we pay?" (255). While Jason and the Scrub Woman may seem callous, they reveal the cold calculus of human worth as determined by eugenics and the economics of state institutionalization.

Pro-eugenic fiction found in the *Birth Control Review*, such as "The Scrub Woman," was reinforced by articles and letters to create a coherent message of birth control as eugenic solution. An excerpt from the Records from the Center for Birth Control Advice at the Maternal Aid Association in New York City lists the case of "Mrs. P. 40 years old. 9 pregnancies—6 living children, 18 to 4 years, one abortion, 2 infant deaths. Two children are mental defectives, the others are subnormal" ("Is Contraceptive Necessary?" 143). Obviously these parents are not "fit stock" to reproduce, and birth control will prevent more defective offspring. Richard Connell's 1922 story "Weeds," set in a shelter for the destitute and mentally defective, illustrates this narrative theme. Talking over the noise of a woman moaning in childbirth, the inmates discuss how her first child had a head "shaped like a peanut" and is now in the "'sylum" (38). A second child, also in the asylum, was "black as soot," indicating miscegenation, and its head "come to a point" (39). Mental defect and constant pregnancy are the norm, as one of the women listening "disremembers" whether she herself had eleven or twelve children, all of whom died except for one now in the asylum. From this nightmarish litany of reproducing defectives the story moves to the office of the Chairman of the State Board for the Guardianship of Orphans, who declares, "Unless we do something about it, that Pinkney woman will people the state with idiots. She's had four already, and she's only twenty-six" (62). While the Chairman decides on sterilization, the Superintendent of the home has something else in mind to make "it impossible for her to have any more illegitimate children"—he marries her to another idiot (62). The Superintendent misses the point, taking morality rather than eugenics as the issue. While this story may seem laughable, with the rambling dialogue of the destitute and the Superintendent's misguided solution, many political leaders feared that the "feebleminded" would overpopulate the globe. Situations such as the one envisioned in "Weeds" led asylum superintendents and others to advocate for involuntary sterilization for mental defectives.

Jack London's foray into the asylum offers a more complex and humane vision of the feebleminded than Connell's "Weeds." London writes from the perspective of an asylum inmate in an early eugenic short story, "Told in the Drooling Ward." The first-person perspective adds complexity to the narrative debate regarding degeneracy, creating a twenty-eight-year-old male character named Tom from which to sympathetically tell the tale. While Tom claims that he is "not a drooler," his happy, repetitive narrative style places him as subnormal, a self-proclaimed "high-grade feeb" (1762). Tom likes to "assist" with the feeding and care of the "droolers," who have something "wrong with most of their legs and arms, and they can't talk" (1762). Tom, who has been in the institution since he was three, proclaims that he likes the asylum better than the outside world and that "they can't get along without me in this institution" (1763). The asylum also houses epileptics and those born with microcephalus and hydrocephalus, all conditions targeted by eugenicists.

Reading this story in the light of the eugenic debate reveals how it questions the great societal fear of feeblemindedness while simultaneously reinforcing eugenic policy. London shows that the gentle, likable Tom prefers the asylum due to his single experience outside of it. "Adopted" to a farm family, Tom was put to work doing hard labor and forced to sleep in the woodshed. He was ostracized, called "Looney Tom," had rocks thrown at him by neighborhood children, and was beaten for being too slow (1765). He was generally feared, and even the mother who had adopted him "was scared to let me play with her children" (1765). As Tom innocently (and London scathingly) remarks, "You never see anything like that in the Home here. The feebs are better behaved" (1765). Thus, London indicts cruelty toward the feebleminded while advocating for their institutionalization. Institutionalization itself was a eugenic measure, as men and women were supervised and segregated. London also comments on another common eugenic measure: marriage laws. Tom, in love with a nurse, "spoke to Dr. Whatcomb about it once, but he told me he was very sorry, because feebs ain't allowed to get married" (1765). While Tom is a sympathetic character, the story reassures readers that the inmates are contained and will not reproduce. Although the story does not explicitly discuss birth control, it contributed to the cultural debate over eugenic policy and the anxiety that led to the growing eugenic thrust of the birth control movement.

Faulkner also touches on the "menace of the feebleminded" in *The Sound and the Fury*. Benjy is mentally retarded, and at the age of thirty-three still needs a constant babysitter to watch and feed him. He is described as drooling and moaning, his condition explained as "born looney" and "deef and dumb" (56). Family studies and other eugenic lore held that the feebleminded were promiscuous and highly sexualized. Benjy is perceived as a sexual menace after chasing a girl, and he is castrated to contain his sexuality. The behavior of the other, "normal" characters heightens the irony of this impression. For instance, Caddy engages in promiscuous behavior, Quentin feels lust for his sister, and Miss Quentin (Caddy's daughter) runs off with a man. The combination of adult male body and childlike mind make Benjy a menace, a mental defective who cannot be allowed to reproduce. His castration is irrevocable, as Benjy is reminded: "*Looking for them aint going to do no good. They're gone*" (84). Faulkner's narrative choice, to have Benjy narrate sections of the novel, creates empathy between reader and "feeb." While London also created this bond through the use of a first-person narrator, Faulkner renders a closer connection by narrating the confusion of Benjy's world and his inability to interpret chaotic stimuli. This largely disallows the easy laughter encouraged in London's tale. While Benjy's castration seems to remove his eugenic menace, the defects represented by other family members are not so easily controlled. Uncle Maury's alcoholism, Caddy and Miss Quentin's promiscuity, and Quentin's melancholy and suicide were all traits that eugenicists considered hereditary. Indeed, Jason Compson remarks that he is scared to have children because "blood always tells" (275). Faulkner references eugenic ideology in his explanation of southern tragedy, reminding readers that hereditary taint can be read through many manifestations.

The "menace of the feebleminded" is largely absent from "Told in the Drooling Ward" due to London's sympathetic portrayal of inmates contained in an asylum and unable to reproduce. Faulkner also defuses this anxiety both by narrating Benjy's direct experience and by having him castrated. Other canonical authors, such as T. S. Eliot, used the trope of the feebleminded as a symbol of the decay of modern civilization. Much of Eliot's poetry displayed such "eugenic anxiety," to use Juan Leon's term, effectively creating the "transcript of a eugenicist's nightmare" ("'Meeting Mr. Eugenides'" 169). Leon notes that Eliot reviewed books with eugenic themes and would have become familiar with eugenic principles by the time he left Harvard in 1914 (170). His recurring themes and images of atrophy, seizures, and physical and moral decay employed the symbolic vocabulary of eugenic discourse. Eliot linked this degeneracy to sexuality and fertility, thus implying a eugenic reasoning of hereditary cause and effect. In the character of Sweeney, Eliot describes a bestial Irishman who, in "Sweeney Erect," sleeps with an epileptic prostitute. This depiction, and anti-Semitic descriptions of Jews, create fear of an overwhelming tide of under-men. Eliot firmly grounded the decay of civilization in mental erosion, such that a feeble mind signals racial inferiority, brute sexuality, and social threat. As Leon notes, Eliot engages in eugenic control by not allowing his characters to reproduce (173). Mr. Eugenides in *The Waste Land*, Eliot's most direct reference to the eugenic debate swirling around him, reiterates the connection between degeneracy and sterility. Thus, a sense of eugenic anxiety rather than univocal contributions to the debate pervades Eliot's work. But the impetus is the same as that which joined negative eugenics and the birth control movement: the reproduction of defectives must be stopped to halt the suicide of civilization.

Eliot's anxiety seems to offer a simplistic view of eugenics, using the trope of mental decay as a gloss for a degenerating civilization. However, his work, and that of London and Faulkner, stand apart from the propaganda used by the eugenics movement. Whereas London and Faulkner add complexity to the characterization of the feebleminded through narrative style, Eliot capitalizes on eugenic imagery to make declarative philosophical statements about civilization itself. His poetic focus is dystopian and far-reaching even as it draws from contemporary concerns. Eliot's work joined a larger discourse to create an anxious mood that had a direct effect on public policy. According to Daniel Kevles, "by 1914 thirty states had enacted new marriage laws or amended old ones" to void or restrict marriages of the feebleminded, the insane, people with venereal diseases, and others (99). Twenty-four states enacted sterilization laws between 1907 and 1929, giving the state power to sterilize criminals, epileptics, idiots, and the insane.[25] This sentiment lasted well into the 1930s, as a 1937 *Fortune* poll revealed that 66 percent of Americans favored sterilizing mental defectives (Kevles 114). Public opinion, influenced by the mass media, fiction, and political debates, declared that society had the right to control the reproduction of the mentally unfit, a sentiment that led to support of birth control.

The issue of mental fitness was inextricably linked to that of economic fitness, as Connell noted in setting "Weeds" in an asylum housing the destitute. As discussed earlier, the upper classes used their access to birth control to limit family size while the poor reproduced at a higher rate. This relationship between class and numbers is what led Theodore Roosevelt and others to thunder about the threat of "race suicide." Birth control advocates used fear of an unbalanced social and economic population to argue that contraception should be made available to the poor. Eugenic pseudoscience supported the belief that poverty was hereditary, caused by lesser ability, lesser intelligence, and laziness. The correlation between social worth and heredity conformed to notions of meritocracy. A practical economic imperative guided eugenic ideas, because the state asked taxpayers to support the maintenance of institutions that cared for the unfit.[26]

25. In February 2001, the Virginia State Legislature publicly apologized for the state's forced sterilization between 1924 and 1979 of over 7,000 white Virginians with "hereditary" diseases such as mental illness, alcoholism, and immorality. Other states have also offered public apologies.

26. As Molly Ladd-Taylor notes, eugenic sterilization often exhibited a strong welfare motive. Ladd-Taylor argues that the economic rhetoric of taxpayer savings was "undoubtedly one reason the sterilization programs achieved more lasting success in the United States than government (i.e. taxpayer-) funded public health services" ("Saving Babies and

FIGURE 10. Arthur Young, "Hell on Earth," *The Masses*, March 1915.

While Sanger had initially argued that contraception would enable working-class women greater freedoms and serve a class revolution, by the 1920s the mainline birth control movement was firmly entrenched in eugenic discourse. The March 1915 issue of *The Masses* contains a cartoon entitled "Hell on Earth" by Art Young, which depicts a man bent over a bill-laden table while his wife holds a baby and several children crowd the background (fig. 10). The subtitle reads "A Question for Eugenicists: In an atmosphere of worry and fear, how can children be developed physically and morally?" This cartoon challenges assumptions of heredity by implying social conditions as causes of poverty, disease, and immorality. But later birth control rhetoric appealed to the wealthy, presenting contraception as a way to lessen the population of those needing tax-supported institutions. Few of the stories in the *Birth Control Review* focus on upper-class characters. Whereas *The Masses*

Sterilizing Mothers" 138).

had satirized rich do-gooders to reveal the futility of philanthropy, the *Review* did not want to alienate an audience of wealth and power. Instead, they dramatized the deplorable conditions of the poor, in effect "othering" the working class. Focusing the fiction on the lives of the poor supports the argument that uncontrolled reproduction leads to overpopulation and poverty. The implicit message here, however, is a eugenic one appealing to professional and upper-class readers: providing birth control to the poor will elevate the race by controlling the growth of the indigent (and largely immigrant or black populations).

Social thought also linked the poor and the feebleminded through the trait of licentiousness. Eugenicists considered both groups to be sexually unrestrained and animalistic. They considered feebleminded women especially prone to lust and used "sexual delinquency" (as evidenced by unmarried pregnancy) to justify sterilization (Doyle 17). The eugenic family studies from 1880 to 1920, by describing inbreeding, "loose marriages," and general immorality in salacious detail, had developed these connections. The degeneracy of these families was linked to mental deficiency and the need to control their promiscuity and consequent reproduction. The state sterilized ("asexualized") or sex-segregated inmates in asylums to ensure that more degenerate offspring would not result. Critics now note that eugenic laws were often administered according to social principles, and "judgments about who was feebleminded or insane—and therefore likely to be sterilized—were fraught with class and race bias. 'Economically dependent' men and women were three times as likely to be sterilized as those who were more prosperous" (Ladd-Taylor, "Saving Babies and Sterilizing Mothers" 144).

Erskine Caldwell's 1932 novel, *Tobacco Road,* illustrates how eugenic discourse lumped together undesirable traits such as shiftlessness and promiscuity. The novel contains characters and descriptions similar to those found in eugenic family studies, which "gave the movement its central, confirmational image: that of the degenerate hillbilly family, dwelling in filthy shacks and spawning endless generations of paupers, criminals, and imbeciles" (Rafter 2). Caldwell would have been familiar with the genre, as his father had written a family study (S. Holmes 243–44). Indeed, one reviewer described *Tobacco Road* as "just another of those 'studies' of agricultural poverty and deterioration becoming degeneration of which we have now had many" ("Review," *Springfield Republican*). The novel focuses on a starving family of cotton farmers, the Lesters, and Lov Bensey, who married twelve-year-old Pearl Lester. Ada and Jeeter Lester had seventeen children, with two living adult children left at home: Dude is "slow" and childlike, while Ellie May has a disfiguring harelip.

In *Tobacco Road* Caldwell uses mythic eugenic images, such as sexual depravity and animal imagery, which Rafter notes as common to the family study genre. Ellie May, for example, drags her bottom across the sand in a kind of sexual heat "like an old hound" (24) and has sex with Lov in full view of her family and several watching Negroes. She embodies the promiscuous female defective prominent in eugenic arguments. Jeeter also enacts the oversexed mythos attributed to the unfit. He admits to fathering numerous illegitimate children in addition to the seventeen fathered with his wife, propositions the widow who marries Dude, and admits to thoughts of incest. Poor, shiftless, stupid, amoral, and riddled with hereditary physical deformities, the Lesters' licentiousness creates an overall eugenic message linking poverty with feeblemindedness with promiscuity, all traits eradicated by a negative eugenics program. These portrayals helped lead to the enactment of public policy measures "to control breeding in the so-called social problem group—those with lives characterized by poverty, loose marriage liaisons, illegitimacy, and dependence on relief" (Haller 140). Control of reproduction was a question of public health.

Although Caldwell credits the farmer's faith in tobacco and cotton as the impetus for his novel, his tone reveals the safe distance of a voyeur. Several contemporary reviewers commented on Caldwell's use of humor, a device that allowed readers to laugh at and thus separate themselves from the dysgenic family. The other potential reaction—disgust—offered the same distancing effect, as *Forum* magazine argued: "Mr. Caldwell recites the orgiastic litany calmly and with a serene detachment. Such detachment is not likely to be shared by most readers, who, if they take the book seriously, will probably finish it—if they do finish it—with disgust and a slight retching; but anyone who considers it as subtle burlesque is going to have a fine time" ("Review"). The narrative style of *Tobacco Road* thus mimics that of the eugenic family studies, using the perspective of an outside observer relating to a distant, voyeuristic audience. This style replaces empathy or sympathy for these "degenerates" with distaste, smoothing the way for restrictive legislation.

The fiction of Meridel Le Sueur provides a more critical reading of the intersections between class, gender, and mental fitness. By using first-person narration, she bridges the pseudoscientific distance between reader and character, insisting on a more intimate reading of the implications of negative eugenic practice. Haller notes that "feebleminded women were considered 'oversexed,' uninhibited, and sexually aggressive" (144). Le Sueur criticizes how a poor woman transgressing traditional gender roles could conveniently be labeled "feebleminded" and thus become a candidate for sterilization.[27] In "Sequel to Love" and *The Girl*, Le Sueur portrays how society applied this (il)logic. She narrates how the state labels a poor young woman, pregnant and unmarried, "feeble-minded" in an attempt to control her sexuality.

In the short story "Sequel to Love," first published in *Anvil* in 1935, Le Sueur shows how poor women were sterilized against their will during the Depression. The story opens with the first-person narrator describing how she got in "the place where they keep the feeble-minded" (36). Her uneducated dialect does not support the idea that the narrator is feeble-minded, however, just that she is young and uneducated. The narrator's first child was taken from her and put in the Salvation Army home because she was unwed, and now "[t]hey won't let me out of here if I don't get sterilized" (36). She is an involuntary inmate, incarcerated until she surrenders reproductive control. But the narrator sees sterilization as a sin and believes it will take away her sexual pleasure, "and that's all the pleasure I ever had. Workers ain't supposed to have any pleasure and now they're takin' that away because it ain't supposed to be doin' anybody any good and they're afraid I'll have another baby" (36).

To the narrator, and to the reader, the enforced confinement and impending sterilization are class-based assaults on her reproductive autonomy. The narrator, who had no access to birth control, had tried to find an abortion: "One month I missed and got nervous and went to a doctor and he wouldn't do nothin' because I didn't have no money. I went to three like that, and then one give me some pills and I took one and it made my ears ring so I was afraid to take any more" (37). These attempts demonstrate the will, but not the resources, to control her fertility. Unable to control her body, she also loses the power to control her offspring: "they [the Salvation Home people] rented it out to a woman and now they got me here" (37). The narrator demonstrates surprising insight into state mechanisms of power enacted upon the classed bodies of women. She views sterilization as a way to control working women and also as a punishment against unwed sexuality: "They keep sayin' I like men but why shouldn't I like men, why shouldn't a girl like a man? But for us girls that work for our livin' we ain't got no right to it" (38). Eugenics provided a justification for sterilizing women such as the narra-

27. Schoen notes that some women in North Carolina with no access to birth control were so desperate to control their reproduction that they submitted themselves for sterilization "even though this necessitated that they be diagnosed as feebleminded" (5; also 112–24).

tor, since promiscuity not only transmitted diseases but was considered a hereditary disease. As Pernick notes, "Homosexuality, masturbation, birth control, sodomy, prostitution, rape, and even too frequent sex within marriage were topics of debate among eugenicists, both as to whether they increased or decreased the propagation of other diseases, and as to whether they were inherited diseases themselves" (*The Black Stork* 68). By naming the organization "Salvation Home," Le Sueur comments on the guise of morality cloaking enforced sterilization. "Sequel to Love" demonstrates the inevitable consequences for poor women with no access to birth control, critiquing the social system that denied these women control over their reproduction.

Le Sueur returns to this theme in her novella *The Girl*, written in 1935 but not published until 1978. The young first-person narrator, referred to only as the Girl, becomes pregnant out of wedlock. Her friend had warned her of what happened to women who transgressed in the city: "They will pick you up, Clara told me, and give you tests and sterilize you or send you to the women's prison" (1). Indeed the Girl's physical display of sexuality earns her suspicion at the Relief office, where her caseworker writes, "*She should be tested for sterilization after her baby is born. In our opinion sterilization would be advisable*" (114). What the caseworker has "read" on the Girl's body is illicit behavior, which she associates with hereditary stain. When the Girl protests, she is taken forcibly to the relief maternity home and housed with syphilitics, epileptics, and other defectives, equating her "sinful" condition with disease. Le Sueur's narrative rescues the Girl from sterilization and has her deliver her daughter in a warehouse full of women, offering a positive alternative to the eugenic fantasy of state control. This socialist-feminist narrative implicitly contrasts a broad spectrum of reproductive options, from enforced surgical sterilization to individual female control through contraception to the welcome acceptance of pregnancy. Le Sueur's writing style, which employs fragmentation and stream-of-consciousness, adds complexity not found in the didactic narratives of the propaganda fiction. Her work adds new layers to the public discourse of economic fitness by questioning popular assumptions. Her sympathetic portrayal of female sexuality confronts a social discourse of sin and punishment. Le Sueur also challenges the application of eugenic policy on economic grounds by demonstrating the harsh financial reality for women of the 1930s. Foregrounding class and sexuality, she layers women's narrative voices to reveal the intersections of class, gender, marital status, and determinations of reproductive fitness.

The Menace of the Diseased Body

Ending the transmittal of inherited diseases was another motivation for negative eugenics. This hidden menace threatened the pure "germ plasm" of a healthy national body. Kay Boyle and Charles Norris explore the dilemma of genetic disease and come to different conclusions in *Plagued by the Nightingale* (1931) and *Seed* (1930), respectively.

Plagued by the Nightingale by modernist expatriate Boyle explores the possibility of transmitting hereditary disease while focusing on the primacy of maternity in the family structure. Critics have ignored the placement of the text in the midst of widespread eugenic anxiety, perhaps taking their critical cues from Boyle herself, who weaves eugenic issues into her text without commentary. The American protagonist, Bridget, is married to the Frenchman Nicolas, who is adamant that they have no children for fear of passing on a hereditary bone disease. The "corruption of the bone," which attacks the legs and brain, is passed through the male line and manifests in male offspring (13). In gendering the disease Boyle gives genetic primacy to women, a structure reinforced by the family dynamics she presents. Nicolas, who is beginning to feel the pain of the disease, returns from the United States to his smothering family in France. His claim, "I have only come into my heritage," resonates on both the genetic and familial level (6).

Nicolas displays a negative eugenic view, believing that he should not reproduce to stop the continuance of the disease. He tells his parents, "I fear . . . that you shall never have the pleasure of distributing boxes of sugared almonds in honour of the baptism of my child" (6). His bourgeois family, however, believes that family is all and pressures the young couple to have children. Marriage and reproduction are paramount goals despite the devastating illness, which they seemingly ignore. Nicolas is incensed by his parents' pressure, spewing bitterness and rage at the family he blames for his condition. He sees disease as his genetic lineage: "Pap says we should have a child," he tells Bridget. "A dear little child to run around and call us mama and papa. I can give it paralysis, what can you give it, my dear?" (19). When Bridget and Nicolas need money, the parents offer it on the condition that they become pregnant. Nicolas resists the insistent pressure, attempting to borrow money elsewhere and, when that fails, attempting suicide. The novel implies that he and Bridget employ an unwritten contraceptive practice, "for nothing on earth would he have a child with his illness in its bones" (76).

In contrast, his sister Charlotte fulfills the family mandate. She is married to her first cousin Jean, in whom the disease has progressed to partial paralysis. The disease is also manifesting in two of her sons, who already show "some weakness in [the] limbs" (13). Nicolas encourages his sister to use birth control and end further inheritance of the disease. Full of despair at his own deterioration and rage at the continuance of this suffering, Nicolas claims, "It would have been better if they had died in my sister's womb!" (32). Charlotte suffers complications during her sixth pregnancy, losing her mind, the baby, and her own life. Her death reinforces the contraceptive and eugenic ideology advanced by Nicolas by highlighting the dangers of reproduction.

Despite their single-minded reproductive advance, the family recognizes the need for new blood. Luc, a family friend, appears as a eugenic savior, and they hope he will marry one of the single daughters. Maman thinks he "must somehow, through the flesh of one of her three daughters, be grafted to them all, be one rich fruitful bough upon the decaying family tree" (94). This language echoes a rudimentary knowledge of agricultural genetics. Rather than cease reproduction of a tainted line, the family hopes to regain its genetic health through the introduction of new blood. However, Luc falls in love with Bridget rather than one of the sisters, with healthy blood attracted to healthy blood. Asked to elope with him, Bridget faces a eugenic dilemma: she wants children, and remaining with Nicolas means either giving that up or risking transmitting a terrible disease. Nicolas himself, in a fit of bitterness, suggests that she have a baby with a different man (110).

In the end, however, Bridget announces that she is pregnant (by Nicolas) and stays with Nicolas and his family. Dianne Chambers reads this ending as a move to set Luc free from the family: "In one action, Bridget both denies the family what it most wants and satisfies its deepest desires" (256). In this context the bone disease stands in for a larger flaw, a "rotten-to-the-bone" bourgeois family that attempts to subsume individual identity. However, reading the novel in the context of ongoing eugenic debates, we can find meanings beyond the traditional interpretation of the female identity quest. *Plagued by the Nightingale* offers a discourse with current social issues. The novel depicts the conflict between the drive-to-family that placed marriage and reproduction as paramount goals against a growing awareness and repugnance of hereditary disease. Boyle presents a eugenic caution in Jean, who is helpless and whose mind is beginning to deteriorate, and Nicolas, whose pain and despair become nihilistic rage. However, Bridget's desire for family and her decision to risk transmitting the disease to her offspring undermines any clear argument in support of eugenic contraception.

Seed by Charles G. Norris more directly interacts with both eugenic

FIGURE 11. Advertisement for *Seed: A Novel of Birth Control* by Charles Norris, back cover of *Birth Control Review,* September 1930. Reprinted with permission of Alexander Sanger.

and contraceptive arguments. Norris envisioned his seventh novel, subtitled *A Novel of Birth Control*, as a conscious exploration of the arguments for and against contraception. His stated purpose was to inform the public, using fiction to instruct and intervene, "feeling that the more thought the public at large gives to the question, the more speedily may come the decision regarding the rights and wrongs of the matter" (qtd. in Davison, "Charles G. Norris, Margaret Sanger and *Seed*" 1). To this end he corresponded with Margaret Sanger, presenting her with galley proofs in 1930. The novel considers how birth control and reproductive choices affected members of an extended family. While the novel makes a comprehensive case for birth control, Sanger judged it too weak and wrote that it "favors the usual Catholic prejudices and upholds them" (qtd. in Davison, "Charles" 3). And while Norris attempted to present balanced views, he does focus the last chapter on a Catholic priest who advocates continence and abstinence from his deathbed. The novel received mixed reviews, both in the *Birth Control Review* and elsewhere, although the *Review* did publish a full-page advertisement for the novel proclaiming it "Fearless!" (fig. 11) [28]

28. John B. Solley, M.D., reviewed the novel in the *Birth Control Review* in Novem-

Seed was a best seller despite mixed reviews. Following the fortunes of the extended Carter family in California, *Seed* focuses on Bart Carter, a novelist, husband, and father of five. Sexually frustrated by his wife, a Catholic who practices contraceptive abstinence, Bart lives for ten years with a more "emancipated" woman who uses birth control. While his aunt and sister are "ruined" from "babies, one after another," Bart's cousin Jane uses birth control and another cousin, Josephine, is "fighting for the establishment of health clinics in all parts of the country and for the repeal of five federal statues and various state laws which class the giving out of contraceptive information along with obscenity" (355, 402). Bart and his brother engage in didactic conversations about the law, but the depictions of women's lives and Bart's own tormented sexual desire for his wife are Norris's most persuasive points about the positive effects of contraception.

The novel's title of *Seed,* the cover image of a full-bodied woman sowing seeds, and the biblical epigraph from Mark 4:3–8 ("Behold, there went out a sower to sow") signal the novel's focus on reproduction. Norris explores eugenic issues as well as the more traditional religious and economic reactions to birth control. The novel supports negative eugenics; even as it recommends birth control to save marriages, women's health, and family financial stability, the novel makes definite claims as to who should and should not reproduce. For example, Bart proclaims that "ours is the very class that *should* have 'em; not the illiterate and unhealthy riffraff down in the Ghetto!" (356). This thinking relies on an association of poverty with hereditary disease. As his sister Josephine argues, "reckless breeding . . . brings hundreds of thousands of diseased or crippled children into the world who never should have been born" (403). Other characters also forward eugenic arguments. Jane rails against a woman who is "positively mentally deficient" and who "welcomes any man that comes along" (189). Is the woman a "disgrace to the community" for her open promiscuity or for all of the "rickety children she's brought into the world. Eight, by the last count" (189)? None of the children are "normal," advancing the image of the relentless reproduction of defectives. The specter of race suicide overshadows Jane's condemnation: she and her husband, ideal genetic stock, decided to postpone children until they were financially stable. Now, however, Jane is too old to reproduce.

The race suicide argument is most strongly made by Bart's brother Josh. A doctor, Josh explains that he and his wife had no children because "Louise is an epileptic, and epilepsy is hereditary. She is much better now,

---

ber 1930. Universal Pictures released a movie version of *Seed* in 1931, starring Bette Davis (Davison, "Charles" 3).

rarely has an attack, but both she and I knew it would be impossible for us to have children. Our problem would have been a serious one without the boon of birth control" (408). The novel thus presents the medical profession advocating birth control for eugenic ends. But Josh goes beyond a disease model to argue against birth control among the upper classes in order to prevent race suicide. He uses Jane as an example, stating, "Unless birth control is stopped among the upper classes, and its use legalized among the lower classes, the best part of our population will die off, and the country will be overrun by incompetents and morons" (409). Josh again associates class with hereditary disorders and mental deficiency, such that the word *disease* takes on multiple valances of corruption.

This congruence of inherited disease with negative traits combining to form a strong eugenic argument is exemplified in the tale of Ossip, "a half-witted, degenerate nymphomaniac" presenting a legacy of mental and physical disease: "She's confined now in a home for women of her type, but before she was put where she couldn't do any further harm she had brought twenty-four diseased and insane children into the world. Half of them died, many are now living in institutions, and the rest are at large, doubtless breeding and bringing more diseased or insane children into the world" (403). Disease begets disease, contributing to the growing social cost of institutionalization. When presented with such degeneracy, sterilization seems to be the answer, and Josh advocates it: "Here in California we are sufficiently progressive to sterilize such people," he tells Bart, "but the harm was done before this woman ever reached the attention of authorities. Such a creature never wanted children; she was a half-witted, ignorant animal, and she would gratefully have used birth control if somebody had told her about it" (403). Indeed, during the 1920s twenty-four states implemented sterilization laws to reduce the amount of spending on public relief (S. Holmes 252). Norris links preventing inheritable disease and birth control; birth control is a viable alternative to sterilization, and knowledge of it may prevent the reproduction of the "unfit" before the state finds them to sterilize. *Seed* is unique in its novel-length attempt to fictionally explore the issue of birth control, and its best-seller status reveals widespread public interest.

The Threat to the "Great Race"

Often remembered today for its racial overtones, the eugenics movement lent a pseudoscientific language and backing to beliefs in biological superiority. In eugenic science the word *race* had multiple meanings, including the broad "human race" and a more specific "Nordic" or white race. Eugenicists considered the Nordic advanced, with immigrants and African Americans as inferior. These beliefs led to public policy such as immigration restriction as well as to racist stereotypes. In the eugenic film *The Black Stork* (later re-titled *Are You Fit to Marry?*) the original taint is traced to Claude's grandfather's affair with a slave.[29] The only identifiable black character in the film is deformed, linking race with disability and ugliness. Demographers forwarded racist assumptions by concluding that the decline in African American fertility during the period was largely due to venereal disease, and that blacks were not intelligent enough to practice effective birth control (McFalls and Masnick 90, 101).[30] Eugenicists recognized established anti-miscegenation laws as eugenic and added scientific credibility to the taboo of racial mixing. They expressed scientific racism not just in demographic studies but also in psychology, criminal justice, and, of course, fiction and popular media.

An early modernist text that invokes racist eugenic stereotypes is Gertrude Stein's *Three Lives* (1909). This work responds to a cultural stereotype of "[t]he imagined fecundity of African American and immigrant women," which "served as a locus of eugenic anxiety in the early twentieth century" (English, "Gertrude Stein and the Politics of Literary-Medical Experimentation" 199).[31] In the "Melanctha" section of *Three Lives*, Stein uses blood to define character, reinforcing a eugenic belief

29. After the release of *Birth of a Nation*, this clear tie between taint and race in *The Black Stork* was considered too inflammatory, and the scene was re-shot to substitute the slave with a white servant, replacing race with class. See Pernick, *The Black Stork*, 56–57.

30. Jessie M. Rodrique strongly counters this claim and argues that black women consciously used birth control and that "blacks were active and effective participants in the establishment of local clinics and in the birth control debate" (138). See also J. Hart. Katz and Stern also note that "[r]ecent work on black fertility rates has challenged the view that the decline in births among post-slavery blacks was due to physiological factors that reduced fecundity, notably venereal disease" and that "black fertility rates reflected the same economic and social variables that determined the fertility patterns of white Americans" (86).

Racist and eugenic ideologies run throughout the history of gynecology and the development of birth control technologies. For example, the "father of gynecology," Marion J. Sims, invented the speculum and techniques of gynecological surgery based on his experiments on slave women, and hormonal birth control was first tested on poor Puerto Rican women. See Kapsalis and Oudshoorn.

31. Many critics have debated Stein's racism. Fleissner notes two interpretive tendencies: condemning the work for its use of racial types that doom Melanctha; or celebrating her sexuality as a "protomodernist ability to slip all determining yokes" (254). I agree with Fleissner that "[t]he strongest readings have been those willing to acknowledge that both of these aspects are present in Stein's text with respect both to its narrative claims and to Melanctha's character, but there has been little attempt to theorize concretely how this can be done" (254). See also English, *Unnatural Selections*.

in the determining power of inheritance. The "half white girl Melanctha Herbert" is "subtle, intelligent, attractive," while her black friend, Rose Johnson, is "coarse, decent, sullen, ordinary, black childish . . . unmoral, promiscuous, shiftless" (Stein 83). Stein exhorts nature over nurture, as Rose was raised by a white family but is described in quintessentially racist terms (training "had only made for habits, not for nature"), while Melanctha benefits from her white blood to become the stereotypic tragic mulatta (she "had been half made with real white blood" [82]). Stein subscribes to the hierarchy of races forwarded by eugenicists, placing the Nordic at the pinnacle of civilized advancement. As Daylanne English notes, Stein eerily echoes Lothrop Stoddard, who describes the result of mixed blood in *Rising Tide of Color*: "These unhappy beings, every cell of whose bodies is a battleground of jarring heredities, express their souls in acts of hectic violence and aimless instability" (*Unnatural Selections* 120). This instability describes Melanctha's sexual wandering, which makes her unable "to fulfill the marriage plot" (English, *Unnatural Selections* 104). Melanctha dies alone and estranged.

Stein's use of racial stereotypes offers a single example of the discursive intersection between fiction and eugenic propaganda. Interestingly, many African American writers, including Nella Larsen, James Weldon Johnson, and Richard Wright, admired Stein's "Melanctha" (Brinnin 120–22). Although Claude McKay found Stein's depiction of "Negro life" unconvincing, his characters in *Home to Harlem* are not dissimilar in sharing Melanctha's sexual "wandering." McKay suggests birth control for the promiscuous working class when the educated Ray encourages Jake to use prophylactics: "Those devices that you despise are really for you rather than for me or people like me, who don't live your kind of free life. If you, and the whole strong race of workingman who live freely like you, don't pay attention to them, then you'll all wither away and rot like weeds" (207). While Melanctha dies alone as punishment for her wandering, both Ray and Jake are paired up at the end of *Home to Harlem*. Jake prepares to leave Harlem with Felice while Ray considers settling down with Agatha and "getting ready to litter little black piggies" (263).

There was no agreement over birth control and eugenics within the African American community. Indeed, much like their white peers, educated black "new women" were "reluctant breeders" (Douglas 98). Marcus Garvey and his followers believed that birth control was being used to eradicate the black race, whereas DuBois supported a program of positive eugenics. As Dorothy Roberts notes, "White eugenicists promoted birth control as a way of preserving an oppressive social structure; Blacks promoted birth control as a way of toppling it" (*Killing the Black Body* 86).

DuBois used the pages of *The Crisis* to fight the scientific justification of racial inferiority but subscribed to a eugenic paradigm in his vision of improving the black race.[32] As he wrote in a 1922 *Crisis* editorial, "birth control is science and sense applied to the bringing of children into the world, and of all who need it we Negroes are the first" ("Opinion" 248). In "Black Folk and Birth Control," DuBois bemoans the fact that "the mass of Negroes know almost nothing about the Birth Control movement, and even intelligent colored people have a good many misapprehensions and a good deal of fear at openly learning about it" (167). DuBois and others viewed birth control as part of a larger eugenics program, inextricably tying together contraception and eugenics.[33]

Although often accused of racism, birth controllers aligned themselves with eugenics to gain the credibility of science rather than to forward a racist agenda. Linda Gordon argues that "[b]irth-control reformers were not attracted to eugenics *because* they were racists; rather they had interests in common with eugenists and had no strong tradition of antiracism on which to base a critique of eugenics" (*Woman's Body* 281). In 1930 the first birth control clinic opened in Harlem. The *Review* included many articles on race and dedicated the June 1932 issue to the topic of birth control for blacks, featuring articles by prominent African American intellectuals in favor of birth control.[34] Articles such as Lemuel T. Sewell's "The Negro Wants Birth Control" argued for a greater number of birth control clinics serving the black population. These articles were often critical of the hierarchy of races proposed by eugenics even as they proposed a positive eugenics program within the ranks of upper- and middle-class African Americans. A debate over the eugenic aspects of contraceptives also surfaced in the *Review*, such as Elmer A. Carter's claim that contraception was dysgenic: "Therein lies the danger, for Negroes who by virtue of their education and capacity are best able to

---

32. See Taylor, English ("W. E. B. DuBois's Family Crisis"), and Doyle.
33. In her study of *The Crisis, Birth Control Review,* and *Opportunity,* Jamie Hart notes that "only male authors expressed opposition to birth control," and they "appear to have subscribed to a rigid understanding of gender roles, a similarity to that found within white ideology, with women serving as 'baby factories' and men in charge of the family and its economic status" (75, 74). Hart argues that the predominance of male voices in this debate is due in part to women's concern with combating negative stereotypes of black women as oversexed. The few women who did contribute "tended to discuss personal cases and appeared to be more concerned with the health and progress of individual African-American women and their families than with 'the race' as a whole" (78).
34. The June 1932 issue also included "A Question of Negro Health" by Charles S. Johnson, who notes that race and "unfit" are often associated. The March 1933 "The Negro and Birth Control" by E. Franklin Frazier refutes the idea that birth control has been dysgenic among African Americans.

rear children shrink from that responsibility and the Negro who, in addition to the handicaps of race and color, is shackled by mental and social incompetence serenely goes on his way bringing into the world children whose chances of mere existence are apparently becoming more and more hazardous" (169). The debate over racial eugenics spilled over into fiction by African American authors such as Nella Larsen and Jessie Redmon Fauset.[35] In her 1928 novel *Quicksand*, Larsen's character James Vayle voices a positive eugenic argument similar to that of DuBois and other members of the black intelligentsia: "Don't you see that if we—I mean people like us—don't have children, the others will still have. That's one of the things that's the matter with us. The race is sterile at the top. Few, very few Negroes of the better class have children, and each generation has to wrestle again with the obstacles of the preceding one, lack of money, education, and background. I feel very strongly about this. We're the ones who must have the children if the race is to get anywhere" (103). The rhetoric of racial uplift rings through in this eugenic plea. Not only does the protagonist, Helga, not reproduce with a suitable mate, denying the call to mother the race, but she marries a poor southern preacher with darker skin. Pregnancy and childbirth follow rapidly, and the novel ends with the implication that Helga will die from repeated childbearing. Larsen sends a mixed eugenic message: she does not advocate positive eugenics, but the bleak ending refuses to romanticize the lower classes. Rather, the implicit message links the successful quest for female sexual fulfillment with access to birth control. Eugenic racial issues are kept apart from and secondary to the exploration of female desire.

Jessie Redmon Fauset's 1931 novel, *The Chinaberry Tree*, also employs the rhetoric of blood and breeding common to eugenic arguments. Laurentine is the product of her mother's love affair with a white man and has "that bad white blood in her" (15); Melissa, her younger niece, is the product of her mother's affair with a married black man. Melissa does not know that she is illegitimate. When she returns to the small town where she was conceived to live with Laurentine, townsfolk describe her as having "vicious blood" (49). Even the local doctor, Laurentine's fiancé, implies that unsavory traits are transmitted in the blood: "a girl with—with that blood in her veins—why there's no telling

---

35. Although her work falls before this period, Pauline Hopkins advocated eugenic marriage in her fiction. According to Nickel, "Hopkins advocated that African-Americans' genetic improvement was necessary for racial advancement and dependent on their marital choices. Calling for the commingling of white and black racial lines, Hopkins asserted that it would produce a genetically superior race and eventually lead to the amelioration of African-Americans' political and social conditions" (47).

what might happen" (318). Fauset and Larsen contributed to the conversation among educated African Americans regarding birth control, eugenics, and their role in reproducing and improving the race. Unlike their male counterparts, these writers focused on the specific role of women in the debate over who should reproduce.

The image of race as disease recurs throughout eugenic texts, fueling beliefs among both black and white populations on the role of reproduction in the improvement of civilization. These texts accrued to shape public views on race and the role of birth control in "balancing the numbers" in a diverse America. The racial eugenic trope still occurs in more recent texts, such as Ben Caldwell's 1968 "Top Secret or a Few Million after B.C." In this play, a racist southern president sitting with his (white male) advisors tries to find a solution to "the nigger problem" (47). The solution is family planning: "We can not only kill the niggers without their knowing it, we can kill them in advance and make them think we're doing them a favor! Niggers love to fuck—we can't stop that, and their women are the most fertile in the universe. We can use this peculiar, animalistic trait of theirs to our advantage. Let 'em fuck all they want. How do we stop the resulting babies? Birth control is the answer" (49). Caldwell's suspicion of the eugenic implications of birth control are reminiscent of those of earlier African American leaders. Toni Morrison's 1977 *Song of Solomon* "flips the script" of eugenic logic through the creation of the "Seven Days," a group of seven African American men whose task is to "keep the ratio the same" by killing a white for every black murdered in racial violence (155). The group's existence rests on eugenic logic, that "[a]ny man, any woman, or any child is good for five to seven generations of heirs before they're bred out. So every death is the death of five to seven generations" (154). The men justify killing whites by their belief that "[w]hite people are unnatural. As a race they are unnatural. . . . The disease they have is in their blood, in the structure of their chromosomes" (156, 157). Morrison's use of eugenic language demonstrates the literary legacy of eugenic discourse.

Conclusion

The popularity of eugenics waned over the course of the 1930s. Haller links this demise to a variety of factors, including a new scrutiny of the accuracy of IQ tests. He writes, "When racism lost its scientific standing in the 1930s and the Nazis showed what use could be made of race prejudice, then a recoil against the racism of the 1920s became the major factor bringing a repudiation of eugenics and destroying the emphasis on heredity that had characterized much of American thought in the previous two decades" (159). The conservative belief that "[m]orons, mental defectives, epileptics, illiterates, paupers, unemployables, criminals, prostitutes and dope fiends" should be sterilized came under fire (Sanger, qtd. in Corea 149). While the birth control movement and the eugenics movement shared aims and fictional representation for a time, this union was always conflicted. Eugenic philosophy called for science to decide who should reproduce and thus found sterilization to be a more efficient solution.[36] Birth control offered too much control to women and left room for misuse. However, the brief union with eugenics greatly affected the movement. As Linda Gordon argues, the shift in focus and name from birth control to Planned Parenthood in 1942 reveals a movement toward incorporating eugenic thinking by emphasizing population control rather than female autonomy (*The Moral Property of Women* 242).

When in *Are You Fit to Marry?* Claude asks, "How did you know?" Dr. Dickey replies, "I'm a doctor—it is written on you. I can read." Heredity is inscribed on the body, encoded in the blood, and written into the body of the text. Eugenicists read social value in race, mental ability, disease, and vice—traits they believed were embedded in the "germ plasm" of each individual and unquestionably available for interpretation. The inheritable nature of this code fueled their desire to "edit" mistakes out of the race, thus improving the American stock. This metaphor of literacy applies not only to eugenic ideology but also to the texts that reproduced its message. Fiction and nonfiction acted as a testing ground for eugenic ideas, providing support for policy. These representations had real material effects on women's lives.

---

36. The use of sterilization to wrest control of female reproduction from women's power is still an issue, as evidenced by recent threats to force welfare mothers to have birth control implants and/or surgical sterilization. See D. Roberts, "Crime, Race, and Reproduction," and Arthur.

6

The Economics of Desire and Despair

Birth Control and the Depression Era

Because it enables parents to limit their children to those they can properly support. Over-large families lead to under-nourishment, overcrowding, child labor, low wages, unemployment; they are one of the most potent causes of poverty.

Because it makes possible the elimination of the unfit, who place such a heavy burden upon the resources of the community. It is estimated that taxpayers spend close to two billon dollars per year for the care of dependency, much of which is preventable.

—Birth Control Review, August 1931

"ONE THING'S SURE and nothing's surer / The rich get richer and the poor get—children," went a popular song of the 1920s. As much of the fiction under discussion reveals, class often determined access to birth control; the wealthy circumvented the law, leading to fears of "race suicide" as the poor and immigrant populations out-reproduced them. Caroline H. Robinson warned of "Collegians' Race Suicide" in 1933, claiming that "the majority of graduates from the big women's colleges never bear a child" (48).

The Depression brought changes not only to the national economy but also to public perceptions of contraception. Many industries declined during the 1920s even as stock market speculation increased, creating an unstable economy that imploded in 1929. In the following four years the "average family's income had fallen 40 percent" (Solinger, *Pregnancy and Power* 103). The birth control movement flourished during the 1930s as economic conditions worsened. While Margaret Sanger lobbied for a "doctors only" bill that would allow doctors to prescribe contraceptives at their discretion, the movement deployed an official rhetoric of economic arguments. The *Birth Control Review* reported, "In April, 1933, a total of 4,445,338 families were being given relief, according to reports of the Federal Emergency Relief Administration" (Bossard 1). Birth control would end the burden of "relief babies" on the taxpayers.

During the Depression, young couples postponed marriage and avoided pregnancy because of the economic conditions. Married women sought relief at the rising number of birth control clinics; in 1932 there were 145 clinics. Alice Dunbar-Nelson wrote, "Negro women are exercising birth control in order to preserve their new economic independence. Or, because of the poverty of the family, they are compelled to limit their offspring" (289). The Depression also affected single women, who often depended on "dates" with men for meals and other gifts such as clothing. More single women worked in industrial centers, which contributed to their greater sense of individual freedom.[1] These economic conditions hastened public acceptance of changes to birth control law. Contemporary polls revealed this growing acceptance; the 1936 Gallup poll "showed that 63 percent favored the teaching and practice of birth control" and a *Ladies' Home Journal* poll revealed that 79 percent of American women "believe in birth control" (Ware 7; J. Reed, "The Birth Control Movement before *Roe v. Wade*" 35). These cultural changes put public pressure on the government to lift legal restrictions, including *U.S. v. One Package of Japanese Pessaries*, the 1936 decision removing the federal ban on the medical profession's dissemination of contraceptives for "the purpose of saving a life or promoting the patient's well-being."[2]

A narrowing of the labor market affected women: soon competition for federal funds was matched by competition for jobs. A 1936 Gallup poll found that 82 percent of respondents thought a wife should not work if her husband was employed (Coiner, *Better Red* 41). But women, who could be paid less than men, often found work more easily.

1. See Peiss.
2. The 1936 *United States v. One Package* decision reinterpreted the Comstock Act in favor of the birth control movement. Judge Augustus Hand ruled that the Comstock Act of 1873 should be applied to "only such articles as congress would have denounced as immoral if it had understood all the conditions under which they were to be used. Its design, in our opinion, was not to prevent the importation, sale, or carriage by mail of things which might intelligently be employed by conscientious and competent physicians for the purpose of saving life or promoting the well-being of their patients" (qtd. in Kennedy 249). An earlier decision, the 1930 *Youngs Rubber Corporation v. C. I. Lee & Co, Inc.*, decided that transporting contraceptive devices under certain conditions was legal.

Paula Rabinowitz argues, "categories of differences—gender, class—are not mutually exclusive but, instead, remain fundamentally implicated within each other as re-presentations of themselves and each other" ("Difference/Different Endings" 65).[3] Families that had once been middle class were now experiencing what the poor had long known: each new child could prove an unwelcome burden to scarce resources. Class and gender, production and reproduction, are mutually constituted in the public discourse and much of the fiction of the 1930s.

The birth control movement continued to make sentimental appeals for why the poor needed contraception. But during the Depression Era the movement fortified this approach with broader appeals to position birth control as a vital part of social policy. We can see this shift in two examples, both of which use a wolf as symbol of the savage effects of poverty. "The Stork and the Wolf," a poem by Florence Wayne Hickey in the April 1925 *Birth Control Review*, offers a first-person account of this problem. The narrative voice of the poem describes a poor mother's situation:

> The stork is at my chimney
> And the wolf is at my door,
> Hush my wailing one!
> My hungry brood is huddled
> In a corner of the floor. (109)

The stork indicates that the woman is pregnant yet again, while the wolf is the danger of poverty that could take the lives of her children. Already there are nine children, including a young toddler. She has "no bread" for "the brood about me pressed," and "no milk" for "the yearling at my breast." Without the ability to control fertility, the economics of poverty, hunger, and despair result. The use of a first-person voice and the woman's isolation create a sense of urgency and despair. A May 1932 drawing in the *Review* also used the image of wolves (fig. 12). This time, multiple wolves not only symbolize hunger but also bear the labels of disease, ignorance, overpopulation, and unemployment. They menace

3. Rabinowitz makes this argument more fully in *Labor and Desire: Women's Revolutionary Fiction in Depression America* (1991). Her stance on women in the economy echoes that of Luce Irigaray in her analysis of women as commodity exchanged among men. Irigaray writes: "all the social regimes of 'history' are based upon the exploitation of one 'class' of producers, namely, women. Whose reproductive use value (reproduction of children and of the labor force) and whose constitution as exchange value underwrite the symbolic order as such, without any compensation in kind going to them for that 'work'" (173).

FIGURE 12. "Bread! Bread! Bread! Hungry all the time," *Birth Control Review*, May 1932: 6. Reprinted with permission of Alexander Sanger.

a group of people huddled behind an opening door. "Birth Control," the caption reads, "will help keep the wolves from the door of the world." The illustration suggests contraception as part of a larger social policy needed during the Depression, and moves beyond appeals to sentimentality to join the scientific and political arguments gaining currency.

While the Depression's effects were felt nationwide, geography exacerbated the ignorance of class and served as another layer of difference within economic strata. Birth control advocates could not reach women in rural and southern communities as quickly. Margaret Jarman Hagood's documentary study of southern tenant farmwomen in the 1930s established that birth control information was not circulating to all women even twenty years after Sanger had begun her fight. By 1936 the American Birth Control League had succeeded in establishing nearly 250 birth control clinics, mostly located in urban areas. Hagood found that "[t]he modal attitude of not wanting children is not accompanied by a modal practice of preventing them. Certain difficulties inhered in the securing of information on contraceptive practices" (122–23). These "difficulties" included neither having private physicians or public clinics to go to nor having the education and money to research the issue. Instead, these women often relied on the oral grapevine for information. Hagood reports, "One woman told how her mother scrimped and saved $10 to buy her a very special sort of "serene" (syringe), which did no good at all. Most have heard that there are effective methods now, but they do not know what they are nor where to go to get reliable information about them" (124). This economic split had racial links as well. Studies conducted in 1938–39 and 1941 revealed that white, urban women with at least elementary-level education reported an 83 to 89 percent contraceptive use: "In all socioeconomic groups, except for the 6 percent with the least income and education, a majority of white women attempted to control their fertility. Black women were much less likely to employ contraception. Poverty and lack of education denied many of them access to information and materials" (Hartmann 171).

For this reason, the birth control movement argued that contraception should be part of federal New Deal programs (Gordon, *The Moral Property of Women* 211). They succeeded in getting birth control into the 1936 Farm Security Administration program. Until the early 1940s, "FSA agents, home supervisors, and public health nurses began to offer contraceptive advice to their clients and to residents in migrant labor camps across the country" (Schoen 37). Individual states such as North Carolina integrated birth control into their public health programs late in the 1930s to aid the rural poor.[4] As the birth control movement entered more fully into policy debates, the *Birth Control Review* ceased publishing fiction, making more space for updates from local birth control leagues and clinics, international news, and conferences.[5] However, American authors such as William Faulkner, Tess Slesinger, Agnes Smedley, and Meridel Le Sueur integrated the issue of contraception into their novels of the 1930s.

When Contraception Fails

Despite a growing acceptance of the necessity for birth control during the

---

4. In *Choice & Coercion: Birth Control, Sterilization, and Abortion in Public Health and Welfare,* Schoen focuses on North Carolina's public health program but provides context on the national picture.
5. Margaret Sanger ceased editing the *Review* in 1929.

1930s, the court system did not overthrow the Comstock Act until 1936. Access to contraception was thus still uneven at best, and the number of illegal abortions rose during the 1930s (Solinger, *Pregnancy and Power* 118). According to Linda Gordon, "Among a thousand women who went to a birth control clinic in the Bronx, New York, in 1931, 35 percent had had at least one illegal abortion, a proportion that applied to Catholics as well as Protestants and Jews" (*The Moral Property of Women* 25). The clinics kept these statistics, among many others, to accumulate data that would appease the scientific community and aid their cause. The movement could use this information to demonstrate that birth control prevented the evil of abortion and provided an economic boon to families and to society at large. But authors such as Tess Slesinger, Kay Boyle, and William Faulkner bring a greater complexity to their explorations of birth control, abortion, and economic necessity, including in their plots elements of ignorance and duplicity, failed contraception, and indecision.

Slesinger, a socialist who traveled in leftist intellectual circles, depicts birth control and abortion within a middle-class marriage in her 1934 novel, *The Unpossessed*. Her characters understand contraceptive practices: the abortion is the result of marital discord and indecision rather than ignorance. The main character, Margaret, has been considering having children ("Twenty-nine! what was the deadline for babies?"), but her Marxist intellectual husband, Miles, believes bringing children into the world is cruel (6). Slesinger undermines his argument, however, by depicting him as self-centered and self-satisfied. Margaret, tempted to have an affair, struggles with both her husband's "revolutionary" thinking and her mother's conventional ideology. She thinks "[c]onvention, her mother's sweet and trustful code, dictated that denial. But it might be one thing for her mother and another for her mother's child" (61). Although Margaret and her friends talk about sex, the intellectual banter covers a fear of mental and physical sterility and male misogyny. For instance, the character Jeffrey thinks "wombs, not souls—that's what women have" (96). The main female characters, Margaret, Norah, and Elizabeth, are childless despite their sexual activity. An exchange between Margaret and Norah reveals this knowledge and use of birth control:

> "oh Norah listen; I've got the silliest thing to tell you: I'm going to have a baby." Norah dropped her arm in alarm and they stood stock still on the fringe of the dancers. "A *baby?* have you tried everything?" "Why, Norah Meadows Blake, you *cynic!* I want it, I did it on purpose." (305)

Norah's reference to "have you tried everything" reveals knowledge of abortion and induced miscarriage, and Margaret's reply that she did it "on purpose" reveals a cessation of normal contraceptive practices.

For these educated, middle-class Marxists, pregnancy is a choice. But they make decisions under pressure from society and from Margaret's husband. The last chapter depicts the abortion.[6] Here we find that Margaret's joy in her pregnancy was short-lived, because her husband, Miles, is "frightened" and convinces Margaret to have an abortion so that they can maintain their economic and intellectual freedom.

> [I]n a regime like this, Miles said, it is a terrible thing to have a baby—it means the end of independent thought and the turning of everything into a scheme for making money; and there must be institutions such as there are in Russia, I said, for taking care of the babies and their mothers; why in a time like this, we both said, to have a baby would be suicide—goodbye to our plans, goodbye to our working out schemes for each other and the world—our courage would die, our hopes concentrate on the sordid business of keeping three people alive, one of whom would be a burden and an expense for twenty years. (349–50)

Miles reduces the baby to economic terms and pressures Margaret to have the abortion.

Class again comes into play when the folk remedies Margaret tries, "jumping off tables and broiling herself in hot water," are unsuccessful. She finds and is able to afford a sympathetic doctor to perform a therapeutic abortion in a hospital: "What's a D and C between friends?" she said. "Nobody at the hospital gave a damn about my little illegality" (350, 344).[7] Recovering in the maternity ward, Margaret is surrounded by women who have had children or miscarried accidentally. They don't understand Margaret's abortion: "*Whatever did you do it for, Missis Flinders Missis Butter was always saying; if there's nothing the matter with your insides*" (341; italics in original). Margaret herself is conflicted

---

6. The final chapter, in which the abortion occurs, also appeared separately as the short story "Missis Flinders" in *Story Magazine*, December 1932. The story had been rejected many times before *Story* agreed to print it, and it was "the first fiction dealing with abortion to appear in a magazine of general circulation" (Sharistanian 377). The novel itself was a critical and popular success and underwent four printings, most recently by the Feminist Press in 1984.

7. A therapeutic abortion refers to an abortion done by a medical doctor in a hospital to "prevent mental or physical damage to the woman" (Luker 88). According to Luker, "between 1926 and 1960, the chance of getting a therapeutic abortion seems to have been almost random: abortions became neither easier nor harder to obtain over time; no geographic area had a monopoly on abortion; and abortion in the most liberal settings was fifty-five times more frequent than in the most conservative settings" (46; see also 257–59).

by what she sees as middle-class motherhood and her own desire for children despite her intellectualism. She resents Miles, and resents their selfish reasons for aborting the child. The abortion is a negative force of male control, "a trope for loss and failed promise" (Castro 17). Birth control as a literary trope can also be both a mechanism of control, if enforced by patriarchal forces, and a mechanism of liberation for women, if freely chosen. With her matter-of-fact presentation of birth control and abortion, Slesinger provides an insightful look at sexual politics and pressures on married women during the Depression.

Like Slesinger, expatriate writer Kay Boyle explores the issue of reproductive control and the links between female biology and maternal destiny. In her 1934 novel, *My Next Bride,* Victoria, a young American living in France, joins an artist's commune and meets the wealthy bohemian Anthony Lister. She becomes pregnant after attending drunken parties and goes to two vaudeville dancers who live at the commune for advice. They procure pills to "bring it off," "the kind the girls at the theatre use" (273). Unfortunately for Victoria, the pills do not induce an abortion but serve only to damage her health. The pills "had fine limber blades concealed which they whipped out and flourished once they had reached the nine miles or yards of entrails coiled secretly in the belly's soft white skin. They removed whatever there was to take, but waltzed in their wary abandonment around the small burden of flesh and blood, leaving it sacred, miraculously untouched. They would have food and spirit and the body's pain, but absolute flesh itself they would not have" (276). Although she keeps increasing the dosage, Victoria is not able to abort the tenacious fetus, "the strange, inhuman kernel of life which sucked blind, featureless, unskulled at what they would not let it have" (281). Victoria experiences unwanted pregnancy as a vampire-like invasion. Anthony's wife, Fontana, takes Victoria to a *sage-femme,* a wise woman or midwife. Fontana promises the *sage-femme* will "do something very quick to you and it will be over right away," but, in fact, the woman only puts up unwed mothers and finds homes for the babies (294).

Still determined, Victoria finds another *sage-femme,* one who "had a reputation," a place "three flights up in the dark and on every flight there was the smell of brussel sprouts, left over from the winter-time, perhaps, but strong and rank in the unswept, sagging stairs" (299). The sordid surroundings presage an unsanitary, back-alley abortion, a dirty coat hanger followed by sepsis and hemorrhage. The *sage-femme* "had seen so much that was secret rot and secret disease and suppuration carried month after month in silence" (300). The woman makes Victoria sign a contract that she won't reveal the abortionist's name and that she'll call in a doctor after the miscarriage begins. Hearing danger in this, Victoria and Fontana leave: "[T]hey were out the door, they were on the landing, and behind them in the silence of the sage-femme's rooms they could hear the dripping, the endless dripping of the life-blood as it left the bodies of those others; the unceasing drip of the stream as it left the wide, bare table and fell, drop by drop, to the planks beneath it, dripping and dripping on for ever like a finger tapping quickly on the floor" (303). In the novel's final pages, Fontana finds a real physician for Victoria, and the novel ends with Victoria crying as they follow the doctor. The implication she undergoes a "therapeutic abortion" is clear. Would birth control have prevented this abortion? Probably not, since the pregnancy was the result of drunken sex, whereas birth control must be planned. Yet, read in the context of the contraceptive movement, both the novel and birth control rhetoric demonstrate the need for reliable methods for women to control their fertility. The description of the pills and abortion evokes public perceptions of quackery and evil that the birth control movement attempted to disassociate from. Boyle's text shows the lengths to which women will go to escape enforced maternity.

William Faulkner also explores female sexuality outside of wedlock, birth control, and abortion in several of his novels of the 1930s. But rather than obliquely criticize the conflict between progressive politics and internal misogyny, as Slesinger does, Faulkner turns his attention to women who are poor and outside of the social mainstream. In his 1930 novel, *As I Lay Dying*, Faulkner presents the seventeen-year-old Dewey Dell Bundren. Dewey Dell has "the female trouble" and seeks an abortion during the family's bizarre trip to bury her dead mother (185). In a series of first-person monologues, Faulkner reveals Dewey's ignorance of birth control and lack of guidance from a distant, unloving mother. Viewing her pregnant body as a repulsive "tub full of guts," she searches for a doctor or druggist who "could do so much for me if he just would" (53). The druggist Moseley represents the self-righteous moral outrage of much anti-abortion rhetoric: "Me, a respectable druggist, that's kept store and raised a family and been a church-member for fifty-six years in this town" (187). He tells Dewey Dell to confess her condition to her father and to find herself a husband.

For Moseley, the solution to Dewey Dell's problem is to follow traditional roles for women as wife and mother. But Dewey Dell, like her mother before her, "rejects the notion that childbirth constitutes the natural fulfillment of feminine collective desire" (Henninger 27). However, Dewey Dell is not a feminist rebel: like the rhetoric of the birth control movement, she reveals that she does want children, just not now: "It's not that I wouldn't and will not it's that it is too soon too soon too soon" (Faulkner, *As I Lay Dying* 106). What Dewey Dell desires is control over her reproductive destiny. Offered no help from Moseley, she continues her quest, this time encountering sexual exploitation rather than fatherly condescension. The druggist MacGowan gives Dewey Dell a false abortifacient in exchange for sex (230–31). Although still determined to abort her child, Dewey Dell remains ignorant of how to do so by the novel's end, ensnared by her lack of knowledge, her dependence upon male institutions, and an inability to mediate her experience through language.

Faulkner's *If I Forget Thee, Jerusalem* (1939) deals more directly with failed contraception and reflects the climate of American anxiety surrounding abortion. Interestingly, while a number of critics focus on the abortion, none mentions the explicit birth control scene.[8] Joseph Urgo states, "Through the choice of abortion, maternity becomes a matter of consciousness, no longer an exclusively natural function" (255). But birth control itself makes maternity a conscious choice for Charlotte before her decision to have the abortion. Faulkner's illicit lovers, Harry and Charlotte, practice post-coital douching as contraception. According to a 1940 survey, antiseptic douching was one of the most popular methods throughout the United States, in part because the necessary materials could be found at any drugstore (Riley and White 898). Douching is effective for Charlotte, but "[w]hen the stove went out my douche bag was hanging behind it. It froze and when we lit the stove again I forgot it and it burst" (172). Isolated in remote mine country, Charlotte cannot replace her equipment, nor can she find any other technological means of contraception. She has to rely on folklore and hope: "I remember somebody telling me once, I was young then, that when people loved, hard, really loved each other, they didn't have children, the seed got burned up in the love, the passion. Maybe I believed it. Wanted to believe it because I didn't have a douche bag any more" (172).

Because of the failed birth control, Harry performs an abortion on Charlotte, which Faulkner describes in metaphoric language: "you just have to let the air in" (185). This phrase, echoing Hemingway's "Hills Like White Elephants" of 1927, demonstrates the existence of a popular legend of abortion rather than practical knowledge of the procedure.

---

8. See Eldred, Henninger, Urgo, and Duvall on abortion in *If I Forget Thee, Jerusalem* (*The Wild Palms*). Perhaps the role of birth control in the text has been ignored because critics such as Urgo have insisted on interpreting the novel as "about abortion" rather than about attempts to control fertility, and then read abortion as a trope throughout the novel (Urgo 262).

Faulkner's text continues the popular discourse that abortion is tragic, as Charlotte dies of hemorrhage and Harry is sentenced to prison. But does Faulkner condemn the lovers, or sympathize? I would argue that he intervenes in the ideology of evil abortion by complicating an easy reading of the lovers as careless or selfish. By depicting the economic despair in the mining communities and elucidating Charlotte and Harry's belief that the world was not a good place to bring a child into, Faulkner adopts rhetorical arguments that would resonate with those still feeling economic effects from the Depression. As Charlotte says, "I can starve and you can starve but not it" (185). The scenes of poverty in the mining community and Charlotte's statement echo the letters in the *Birth Control Review* and Sanger's arguments regarding bringing children into the world to starve.

But if Faulkner is sympathetic toward abortion, why kill Charlotte and condemn Harry? As Eldred notes, the novel reflects "the reality of abortion in the 1930s," a time when therapeutic abortions were legal and there was growing acceptance of abortion in general (141). The fate of Harry and Charlotte reflects the contemporary reality. Ware reports that couples could find an illegal abortionist who charged $100–150, but that between 8,000 and 10,000 women died each year from abortions during the 1930s (63). The high mortality rate of abortion was another reason birth control advocates fought it—birth control, they argued, would protect women's health and allow them to bear more children. Charlotte's death after her abortion fits the odds. Harry's fate also aligns itself with reality, although in a more complicated manner. Through the 1930s, the state prosecuted abortionists after the death of the woman, but more so if the woman was unwed. Regan cites a case that is strikingly similar to the tale of Harry and Charlotte: "In 1916 Chicago and Denver newspapers published Ruth Merriweather's love letters to a Chicago medical student, who was on trial for his involvement in her abortion related death" (1257). Faulkner's text is significant for its development of this cultural narrative, exploring the consequences of unmarried sexuality, failed contraception, and the resulting unwanted pregnancy.

If I Forget Thee, Jerusalem contains an implicit pro–birth control message, both in depicting Harry and Charlotte's attempt at douching, and in the knowledge that if it had succeeded abortion would have been prevented. Faulkner's text does not take a definitive stance on abortion. While Faulkner punishes both Charlotte and Harry, despite his seeming sympathy for their illicit love, he does not punish Billie Buckner, on whom Harry performs an earlier abortion. While aligned with the position that birth control would prevent abortions, the text does not explicitly valorize marriage and motherhood. This is reinforced by Charlotte's abandonment of her two daughters, as well as by the plot of the "Old Man" narrative interwoven into *If I Forget Thee, Jerusalem*. The main character of "Old Man," a convict, is trapped in a flood with a pregnant woman. He views her pregnant body as "monstrous" and "a mass of female meat" (137, 144). Although Faulkner's text resonates with some arguments of the birth control movement, it goes beyond the conservative values of the birth control rhetoric. Because he was not involved with the political movement to repeal the law, Faulkner had greater latitude to challenge social norms and gender roles. This greater license of topic paralleled Faulkner's ability to write outside traditional literary styles, employing modernist experiments such as interwoven narratives. The novel engages with issues of birth control, abortion, and sexuality that were circulating in pubic discourse during the 1930s, including a growing acceptance of economic factors in abortion.[9]

Contraception and Communism

AGNES SMEDLEY AND MERIDEL LE SUEUR

While the official birth control movement cut its overt ties to radical politics, the Socialist and Communist Parties incorporated contraception into their vision of social revolution. The Communist Party USA advocated birth control during the 1930s, and the party magazines *Woman Today* and *Working Woman* carried articles by Sanger and others.[10] This message found its greatest foothold during the Depression. The economic conditions of the 1930s attracted many people to the political left and the Communist and Socialist Parties. While these political groups

---

9. The critical reception of *If I Forget Thee, Jerusalem* demonstrates Faulkner's engagement with social attitudes. See Eldred, especially 140, 146.

10. Many historians of the American Socialist and Communist Parties note the ideological fragmentation that prevented these groups from a consistent message. The Socialist Party itself offered different views on birth control. Miller writes of Socialist women: "A majority appeared to support birth control as a necessary factor in the emancipation of human beings, while a minority—perhaps influenced by Clara Zetkin—viewed increasing numbers of workers' children as assets in the class struggle" (109–10). The December 1936 issue of *Woman Today* published "The Soviet Union's Abortion Law" by Margaret Sanger, where she argues against "any woman having children if and when she does not want them" (30). Margaret H. Irish argued for "free clinics with scientific contraceptive information" in her article "Childbirth—A Woman's Problem" in the May 1933 *Working Woman* (17). Nadezhda Krupskaya's "Sane Birth Control" appeared in the *Sunday Worker Magazine* in July 1936.

subordinated "the Woman Question" to class revolution, they welcomed women as members. Sally Miller reports that roughly one-tenth of the membership of the Socialist Party was female, mostly white, middle class, native American, and college educated (97). Many American women writers of the 1930s, including Meridel Le Sueur, Tess Slesinger, and Josephine Herbst, participated in these political movements.[11] They acted as journalists, writing for the New Masses and others, and wrote their fiction in the tradition of "Proletarian Realism."

The Third Period of the Communist Party USA (roughly the 1920s and 1930s) witnessed a boom in fiction by, for, and about workers. However, as Paula Rabinowitz argues, radical women's texts are marked by the intersection of gender, class, and sexuality, and thus differ from traditional proletarian fiction, with its formulaic plot of the worker's evolving revolutionary consciousness. Rabinowitz argues that "women's revolutionary writings foregrounded the need for contraception and abortion, the terrors of forced sterilization and rape, and the repression of sexuality as primary determinants of class consciousness among working-class women" (Labor and Desire 61). Tillie Olsen's Yonnondio, for example, follows a growing family from the mines of Wyoming to tenant farming in South Dakota to the sewers and meatpacking plants of Kansas City. Their poverty and despair lead both parents to be "bitter and brutal" (9) to their children, and repeated childbearing leaves Anna broken: "In her great physical pain and weariness Anna stumbled and lost herself. Remote, she fed and clothed the children, scrubbed, gave herself to Jim, clenching her fists against a pain she had no strength to feel" (80). In a wrenching scene young Maizie overhears her mother try to refuse sex: "It hurts too much. No, Jim, no." "Cant screw my own wife. Expect me to go to a whore? Hold still" (108). Olsen's unfinished novel demonstrates leftist women writers' focus on working-class women and the negative effects of their uncontrolled fertility.[12]

My reading of work by Le Sueur and Smedley supports Rabinowitz's conclusions, but I extend her analysis of the sexualization of hunger and

11. Radical women writers of the thirties (Le Sueur, Herbst, Slesinger, Olsen, and others) were virtually ignored by literary and political history, such as Walter Rideout's The Radical Novel in the United States, 1900–1954 and Daniel Aaron's Writers on the Left: Episodes in American Literary Communism. They were virtually unknown by literary critics until the 1970s, when feminist scholars "rediscovered" them. Much of the critical focus has been on the relationship of these women writers to the Communist Party. I do not discuss this relationship but instead concentrate on the conversation between the texts and the rhetoric of economics in birth control propaganda.

12. Claire M. Roche reads Yonnondio alongside some writing by Margaret Sanger and argues that both authors participate in eugenic discourse through their stereotypic representations of the poor.

labor through the politicized female body. Smedley, a friend of Sanger, worked for the *Birth Control Review* and wrote articles on birth control in China and India. Her autobiographical novel, *Daughter of Earth* (1929), should be read in the context of the movement. While Meridel Le Sueur was never an active part of the birth control movement, her writing invokes both feminist and economic themes of women, sexuality, and class. Like Smedley, Le Sueur's novel *The Girl* (written in 1939 but not published until 1978) is based in reality, her own experience and the stories she heard from other women during the Depression. Le Sueur and Smedley, both from working-class backgrounds themselves, offer a complex rendering of the intersections of economics and female sexuality during the Depression. Both the body of Le Sueur's "Girl" and Smedley's Marie Rogers act as sites for cultural critique of economic and reproductive policy.

Agnes Smedley's autobiographical novel, *Daughter of Earth*, invokes many themes of the birth control movement. Although Smedley's main political focus was the nationalist movement for Indian independence, she also became involved with birth control after hearing Emma Goldman lecture, and met Margaret Sanger in 1916 when both were active in the Socialist movement and in liberal Greenwich Village circles.[13] Smedley struggled with her own sexuality throughout her life, and in 1916 "[r]ecently acquired information on birth control gave her the means with which to deal with it physically. She channeled her personal anger in a political direction by blaming the state for keeping the liberating knowledge of birth control out of the hands of poor women" (MacKinnon and MacKinnon 27). On April 1, 1918, Smedley was charged with distributing birth control information in New York; Sanger rallied the movement to try to raise the $10,000 bail. After her release from prison, Smedley worked on the *Birth Control Review* from January 1918 until December 1919. Sanger and Smedley remained correspondents, especially from 1928 to 1931, and Sanger paid for Smedley's psychoanalysis in 1924. In return, Smedley advised Sanger on how to introduce birth control in India, and she worked on establishing birth control clinics in Japan, Germany, and China. She also wrote pieces for the *Review*, including "Babies and Imperialism in Japan," "Margaret Sanger Comes to Berlin," and "Birth Control in Germany."

Daughter of Earth follows Smedley's own life so closely that most critics read it as autobiography. The novel opens with an immediate claim

---

13. See MacKinnon and MacKinnon. For the place of *Daughter of Earth* in proletarian fiction, see Rabinowitz, especially *Labor and Desire*.

to realism rather than aestheticism: "It is the story of a life, written in desperation, in unhappiness" (7). But it is not just any life, but both a "lowly" or poor life and specifically a woman's life, indicating the simultaneous experience of class and gender. Smedley infuses the novel with the concerns of poor women, of unhappy marriages, abusive husbands, menial labor, and numerous children. Smedley recounts the story of her own mother, a woman who was once beautiful but whose frail hands have turned black from the labor of other people's laundry. Repeated childbirth causes such physical depletion and weakness that the character Marie believes it contributes to her mother's death. Her mother takes out her frustration from increasing poverty and repeated childbirth on her children: "As the years of her unhappy married life increased, as more children arrived, she whipped me more and more" (11). As in *Yonnondio*, the father moves his wife and children from one failed venture to the next. Unable to provide for his family, he slips into alcohol, abuse, and despair, while the labor of women (the money earned from the mother's laundry and aunt's prostitution) keeps the family alive.

Smedley suffered from a fear of sex due to watching her mother's life and death—constant pregnancy, ill health, and an abusive husband. She feared and despised marriage, equating it with sex and childbearing, and idolized her Aunt Helen, a prostitute who earned her own money and helped the family while the father spent his wages on alcohol. To the character Marie, marriage stripped women of any power and left them as chattel to their husbands, economically and physically at their mercy. Her feelings echo Emma Goldman's arguments about marriage and prostitution in "The Traffic in Women" and "Marriage and Love." As Marie states, "I was proud of Helen. To me her profession seemed as honorable as that of any married woman—she made her living in the same way as they made theirs, except that she made a better living and had more rights over her body and soul" (142). The true evil is not prostitution but an economic system that leaves women at the mercy of men. In Smedley's novel, marriage is no better alternative. To be "married to some working man, borne him a dozen children to wander the face of the earth, and died in my early thirties" was "the fate of all women about me," a fate Marie was determined to escape through education.

Daughter of Earth details the debilitating effects of uncontrolled fertility on female sexuality through its protagonist, Marie. To Marie, education would enable her to leave the crushing poverty of her childhood. She leaves her family to work and go to school, eventually marrying a friend. Her vision of marriage is without sex: "Sex had no place in love. Sex meant violence, marriage or prostitution, and marriage meant children, weeping nagging women and complaining men" (188). Twice she becomes pregnant, and twice has an abortion. After the second abortion she divorces her husband and devotes herself to her studies and to political causes. Later she marries a compatriot in the Indian nationalist movement. Because she denies her sexuality in an effort to control her fertility, Marie never enjoys a fulfilling relationship. Smedley's text thus reveals the psychological effects of poverty on developing female sexuality.

But what is the role of birth control within the novel? In the July 1929 *Birth Control Review* a reviewer praised *Daughter of Earth* extravagantly, calling it "a prayer for freedom": "Probably the cause of Birth Control will never find a more frightful and dramatically perfect argument in its favor than that of the conditions in coal-mining communities [depicted in the novel], where swarming human lives are worth a few dollars a head to a bloated and sprawling industry" (Pangborn, "Book Review" 196). Although the *Review* rather conveniently read the novel as a direct argument for birth control, this is true only in regard to the larger economic arguments the movement was using. Smedley herself never mentions contraception, and her involvement with the movement is glossed over in a single page (Smedley, *Daughter of Earth* 340). The novel focuses on how one woman overcame economic restraints to educate herself and join in a larger political movement. However, in another sense, the novel is entirely about the prevention of childbearing. Walt Carmon's review in the *New Masses* reads the novel as a straight "class novel," and on these grounds criticized it for being divisive and affected by "the bitterness of a woman" (17).[14] Both reviewers miss the synthesis that Smedley accomplishes: class and gender are inseparable in her experience and in her work, just as they are in the fight for birth control.

Like Smedley, Meridel Le Sueur simultaneously addresses class and gender in her work. Le Sueur joined the Communist Party in 1924 and became known in the 1930s for her reporting and fiction focusing on working women published in magazines such as *Dial*, *Scribner's*, and *Pagany*. While Le Sueur did not write explicitly about birth control, we can better understand her fiction, and particularly her novel *The Girl*, by placing it in the context of contraceptive and economic arguments during the Depression. Le Sueur was certainly aware of the controversy surrounding contraception: her mother, Marion Wharton, had lectured on birth control before World War I and was arrested for disseminating contraceptive information. Through her parents Le Sueur met such birth

14. This review exemplifies early attempts to fit radical women's fiction within the proletarian genre. These reviewers saw women's writing as failed attempts at the genre, seeing only that it was "about sex" and missing the intersection of gender and economics.

control activists as Margaret Sanger, Emma Goldman, and Theodore Dreiser. Le Sueur's message of female community and birth/rebirth participates in the exchange between leftist politics, feminist theory, and the cultural moment of the American Depression.[15]

Le Sueur depicts the body of the working class, and specifically of working-class women, as innately figured by capitalist exploitation. Working-class women, in their dual roles as workers and the producers of workers/mothers, "pick it up at the source, in the human body, in the making of the body, and the feeding and nurturing of it day in and day out.... In that body ... resides the economy of the world" (Le Sueur, "Annunciation" 172). Working-class women are organically essential to the maintenance of the world economy. If, as Anthony Dawahare argues, Le Sueur writes of a working class with "an unmediated relationship with socio-economic and political knowledge: the working class reads itself to learn about politics and the world economy," how would birth control change the dynamic of this reading (412)? Le Sueur's rendering of the political body focuses on the reproductive aspects of capitalist exploitation and female biology. Through the figure of the Girl, she privileges pregnancy as the site of communal experience. So why read this text in a discussion of birth control? In her exploration of economic conditions and female experience, Le Sueur articulates the issues at the heart of the drive for birth control in the 1930s, thus enabling a contextual reading situated in leftist politics.

Le Sueur's single novel, *The Girl*, is the story of an unnamed "everygirl" coming into womanhood and experiencing sexual desire, pregnancy, and childbirth during the Depression. Critics often read the novel as a powerful narrative of female desire and collectivity, which presents an essentialist view of women as mothers and daughters. Rabinowitz argues that "it invokes women's biological capacity to bear children without interrogating the cultural platitudes surrounding motherhood" ("Maternity as History" 544). Nora Ruth Roberts charges Le Sueur with a "thoroughgoing indigenous feminism" and "identification with all aspects of the wom-

---

15. Some critics have labeled this vision of female community as "essentialism" or "organicism," "a view of women that relates birth-giving, nurturing and the life-giving forces of organic nature in a way that Le Sueur sees as anti-bourgeois and particularly feminine" (Nora Ruth Roberts, *Three Radical Women* 36; Coiner, *Better Red* 109). See also Coiner's "Literature of Resistance: The Intersection of Feminism and the Communist Left in Meridel Le Sueur and Tillie Olsen." Coiner sees Le Sueur in opposition to Communist Party hierarchy, while Nora Roberts argues that the party had a "rich discussion" on "the woman question" and that women were active in this; therefore Le Sueur's work can be seen as within the party rather than in opposition ("Radical Women Writers of the Thirties and the New Feminist Response" 89).

anly experience" ("Radical Women Writers" 85). While *The Girl* clearly celebrates pregnancy and birth into a community of women, the novel also offers a more complex message of reproductive control, a message that most critics overlook in their call to "essentialism." By looking at the economic conditions in which the Girl finds herself, and examining the other female characters in the novel, we can expand this identification to include control of reproduction. Le Sueur creates a naive character in the Girl and invites the reader to celebrate her youthful ideas of love and birth. But Le Sueur also builds into her narrative a rhetoric that is not so celebratory. Through the stories of the other female characters, we receive a cautionary tale of the economic hardships and abuses suffered by women. In Belle, Clara, and Amelia, Le Sueur embeds the thread of female struggle for reproductive control, strengthening her claim through overlapping variations on the same theme.

Le Sueur paints a poignant picture of the harsh economic reality for women during the Depression. Living in an abandoned warehouse, the Girl survives her conditions only through the support of the community. The stark poverty shadows the notion that community is all one needs; Amelia, the Socialist activist, repeatedly rages that "you can't make bones without milk," referring to the Girl's lack of proper nutrition and its possible effects on her baby (109). This foregrounding of struggle and loss, of hunger and deprivation, darkens any purely "pro-childbirth" reading of the text. While it surely celebrates the power of women to reproduce, the text's criticism of economic conditions inherently supports a contraceptive argument against having children who cannot be fed. Critics such as Roberts have argued that Le Sueur fetishizes the maternal body, yet in this novel it is also a poor, starving body, one grounded in economic lack. While the novel privileges the Girl's pregnant body as the focal point, this suffering body is situated throughout the text among other women. Rather than pregnancy as the site of female community, these women all share a battle for control over their reproductive bodies.

To fully understand the Girl's pregnancy we must first examine the reproductive lives of Clara and Belle, the novel's other two main characters. Le Sueur's presentation of these women is consistent with her earlier writings in which she acknowledges the economic and physical reality of women. In "Women on the Breadlines," Le Sueur states matter-of-factly that the only commodity many women control is their own body and that they often turn to prostitution to survive.[16] Clara, the Girl's first friend in

---

16. "Women Are Hungry" and "Women on the Breadlines" echo scenes from *The Girl*. "Annunciation" also depicts a pregnant woman during the Depression struggling with poverty and lack of food. These pieces are collected in *Ripening* ("Annunciation" 124–32,

the city, works as both a waitress and a prostitute, feeding men's double desires. Clara clearly has some means of keeping childless: despite her sexual activity she is never pregnant. Le Sueur does not condemn Clara's prostitution but presents her sympathetically as occupying a legitimate place in the labor economy. A runaway, Clara was one of eight children, four of which were taken away from her mother by social workers. This pattern is repeated: women have little control over their bodies or the children they have borne. Clara began work in a sweatshop when she was twelve, the same time she started fooling around with men for attention and presents (8, 49). Thus Clara associates sexuality with labor from a very precocious age. To Clara, her body is "the only thing you got that's valuable" (49). While Clara sells her body for economic gain (for survival as much as for trinkets), the Girl in contrast is a virgin until she falls in love with Butch. Clara also acts as a foil for the Girl in the novel's concluding pages. Weak and suffering from venereal disease, Clara is given electric shock therapy to "cure" her prostitution. She dies in the same moments as the Girl gives birth. Clara's pathetic life and death dramatize the plight of women whose only market value is their sexualized bodies.

The Girl is surrounded by women who attempt to control their bodies in different ways. Besides the dark choice offered by Clara, Le Sueur presents the older character, Belle. During the first half of the novel Belle is jolly, happy in her proprietorship of the bar where Clara and the Girl work, and satisfied in her marriage to Hoink. Indeed, Le Sueur clearly presents a mature couple with an active sex life. But Belle's outward demeanor hides her own dark story of abuse and her struggle to control her sexuality. As a child Belle was abused by her father's friend, resulting in pregnancy and abortion: "He gave me a little money and I come to St. Paul where for ten bucks they'd stick a huge vet's needle into you and start it and then you were on your own" (47). Belle's matter-of-fact statement of a brutal and illegal procedure allows for no escaping from the reality of women's lives. An unwritten condition of her marriage is that she remain childless, and Belle admits to having thirteen abortions. The Girl relates that "Belle says this is a rotten stinking world and for women it is worse, and with your insides rotting out of you and men at you day and night and the welfare workers following you and people having to live off each other like rats" (9). Belle's body is inscribed by her reproductive history and her labor. Birth control could help separate human from rat by dividing female sexuality from pregnancy, raising poor women above the condition of animals.

"Women on the Breadlines" 137–43, "Women Are Hungry" 144–57).

The Girl's full story, including her pregnancy, must be understood within this context. In many ways it echoes the other female voices: a childhood of poverty, constant motion, and abuse as "papa was driven to a fury sitting down with all the mouths to feed. We had to eat in relays" (26). Like Clara, the Girl was sent to work young (age eleven), and like Belle, was sexually assaulted by an adult. With an abusive father and ten siblings, the Girl escapes to the city for employment, where she meets and falls in love with Butch. Ignorant of birth control, their sexual activity leads to a pregnancy that Butch wants to abort. "I could do it myself with a pair of scissors, there's nothing to it," he tells her (70). Although she resists the abortion, the Girl's loses her belief that she controls her own body when she is raped by two men.

If, as I have argued, these women are struggling for reproductive control of their own bodies, whom are they struggling against? Economic conditions also trap the male characters (Butch, Hoink, etc.), and they exit the novel after a failed bank robbery, leaving the female characters to form their own community. But within this female enclave the women still struggle against a "relief system" that seeks control. Thus, a larger economic system, not men in particular or in general, threatens their bodily control. The threat is not class or gender but the conjunction of both. In *The Girl* it is dangerous to be unemployed and a woman, dangerous to walk alone in the city streets. The authorities assume such women are prostitutes without rights to their bodies or their sexuality: "They will pick you up, Clara told me, and give you tests and sterilize you or send you to the women's prison" (1). In both options the state takes bodily control of the working-class woman. Seeking work and milk, the Girl visits a relief office where the worker writes in a report, "She should be tested for sterilization after her baby is born. In our opinion sterilization is advisable" (114). When she protests, the Girl is forcibly taken to a Salvation Army home for unwed mothers. Scheduled to be sterilized immediately after giving birth, the Girl is rescued by Amelia, literally saved by socialism. Her future fertility salvaged (for now), the Girl gives birth on the floor of an abandoned warehouse, surrounded by other women. The social welfare system does not help these women but takes away their control over their own bodies.

Amelia, the voice of the Workers Alliance, articulates the party line with a feminist slant: "What are we? Just goods to be bought and sold? Yes, she answered herself cursing, that's what they think, buy and sell you and then use your body after you're dead! It's too bad, it's too bad they can't kill our babies and eat them like suckling pigs" (120). Amelia herself has had six children but leaves unclear whether they are alive or still in her care. This articulation of the female body as a product corresponds to the economic conditions of the characters to reinforce the idea that women are objectified by economic means, losing all subjectivity and power. Thus, to Amelia, the threatened sterilization is both an economic and eugenic measure dependent upon the whim of the ruling class: "It's because they don't need any more children from workers. They don't need us to reproduce our kind" (124). One could easily read this and other comments made by Amelia as pro–birth control. The high value Amelia places on life is consistent with the arguments of birth control advocates regarding morality, especially when read in the context of the devastating effects of poverty on childbearing.

Both Meridel Le Sueur and Agnes Smedley made explicit the relationship among gender and class, politics and experience. They develop implicit arguments for contraception through and on the bodies of women. Embedded in a larger politics, *The Girl* and *Daughter of Earth* reveal traces of the conflict over birth control. The effects of economic conditions on the control of women's bodies and lives implicate this "proletariat" or "revolutionary" fiction in the larger argument for contraception as empowering to women.

Conclusions

THE ECONOMICS OF DESIRE

The issue of birth control cannot be separated from economics and politics during the Depression.[17] Even as birth control advocates lobbied to change the law, commercial enterprises saw money to be made in contraceptives. What had once been a moral issue grew more acceptable as practical economic pressures became mainstream. Elizabeth Garrett stated in 1934, "the contraceptive business has outgrown the birth control movement" (271). Despite repressive laws, "an extensive

---

17. Birth control remains grounded in economics. This logic of controlling reproduction for economic reasons still circulates in public rhetoric today. In December 1990, following FDA approval of Norplant, an editorial in the *Philadelphia Inquirer* called Norplant a "tool in the fight against African American Poverty" (quoted in Kapsalis 54). This logic is now being turned on male bodies as well. In July 2001 the Wisconsin Supreme Court "upheld a probation order that bars a man convicted of failure to pay child support from having more children unless he shows that he can support all his offspring" (Lewin A14). Interestingly, the court split along gender lines, with male justices finding the condition reasonable while the female justices "opposed it as an unconstitutional intrusion on a basic right to procreate" (Lewin).

and thriving business is being done in every variety of contraception," and contraceptives were being sold under the moniker "prophylactic" and "feminine hygiene" (269).[18] The birth control business boomed, and "preventatives" found their way into the Sears and Roebuck catalog and the local five-and-dime shop (Solinger, *Pregnancy and Power* 126). By 1934 over three hundred manufacturers were producing contraceptive devices, in addition to druggists, doctors, and firms selling door-to-door and by mail order, and *Fortune* magazine reported the annual sales of the birth control industry at over $250 million in 1938 (Garrett 269; "Accident of Birth" 84). The harsh economic reality of the Depression Era had a direct influence on public opinion regarding birth control. And the fiction of the period, whether explicitly propagandistic or more nuanced, helped bring the economic effects of birth control into public discourse. However, despite growing commercial availability, ignorance and poverty kept contraceptives out of reach of many women such as Faulkner's Dewey Dell. According to Andrea Tone, in the 1930s, "[w]hile the going rate for a diaphragm and a companion tube of jelly ranged from four to six dollars, a dollar purchased a dozen suppositories, ten foaming tablets, or, most alluring of all, up to three douching units, depending on the brand" ("Contraceptive Consumers" 492).

Birth control has the potential to disrupt a sexual economy that values the female body only for its reproductive capacity. It also has the potential to disrupt conditions of female sexual passivity. However, one of the many contradictions of the birth control movement is that advocates often ignored its revolutionary potential in favor of a rhetoric that reinscribed cultural norms. Thus, the movement marketed contraception both as a way for poor women to escape the cycle of poverty and for the wealthy to control the number of people needing social welfare.

By the time the United States emerged from the Depression in 1939, the once-radical movement for birth control had been replaced by the Birth Control Federation of America, an organization dedicated to family planning and the interests of public health. Women were safely inscribed as mothers who scientifically planned their families with the aid of clinics and physicians. As the caption for a 1937 photograph in the *Birth Control Review* promises, "We want another as soon as we can afford it" (fig. 13).[19]

18. See Tone, *Devices and Desires*, for a discussion of how manufacturers created a mass market for contraceptives during the Depression despite the laws. For an analysis of feminine hygiene and birth control marketing in the 1920s and 1930s, see Sarch.

19. Recent contraceptive ads echo this assumption that women naturally want children and want to space them. A Norplant ad depicts a woman holding a smiling toddler with the caption, "I'd like to have another child, but we also want some time before the next one."

The Economics of Desire and Despair · 167

> "We want another as soon as we can afford it"
>
> A happy young mother with her "planned baby" at one of the twelve medically directed birth control centers maintained in settlement houses by the New York City Committee of Mothers' Health Centers. These centers have had more than 14,000 new patients since the first one opened in 1930. The Committee's annual theatre benefit, to take place the last week in October, will raise funds to continue this work for the health, happiness and security of New York families.
>
> *Photograph by Ruth Rozaffy*

FIGURE 13. Ruth Rozaffy, "We want another as soon as we can afford it," *Birth Control Review* 12.1 (1937): 12. Reprinted with permission of Alexander Sanger.

The image shows a smiling young mother leaning over a baby's crib, but the caption is more telling: "we" indicates a decision made within a happy marriage, "want" shows the natural attitude of couples toward children, and "afford" highlights that the couple is planning their family with an eye toward economic responsibility. But while the *Birth Control Review* stopped running fiction and moved toward science and public policy for its own increasingly mainstream message during the Depression, a wide variety of authors explored the complications of contraception, sexuality, and economics. The topic fit the two main literary modes of the period: modernists such as Faulkner developed new narrative techniques to capture the current psychological and sexual reality, and the leftist writers of the 1930s, such as Smedley and Olsen, employed social realism to elicit political change for the working class. This fiction provided another vehicle for contraceptive arguments to enter public consciousness.

7

Conclusion

Textual Contraception

> It follows, if literature is the voice of life, that modern literature will direct an overwhelming amount of its effort toward sexual freedom of speech. Certainly modern literature is doing just that.
> —Pangborn, "The Probation in Literature," *Birth Control Review*, January 1929: 13

"AMERICAN MEDICINE Accepts Birth Control" announced a headline in the 1937 *Birth Control Review*, celebrating the American Medical Association's official recognition of contraception as "as a legitimate part of medical practice" on June 8 (1). This begrudging approval came only after growing support in the media and general public and legal success with the 1936 *United States v. One Package* decision, in which a federal appeals court ruled that doctors could prescribe contraceptives at their discretion. Margaret Sanger had won a victory, albeit a limited one compared to her original goals in *The Woman Rebel*. Birth control was no longer radical, and in 1938 the once scattered factions merged to become the Birth Control Federation of America, which four years later changed its name to the more familiar Planned Parenthood Federation of America (Gordon, *The Moral Property of Women* 242). According to a 1944 survey, three-quarters of physicians trained after 1937 were instructed in contraceptive methods, a substantial increase from the 10 percent receiving this training before 1920 (Solinger, *Pregnancy and Power* 135). By the time World War II loomed on the American horizon, the move away from feminist and leftist ideals was complete, and contraception was an issue of family planning, ensconced within marriage and prescribed by a physician.

In 1932 Dr. Hannah M. Stone, birth control activist and clinic director, wrote in the *Review* of a great change in American attitudes toward birth control: "The cumulative effect of the various social, economic, educational and scientific forces on birth control thought is now becoming manifest, and a significant change is taking place in the attitude of the public, the church and the medical professional" ("Birth Control in America" 188). Recent scholars such as Katrina Irving have speculated that the shift to a consumer-based economy, which "valorized spending, enjoined the satisfaction of ever-expanding material desires, and encouraged indulgence in leisure pursuits and other nonessential commodities," accommodated the acceptance of birth control (55–56). This work's previous chapters have demonstrated that American writers engaged with shifting social values and contributed to this changing social acceptance. This modern American literature thus fulfills the function described by Charles Glicksberg: "Literature, prophetic or rebellious in its insights, is often a harbinger of values that are only gradually and reluctantly accepted by society at large" (9). As a rhetorical force permeating public consciousness, fiction contributed to public attitudes, using economics, traditional views of marriage and motherhood, and scientific eugenic thought to rewrite contraception's role. This gradual liberation of sexual discussion corresponded to new forms of writing: as birth control allowed women to rewrite the biological narratives of their lives, adding diversity to the imperative of virginity—marriage—sexuality—motherhood, American authors found a new liberation to "write beyond the ending" of genre conventions.[1] These texts are "contraceptive" in their disruption and rewriting of the traditional biological plot, interrupting the generic plots of fiction that tend to repeat marriage and motherhood as the most plausible roles for women.

By 1945, the birth control movement had spawned more than eight hundred clinics across the nation, and in the 1950s Gregory Pincus, a scientist in the field of sex hormones, began to research hormonal efficacy as a contraceptive. Social attitudes toward birth control have changed significantly since Sanger's day, as has legislation. In *Griswold v.*

1. Rachel Blau DuPlessis coined the phrase "writing beyond the ending." She writes, "It is the project of twentieth-century women writers to solve the contradictions between love and quest and to replace the alternate endings in marriage and death that are their cultural legacy from nineteenth-century life and letters by offering a different set of choices. They invent a complex of narrative acts with psychosocial meanings, which will be studied here as 'writing beyond the ending'" (*Writing beyond the Ending* 4).

FIGURE 14. "I'll need to see a marriage license," *Ms.*, Summer 2005: 31. Reprinted with permission by the National Family Planning and Reproductive Health Association.

Connecticut (1965), the U.S. Supreme Court overturned a Connecticut statute prohibiting contraception on the grounds that it violated the right to marital privacy.[2] Seven years later, the court extended this right to the unmarried in *Eisenstadt v. Baird,* invalidating a law that prohibited the distribution of contraceptives to the unwed. The issue of privacy in reproductive decisions came into play again in *Roe v. Wade* (1973). Although the Supreme Court has heard numerous cases regarding abortion since 1973, contraception itself seems to have escaped further legal battles. This right is not guaranteed, however, as the National Family Planning

2. For a comprehensive discussion of *Griswold v. Connecticut*, see John W. Johnson.

and Reproductive Health Association acknowledges in a recent advertisement warning that "a powerful minority wants to turn back the clock on reproductive rights" (fig. 14).

Just as women have always fought to control their bodies, citizens have disagreed about reproductive control. The original movement to make birth control legal and available has been won, but many battles remain: consider the recent cases of health insurance coverage and FDA approval for Plan B. The relationship between American fiction and birth control discourse did not end after the acceptance of contraception by the American Medical Association in 1937, or the American entrance into World War II, or any other arbitrary date. American writers have continued to write about contraception and its effects on women's lives. To conclude, this chapter will consider several texts published after the heyday of the birth control movement and address the continued legacy of textual contraception.

In her 1942 best seller, *The Prodigal Women*, Nancy Hale rewrites the old story of a woman using her sexuality to gain the security of marriage and of a freewheeling man "tricked" into an unwelcome commitment. When Maizie becomes pregnant by her wealthy beau, their vastly different visions of the relationship become clear. The novel reveals the continued privileging of marriage despite ideological shifts regarding women. Maizie demonstrates this tension as she practices unwed sex but falls back on the "old pattern" unconsciously "put in her mouth" as the expected response of a "good" girl in the face of pregnancy. Accused of trying to trap Lambert, Maizie replies, "I couldn't help this happening to me" (Hale 72). She apparently had no recourse to birth control and no control over her body. The young lovers are left with few options: Maizie's public disgrace, the social sanction of marriage, or Lambert's suggestion of abortion. "I know a man that knows. . . . It isn't such an awful thing, you know," he said. "Other women have done it" (72). This beginning, fraught with distrust and disagreement, predicates a disastrous marriage filled with psychological abuse and the ruin of Maizie's emotional and physical health. The exchange reveals the tension between love and marriage, sex and reproduction that continued well beyond the legalization of birth control.

Herself married three times, Hale depicts three women and their disastrous marriages in *The Prodigal Women*. Maizie endures an emotionally abusive marriage to her artist husband; Betsy, a "New Woman" experimenting with relationships, engaging in premarital sex and "open marriage," finds herself in an abusive second marriage; and Leda marries for money and never finds love. None of these women are sexually fulfilled or successful in marriage. While Maizie and Betsy degrade themselves to their abusive husbands, Leda finds herself estranged from her only son. How is birth control implicated in this dynamic? In her depictions of female sexuality, Hale implies, for Betsy and Leda at least, a level of contraceptive knowledge. The first mention of birth control occurs when Betsy loses her virginity:

> "Look, do you know what to do?"
> "No."
> "God."
> They drove back into town and stopped at an all-night drugstore.... Nothing untoward came of that night. (350)

Throughout the novel Betsy gains additional knowledge, obliquely revealing her sexual development to her family in the riddle

> There was an old woman who lived in a shoe
> And had so many children she didn't know what to do
> But there was a young woman who lived in a shoe,
> And she didn't have any children, for she knew what to do. (379)

"—that'll be me, if I ever get married!" Betsy declares into the shocked silence. Nancy Hale inscribes female characters using birth control into public discourse, challenging a previous narration of absence. Such an open discussion of contraception, female sexuality, and marriage demonstrates shifting literary standards and a growing public discussion not possible thirty years earlier.

Maizie, the character with no contraceptive knowledge, becomes pregnant, marries, and then succumbs to her husband's coercion and has an abortion. Maizie is adamantly against abortion, saying, "I'd rather die than do that, go to one of those people" (72) but finally agrees to the abortion while they are traveling in South America on their honeymoon. She experiences a series of complications leading to a second operation, regular diathermy treatments, constant pain and weakness, and then a nervous breakdown. While Hale depicts the dangers of abortion through Maizie's experience, she also shows a safe abortion when Betsy undergoes the procedure: "Willy found out the name of a doctor, and one cold morning in January they had driven through the snowy stretches of Central Park, in a taxi, to an address far up in Manhattan, where the doctor had operated on Betsy" (434). The point of Hale's critique is not abortion itself but how female sexuality and fertility act as a battle line in unhealthy relationships. The reader is left to wonder how cheap and accessible birth control would change these women's experience.

Inserting the Diaphragm
RE-WRITING THE ROMANCE

As birth control became more socially acceptable and a new sexual explicitness entered fiction, authors such as Mary McCarthy and Philip Roth added specific references to contraception as an integral factor in modern sex, particularly in unmarried sexuality.[3] McCarthy's 1954 story "Dottie Makes an Honest Woman of Herself" and Roth's 1959 novella "Goodbye, Columbus" center on sex and the diaphragm, at the time the most popular form of birth control. Both narratives offer insightful answers to the question, what are the effects of contraceptive technology on romance?

McCarthy's texts and Roth's novella can be read as examples of the rhetorical function of fiction, educating and influencing readers about birth control, and as artifacts of cultural memory, reenacting history. Both authors use synecdoche, referencing Sanger to stand in for all of birth control, and write against the literary genre of romance to explore the role of technology in modern relationships. Their focus on the increasingly public role of contraceptive technology in heterosexual romance relocates the female as both subject and object of birth control. Their narrative rendering of this technology provides fictional evidence to the claims of recent feminist critics who argue that reproductive technology simultaneously oppresses and frees women. As Adele Clarke has shown, reproductive science is grounded in an ideology of control: control over materials, over bodies, and over life itself. In their fictional depiction of birth control, McCarthy and Roth reveal the contradictions of control with the diaphragm acting as what Foucault called "disciplinary technology" (Rabinow 17). On the literary level, the presence of the diaphragm disciplines the texts by limiting their romantic potential.

According to Gillian Beer, the traditional romance invokes the past

3. Perhaps because of their foray into "shocking sex," these two works also share public acclaim and were made into movies. Scholarly attention to Roth far outweighs that paid to McCarthy, although no critic focuses on the role of birth control but instead tend to examine their use of humor, their work as autobiography, and their role as ethnic writers. Both the 1964 movie version of *The Group* and the 1969 Paramount version of *Goodbye, Columbus* received mixed reviews and never reached the popularity of the texts. See Kael.

to present a story of courtly and sexual love concerned with the ideal. Although written to entertain, these texts are also implicitly instructive (2–3, 9). Beer differentiates the romance genre from modern romance novels, which she characterizes as "subliterature . . . lightweight commercial fiction deliberately written to flatter daydreams" (1). According to DuPlessis, the romance uses "conjugal love as a telos and the developing heterosexual love relation as a major, if not the only major, element in organizing the narrative action" (*Writing beyond the Ending* 200). However, in her study of the modern romance novel, Janice Radway argues that these texts serve an important psychological function for their female readers. The popular romance is characterized by a heterosexual relationship developing into marriage and features romantic and passionate sex, a dashing hero, and a happy ending. Both McCarthy and Roth write within and against these romance conventions. They invoke a past that is less than ideal to instruct readers on birth control method and its role in relationships. Their failed romances could be described with this pitch: "imagine what could happen when you send modern romance on a blind date with contraceptive technology."

"Dottie Makes an Honest Woman of Herself" originally appeared in the *Partisan Review* in 1954 and ultimately appeared with minor revisions as chapter 3 of McCarthy's controversial 1963 best seller, *The Group*. According to Frances Kiernan, "the story of Dottie's getting herself fitted for a diaphragm created a sensation" (510). This controversy was the result of McCarthy's explicit and humorous approach to what most perceived as a private medical matter. McCarthy sets her story in the past, focusing on a group of (white) 1933 Vassar graduates, thus situating her characters in the midst of the American birth control movement. By 1933, Sanger's American Birth Control League had opened birth control clinics across the nation, and the National Committee on Federal Legislation for Birth Control was feverishly lobbying for repeal of the Comstock Act. Setting her story in an earlier period, McCarthy corresponds to the romance convention of invoking the past. However, she reveals the depths of uncertain sexual relations beneath the nostalgic veneer of the New Woman's liberation. "Dottie" is more than simply a nostalgic or didactic rewriting of history because it reveals the fear of pregnancy that remained a common thread in women's lives even as McCarthy was writing.

Published just a few years after the Pill won FDA approval, the novel capitalizes on more relaxed attitudes towards birth control to depict an era of controversy over contraception. *The Group* and "Dottie Makes an Honest Woman of Herself" contain a much franker, more explicit discussion of birth control than works of earlier American writers such as Djuna Barnes, Agnes Smedley, and Theodore Dreiser, who were themselves constrained by the same Comstock Act that made the dissemination of contraceptive information illegal. Writing almost half a century later, McCarthy and Roth enjoyed a greater freedom to discuss contraception explicitly and humorously. By setting her story and novel in 1933, McCarthy revisits a time when she would not have been able to write so openly and in so much detail about birth control. This work demonstrates the complexities of inserting realistic contraception into heterosexual romance.[4]

The morning after losing her virginity, Dottie is commanded by her new lover to "[g]et yourself a pessary" (34). Dottie originally mistakes "pessary" for "peccary," "a coarse, piglike mammal" she had studied in zoology (34). This humorous mistake hints at Dottie's innocence and her romantic tendencies. Her confusion of the natural and technological reveals an ideological grounding in the premise that sex is "natural" and human relationships are animalistic in their simplicity. Dick clarifies his order by redefining his term, much to the relief of Dottie and the reader, with the modifiers "[a] female contraceptive, a plug. . . . You get it from a lady doctor" (34). Dick's specification of a "lady doctor" is wonderfully vague and could be read as a female physician (such as those who often staffed birth control clinics, like the "white-coated, olive-skinned woman with a big bun of black hair" that Dottie sees) or a male physician specializing in "lady's problems," a gynecologist (49).

To further distinguish between a peccary and a pessary, Dottie goes to a birth control clinic for information. Birth control clinics were spreading across the nation during the 1930s: in 1930, there were 31 clinics; in 1935, 150; and by 1936, nearly 250.[5] Here Dottie obtained

4. Differences between the *Partisan Review* story and chapter 3 of *The Group* are minor, especially in terms of the discussion of the diaphragm. Some names are changed (Harald in the novel is John in the story, for example), and the novel expands upon the story. Since Roth's 1959 novella references the 1954 "How Dottie Makes an Honest Woman of Herself," I refer to quotes and page numbers from the *Partisan Review* story unless otherwise indicated.

While McCarthy enjoyed more freedom than Dreiser and earlier writers, this was not without its repercussions. The *Partisan Review* editors "were prepared to print the pessary story and run the risk of coming up against the postal authorities" (Kiernan 357). While *The Group* was an immediate public success, critics faulted the book as being too "trivial" in its detail, a symptom of "the profound materiality of women" (Mailer), lacking in focus, and not coming together as a novel. See Bennett and Hochmann for annotated reviews. The novel was banned for obscenity in Ireland, Australia, and Italy, "thanks largely to the chapters about Dottie Renfrew" (Brightman 486).

5. Clinic numbers taken from "Birth Control Centers in the United States." See also "One Hundred Contraceptive Clinics" for demographic and attendance data.

"a doctor's name and a sheaf of pamphlets that described a myriad of devices—tampons, sponges, collar-button, wishbone, and butterfly pessaries, thimbles, silk rings, and coils—and the virtues and drawbacks of each" (37). Such pamphlets, likely based on Margaret Sanger's "Family Limitation," were often the first (and only) frank, detailed material available for women.[6] The pamphlet described and pictured methods, even telling women where they could obtain materials and how much they were likely to cost. The practicalities of contraception, with its myriad accoutrements, conflict with the ideal notion of romance by foregrounding the base physicality of sex and its possible consequences. While Dottie never seems concerned about pregnancy, Dick's insistence that she be fitted for a diaphragm reveals his practical rather than romantic view of the relationship. Radway argues that the popular romance leads to marriage, but Dick is already married (though separated from his wife) and is careful not to be tied to Dottie through pregnancy. Disqualified as a male romantic hero, he insists on inserting the diaphragm into their relationship.

While attention to detail is a common aspect of the romance genre (Beer 3), McCarthy chooses to detail the history and method of the diaphragm. This technical specificity relocates attention from the developing relationship between Dick and Dottie to the diaphragm itself, which becomes the third player in this "love" triangle. Three days after her clinic visit Dottie and her friend Kay are fitted for a diaphragm pessary, which the bureau had suggested: "The new device recommended to Dottie by the bureau had the backing of the whole U.S. medical profession; it had been found by Margaret Sanger in Holland and was now for the first time being imported in quantity into the U.S.A., where our own manufacturers could copy it. It combined the maximum of protection with the minimum of inconvenience and could be used by any woman of average or better intelligence, following the instructions of a qualified physician" (37). The diaphragm was the method recommended by Sanger and the birth control clinics, due in part to its high effectiveness when used correctly and also because it needed to be fitted, thus keeping women in contact with a clinic.[7] Thus, access to this method was under direct control and supervision of the medical profession. Dottie gains power through her knowledge even as a physician limits her access

6. The pamphlet, originally published in 1914, was revised several times. See Jensen.
7. The percentage of diaphragm users grew in the 1930s, but according to Dawson, Meny, and Ridley, while 71 percent of the educated, white, urban women in their sample used birth control, only 17 percent used the diaphragm. The study surveyed 1,049 white married women of childbearing age during the 1920s and 1930s. The majority of women used condoms, withdrawal, or the rhythm method.

and she submits to physical and psychological surveillance. In educating her reader on the diaphragm's history, still a widely used contraceptive in the 1950s, McCarthy also reveals the forces that regulate its use and the diaphragm's own power over the female body.[8] In an almost documentary fashion, McCarthy details Dottie's experience with birth control rather than the niceties of her relationship with Dick. Indeed, Dottie and Dick's relationship, based on a single night of sex, never really develops and thus does not meet a basic requirement of the romance genre. However, Dottie *does* develop a courtly relationship with the diaphragm. Thus in this triangle Dottie's physical association with contraceptive technology supersedes her emotional attachment to Dick; her location as an object within the medical system seems to foreclose on her becoming an object of patriarchal marriage (the traditional ending of the popular romance).

Viewing her relationship to Dick through traditional romantic lenses, Dottie integrates her new knowledge of birth control into a loving fantasy. In what can be read as an attempt to fulfill the popular romantic conclusion, Dottie envisions the "ring" shape of the diaphragm as wedding her symbolically to Dick. She tells herself "he had sent her here, to be wedded, as it were, by proxy, with the 'ring' or diaphragm pessary that the woman doctor dispensed" (37). Indeed, the story emphasizes the marital status of the woman doctor herself: "the broad gold wedding ring on her hand shone like a talisman, a Hippocratic band" (49). The doctor's wedding band becomes entangled with her ability to prescribe a diaphragm, conflating the gold wedding ring with the ring of the pessary. To Dottie, the symbolic wedding ring transforms her illicit affair into socially sanctioned sex within wedlock. She reads herself as a character in a romance, involved in a developing relationship leading to marriage. But her relationship with Dick violates the basic description set forth by Radway of "a relationship characterized by *mutual* love and by the hero's quite unusual ability to express his devotion gently and with concern for his heroine's pleasure" (70). The clinical tone employed by McCarthy to describe the situation reveals Dottie's fancy for what it is: a naive romanticization of her entry into sexual politics. Dottie's matrimonial fantasy, at odds with her clinical knowledge, reveals yet another layer of control in the social fabric as Dottie unconsciously idealizes traditional marriage and the gendered power relations it entails. Indeed, her brief interactions with Dick already have established her role as one of submission and appeasement.

8. According to Piccinino and Mosher, diaphragm use has decreased in the United States since the 1980s, largely due to concern over preventing HIV and other STDs.

McCarthy's text is not "implicitly instructive" in the traditional romantic sense of how to find and keep the ideal man. However, the choice of detail does create a text that instructs in almost documentary fashion. In her description of the clinic, and her enumeration of the various contraceptive methods available (including withdrawal, suppositories, condoms, and douching), McCarthy educates her readers about the clinic system and birth control technology. Women used many of these methods in the 1950s and 1960s, and the step-by-step directions on diaphragm insertion could still be followed today. Because of her clinic visit, Dottie knows exactly what will happen when the doctor sees her. Because McCarthy details a diaphragm fitting, in clinical detail, the reader soon knows as well:

> This article, a rubber cap mounted on a coiled spring, came in a range of sizes and would be tried out in Dottie's vagina, for fit, wearing comfort, and so on, in the same way that various lenses were tried out for the eyes. The woman doctor would insert it, and having made sure of the proper size, she would teach Dottie how to put it in, how to smear it with contraceptive jelly and put a dab in the middle, how to crouch in a squatting position, fold the pessary between thumb and forefinger of the right hand, while parting the labia majora with the left hand, and edge the pessary in, so that it would snap into place, shielding the cervix, and finally how to follow it with the right middle finger, locate the cervix or soft neck of the uterus and make certain it was covered by rubber. (37–38)

Dottie would then be taught how to douche and how to care for all her equipment. The technical detail, which could have been excerpted from a medical textbook, contrasts with Dottie's matrimonial vision of the diaphragm. Dottie herself is the object of this scene as much as the diaphragm is: she herself could be inserted into a textbook.

This disparity between Dottie's romantic vision and the clinical contraceptive details emphasizes the gulf between scientific aspects of contraception and how American society shapes the deployment of this knowledge. The diaphragm's physical presence could not be reconciled with passionate visions of carefree love. As the diaphragm embodies the potential to separate sex from marriage and women from reproduction, society reinscribes matrimonial ideals to contain this threat. The diaphragm's prominence signifies the failure of Dottie's romance. Radway refers obliquely to this possibility in her discussion of failed romance novels: "When another text portrays a heroine who is neither harmed nor disturbed by her ability to have sex with several men, I suspect it is classified as 'bad' because it makes explicit the threatening implications of an unleashed feminine sexuality capable of satisfying itself outside the structures of patriarchal domination that are still perpetuated most effectively through marriage" (74). Because birth control offers the potential for expressing female sexuality outside of marriage, it complicates the traditional trajectory of romance and exemplifies the tensions of the contraceptive text. The conflict inherent in Dottie's romanticism and McCarthy's choice of detail foregrounds the idea that the sexual freedom inherent in birth control is always tempered by cultural context. In the 1930s and the 1950s, the female body is subject to moral codes that mandate marriage.

The conflict between Dottie's romantic vision and the stark reality of the diaphragm fitting create a humorous tone. Reading Dottie as developing a relationship with the diaphragm, rather than with Dick, creates the sense of a tragicomedy of misunderstanding, mistaken identity, and physical humor. For instance, Dottie's original misunderstanding of "peccary" for "pessary" was a bit of harmless absurdity. Her supervised attempt to insert her newly fitted diaphragm adds a note of physical farce: "As she was trying to fold the pessary, the slippery thing, all covered with jelly, jumped out of her grasp and shot across the room and hit the sterilizer. Dottie could have died" (73). More tragic in its result are the cases of mistaken identity: Dottie mistakes her own identity as love interest to Dick, and Dick's identity as a romantic hero. She also misreads the diaphragm as a minor object in the normal course of natural love rather than as a subject, a silent third partner, in the relationship.

The accumulation of technological detail forcing a reconsideration of male/female relations undermines Dottie's construction of herself as a "natural," romantic subject. As Dawn Trouard has noted, McCarthy provides "complete instructions on inserting a pessary. . . . By the time Dottie has been fitted, the reader knows that McCarthy knows that there are at least nine designs in diaphragms and that she knows all the Latin terms for female anatomy" (106). Trouard argues that this attention to detail is a part of McCarthy's satiric elitism.[9] However, when read simultaneously in the context of the period it was created and the period it represents, McCarthy's display of knowledge acts as more than either satire or elitism. In addition to the technical information of how to insert

9. Trouard argues that "McCarthy appears magisterial and smugly resolute as a defense against uncertainties that plague her values," and that "[t]he elitist vacillation combined with an assertive need to glorify and destroy characters, in the same sentence, stems from a dilemma rooted in McCarthy's own life concerning peer group standards" (98, 101).

a diaphragm, McCarthy also describes the social context of its usage. This technology is at once liberating and restrictive, contingent upon the subject position of woman as married/unmarried, rich/poor, fit/unfit.

Social forces that considered marital status, morality, and class in the equation determining contraceptive access contained women's reproductive freedom. As a well-to-do woman, Dottie could find a sympathetic doctor willing to prescribe a pessary for "female troubles." As Dottie tells her friend Kay, birth control is "legal and aboveboard, thanks to a court decision that allowed doctors to prescribe contraceptives for the prevention or cure of disease" (42).[10] Through the character Kay we get a glimpse of the social significance of Dottie's brazen act.[11] Kay is horrified that, as an unmarried woman, Dottie made the appointment in her own name, when "the office might be raided and the doctor's records impounded and published in the papers, which would be terrible for Dottie's family" (42).[12] McCarthy might be referring to the 1929 raid on the Birth Control Clinical Research Bureau in which authorities seized private medical records. Such public advertisement of illicit sexuality would destroy the reputation of a respectable, well-to-do girl and ruin her prospects for an advantageous marriage. Kay represents social hypocrisy and the double standard of sexuality: although she herself had sex before marriage, she believes "[o]nce a [single] girl got a pessary, it cheapened her" (41). Even the practical Kay indicates that sex out of wedlock is acceptable as long as it is not technologically controlled. That is, the diaphragm takes the risk and romance out of sex. By writing through the voice of Kay, McCarthy touches on the complex role of birth control in the changing conception of female sexuality, as she adds humor and

10. Dottie is referring to a 1919 New York decision that allowed doctors to prescribe birth control only to prevent or cure disease. Not until 1936, in the *United States v. One Package* decision, were doctors legally allowed to prescribe contraception for contraceptive purposes.

11. McCarthy discusses her use of different narrative voices in "Letter to a Translator about *The Group*." In "Dottie Makes an Honest Woman of Herself" and chapter 3 of *The Group* there are three main strands: Dottie's idealistic voice, Kay's cynical voice, and the instructional voice in which Dottie relays her birth control knowledge. McCarthy writes, "The *style indirect libre* makes it possible for each girl to be heard in *her own words*. Yet out of this an irony develops. This is that her own words, in most cases, are everybody's words—clichés pronounced with an air of originality" (74).

12. Interestingly, McCarthy changed this phrasing in the novel to "would *kill* Dottie's family" (64). This hyperbole more clearly indicates that the narrative is in Kay's voice here by referring to her concern for social acceptance. Kay's practicality and concern for material goods contrast with Dottie's idealism throughout the story. Dottie even envisions a future as a birth control advocate: "In the back of Dottie's mind was a plan, not yet fully matured, of coming to New York and working as a volunteer for the birth-control people" (48).

texture to the narrative.

Kay plays a central role in recasting the romance by narrating a section on the "Etiquette of Contraception," which effectively pays homage to the frequent reality of sex outside of marriage. By detailing the implicit power of the diaphragm to enable illicit sexuality and therefore undermine marriage, McCarthy violates another convention of popular romance: a strong stance against "bed hopping" and multiple sexual partners. Her husband tells Kay, who had introduced Dick and Dottie, that this contraceptive etiquette is "well understood by all the young men of his acquaintance" (39). Kay therefore reads Dick's request to Dottie as confirmation that he is serious about the relationship: "If it were only a casual affair, he would feel himself bound to use condoms or practice coitus interruptus. The expense was a determining factor: no gentleman would expect a girl to put up the doctor's fee, plus the price of the pessary and the jelly and the douche-bag, if he were not going to sleep with her long enough for her to recover her investment" (39). Kay's terms are those of exchange and investment, indicating that she understands the true foundation of the relationship and is without Dottie's romantic notions of love and marriage. Courtship and romance, then, are firmly grounded within a consumer economy of supply and demand, investment and profit. The physical presence of the diaphragm foregrounds this expense as a reminder of the manufactured goods bought in the sexual marketplace. Kay goes on to detail the arrangements for who keeps the diaphragm in affairs, the possibility of discovery, and the problem of disposal. In all, McCarthy presents what Joseph Epstein calls a "sociology of the diaphragm" that satirizes sexual relations while revealing how power flows among men and women, married and unmarried (45).

Although Dottie occupies a powerful position as white, upper-middle class, and educated, her unmarried status still restricts her possession of birth control. The unromantic resolution emphasizes Dottie's precarious position, demonstrating the social constraints on female sexuality despite access to the technology. After going through her exam and fitting, Dottie never uses the new diaphragm, jelly, fountain syringe, or douche bag. Leaving the doctor's office, she calls her lover but is unable to reach him. The bag begins to represent risk rather than promise, and Dottie realizes that she does not control her sexuality: Dick does. She bought the diaphragm at his command and its presence now binds her to him: "She had no wish ever to see Dick again, but the possession of all this machinery left her no choice. . . . She had nowhere to go but Dick's" (52). The story ends with Dottie alone on a park bench, not with the traditional romantic conclusion of a happily married couple.

How, then, does Dottie "make an honest woman of herself?" Does the pessary make her honest, or does this title refer to what happens beyond the scope of the story, after she leaves the park bench? The novel adds to this ending in interesting ways. In chapter 3 of *The Group*, Dottie waits in Washington Park for several hours before leaving her bulky bag of contraceptives under a bench and walking off alone. Why would Dottie abandon the promise of sexual freedom in that nondescript brown paper bag? Without a real wedding ring on her finger, Dottie has no place to keep her symbolic ring. Even sitting alone in Washington Square in the growing dark makes Dottie's sexual status questionable: she is accosted by strange men and "a policeman had stared at her curiously" (76). Dottie's interpellation as a "loose woman" reinforces the message that the diaphragm cannot bestow sexual power as long as she remains socially marked by her marital status. "Cheapened" by her possession of the diaphragm, she "makes an honest woman of herself" by leaving it behind. In the novel, this experience leads to a nervous breakdown, and Dottie conforms to social stereotypes of womanhood by becoming engaged to a man she doesn't love. Thus, the story is not only a failed romance but a failed contraceptive text that cannot, to use DuPlessis's phrase, "write beyond the ending" of marriage.

While Dottie falls in love with the married man who seduces her, Kay thinks in practical terms of material gains and reputations lost. Her consumer mentality and quest for upward mobility complement the economic mechanism of control over female access to birth control. Dottie's desire to experience a love affair was quite common, according to an "Unofficial Questionnaire" of college women published in the 1930 *Birth Control Review*. However, she did not represent the average birth control clinic demographic. A study of 100 representative contraceptive centers in 1936 revealed that the average woman instructed in birth control clinics was "28 years old with three living children; in poor circumstances or receiving public relief" ("One Hundred Contraceptive Clinics" 3). Dottie views birth control as a right, a symbolic marriage, but as I've shown, during the 1930s it was a discourse of economics and eugenics that helped birth control gain social acceptance. McCarthy points to this tension by contrasting Dottie and Kay to the surrounding doctor's office: "On the walls were etchings showing overcrowded slums teeming with rickety children and a lithograph of an early hospital ward in which untended young women, with babies at their side, were dying, presumably of puerperal fever" (42). The description of these pictures corresponds with much of the artwork found in the *Birth Control Review*, which pictured large families in extreme poverty, with dirty, skinny children in the foreground. The message, made explicit by birth control advocates, is that contraception will control the indigent population. While this rhetoric led to a growing public acceptance of birth control, the reality was that women like Dottie and Kay, white middle-class college graduates, were successfully using birth control, leading some to fear a "race suicide" (Robinson 48).

The Group expands on the waiting room scene to further depict how class acts as a mechanism of control. Surrounded by pictures of the poor, Kay silently accuses herself of "'profiteering' on the birth-control crusade. Mentally, she defends herself. Birth control, she argued, was for those who knew how to use it and value it—the educated classes" (69). The nurse further elaborates this class bias, implying that those who need birth control most are too ignorant to follow directions (an attitude that often justified forced sterilization) (73). The attitudes of Kay and the nurse reveal another level of restriction on birth control technology. Despite clinics being opened to serve a poorer population, policy on information dispersal was in the hands of the medical profession and the economically powerful. Birth control was firmly situated in a consumer culture, with the diaphragm a dear commodity. The simple fact of technological progress, of effective contraception, does not guarantee social progress. As she told Elisabeth Niebuhr in a *Paris Review* interview, McCarthy wrote her novel to demonstrate a loss of faith in the idea of progress, including sexual progress, "a deliberate exposure of the fantasy of the educated American woman's freedom" (qtd. in Showalter 345). Neither technology nor education can free women trapped by romantic ideology.

Philip Roth echoed McCarthy in his use of the diaphragm as a focus of young sexuality in "Goodbye, Columbus"; this daring treatment helped his work receive public and critical acclaim, leading to the National Book Award for Fiction. This novella invokes McCarthy as a source of birth control knowledge and follows her lead in using Margaret Sanger as synecdoche for the larger social movement. But an evaluation of the relationship between these texts reveals more than the flip salute of one author to another. The connection acts as much more than the romantic genre convention of recycling plotlines (Beer 3). In his description of the relationship between Neil and Brenda, Roth builds upon McCarthy to examine the role of the diaphragm in romantic and sexual relationships.

Although Roth uses younger characters, both authors focus on an unmarried, well-educated white couple, and both reinscribe a sexual dynamic of male control and place birth control firmly within this relationship. McCarthy's Dottie and Roth's Brenda are fitted for diaphragms not on their own motivation, but because their lovers tell them to. Dick's command to "Get yourself a pessary" reminds Dottie of Hamlet's order to Ophelia to "Get thee to a nunnery" (34). The tone of mandate and the sentence structure are not the only echoes here. Janet Adelman has interpreted Hamlet's "task as the disruption of marriage itself," his relationship with Ophelia tainted with a misogyny caused by his mother's sexual behavior (14). Indeed, Hamlet's command is contraceptive in implication, followed as it is by the question "Why, wouldst though be a breeder of sinners?" (3.1.121). Relocating Ophelia to a nunnery removes her from the cycle of romance, sex, and reproduction. Dick and later Neil use the diaphragm to remove the threat of breeding from their sexual liaisons.

Dick's command also echoes Hamlet's in its reproduction of gendered power relations that assume male control over the female body. Like Dick, Roth's Neil introduces the diaphragm into his relationship with Brenda. Although he is less immediately commanding than Dick, Neil resorts to mandate when persuasion fails. The following conversation is a textbook case of rhetorical manipulation. Neil first expresses his desire and then uses the logical argument of effectiveness against pregnancy:

> "I know this is out of the blue, though really it's not. . . . I want you to buy a diaphragm. To go to a doctor and get one."
> She smiled. "Don't worry, sweetie, we're careful. Everything is okay."
> "But that's the safest."
> "We're safe. It'd be a waste." (Roth 79)

The appeal to safety is meant to resonate with female fears of pregnancy. But Brenda is unaffected and indeed seems unconcerned with possible pregnancy. She counters Neil's argument with her own reassurance of safety and call for economy, indicating satisfaction with their previous method (most likely withdrawal or condoms). When Brenda rejects both arguments, Neil takes a new path, arguing for his own sexual pleasure:

> "Brenda, I want you to own one for . . . for the sake of pleasure."
> "Pleasure? Whose? The doctor's?"
> "Mine," I said. (79)

Neil's concern for his own pleasure rather than Brenda's makes him unfit to play the role of romantic hero. When Brenda resists this argument, he calls her selfish and then resorts to command: "I'm bothering just because I want you to go to a doctor and get a diaphragm. That's all. No explanation. Just do it. Do it because I asked you to" (81). The command to "Just do it" reveals that, to Neil, Brenda should need no other reason but the fact that he has told her to. Men command women, and they command their sexual choices. As Alan France notes, the diaphragm is a symbol of Neil's larger attempts to impose his will upon the relationship and retain control (87). Neil's multiple, unsatisfactory reasons may hide a deeper motive, a resistance to the marriage that would likely result if Brenda became pregnant. Both Dick and Neil are unfit for marriage and thus unfit to play the role of romantic hero. While the command of Dick and Neil to buy a diaphragm is the sexual opposite of taking up residence in a nunnery, both imply female passivity and a lack of bodily control.

Seemingly unconcerned about pregnancy, both Dottie and Brenda are physically examined and fitted for the diaphragm at the command of a man. The diaphragm is the responsibility of the female partner with no outward signs to the male that it is in use. Birth control as the women's responsibility upholds normative ideologies of the female as reproductive body, responsible for her fertility and for any results, at the same time that it potentially undermines the idea of female sexual passivity. As technology offers the potential for women to control their reproduction, it enters the power structure as a tool for men to control women. The diaphragm's insertion into the relationship foregrounds the gender relations inherent in popular romance, which constructs "a particular kind of female self, the self-in-relation" to the male (Radway 147). In its effect, in these novels the diaphragm becomes another mechanism of emotional and physical control.

For McCarthy and Roth, the diaphragm acts to discipline the female body in the modern romance, embodying the intersection of technology and sexuality. They use the literary device synecdoche to demonstrate how technology became inserted into cultural discourse. As in McCarthy, the name of Margaret Sanger stands in for birth control and the entire clinic system. Neil tells Brenda, "You can go to Margaret Sanger, in New York. They don't ask questions" (82). Read literally, this sounds as though Brenda will knock on the door of Sanger's personal residence and request a diaphragm. Brenda also uses this figure of speech, telling Neil, "I called Margaret Sanger Clinic" (97). The lack of a "the" or "'s" elides the difference between the individual, Margaret Sanger, and the clinic system. It is not *the* clinic named for Sanger, or Sanger's clinic: the individual and the structure are one and the same. Ironically, Sanger fought to put birth control into the hands of physicians rather than directly into the hands of women. Invoking birth control in the name of Sanger directly references the conservative ideology of contraceptives as belonging to the realm of science and medicine.

Roth reveals his debt to "Dottie" by using McCarthy's name as synecdoche for illicit birth control knowledge. When an indignant Brenda asks Neil if he has "done this before," Neil replies, "I just know. I read Mary McCarthy" (82). To read "Dottie Makes an Honest Woman of Herself" is to gain an essential education in how to find and use birth control. It also stands in, however, for doing so under questionable terms. Brenda replies to Neil, "That's exactly right. That's just what I'd feel like, somebody out of *her*" (82). This comment reveals an interesting anachronism: while McCarthy depicted women in 1933, she was really writing about women in the 1950s. The social code of morality regarding unmarried women, sexuality, and reproduction was still largely operative. Dottie inhabits cultural memory for her possession of the diaphragm and her romantic failure. This identification of McCarthy with illicit sex is made again when Brenda and Neil register at a Boston hotel as a married couple. Indeed, the earlier conversation is repeated almost verbatim, but with the speakers reversed:

"Have you done this before?" I [Neil] said.
"I read Mary McCarthy." (125)

Unmarried sexuality, birth control, the diaphragm, Margaret Sanger, and Mary McCarthy become synonymous in Roth's novella and in the larger cultural discourse. Each references a narrative that questions notions of fulfilled romance through female sexuality. This intertextual re-invocation rewrites birth control as antithetical to female autonomy.

Another intertextual echo is the symbolic significance of the diaphragm, its indication of a serious relationship akin to marriage. Roth twists McCarthy's use of this trope, as the male character Neil sees the diaphragm, like Dottie, as a kind of marriage. He waits for Brenda in St. Patrick's Cathedral, conveniently across the street from the "posh gynecologist," and thinks, "Now the doctor is about to wed Brenda to me" (100). Neil's location trying to pray in a Catholic Cathedral, when he is himself Jewish, points to the dissonance between Neil's thoughts of marriage and his relationship to Brenda. In a socially sanctioned wedding bride and groom would be together awaiting public declaration of their legal status as husband and wife. The matrimony of the diaphragm is one of secrecy, separation, and sex. This is further made clear by the continuation of Neil's thought: "and I am not entirely certain this is all for the best" (100). Neil lacks Dottie's naive romanticization of sex as marriage but rather dreads the implications of this secret nuptial.

Unlike Dottie, Brenda leaves the doctor's office carrying nothing, "like a woman who's only been window shopping" (101). Neil's brief vision of Brenda as a wealthy cosmopolitan consumer is, indeed, not at all dissonant with her purpose. Brenda's ability to be fitted for the diaphragm is, like Dottie's in 1933, in large part a result of her wealth. The location of the gynecologist's office across from Bergdorf Goodman's emphasizes this consumer power. Indeed, shopping was the motive given for the trip from Newark to New York, and the doctor's location in an upscale commercial district "was a perfect place for Brenda to add to her wardrobe" (99). Neil compares Brenda to the idle female consumer, and the gynecologist's remark—"shall I wrap it or will you take it with you?"—parallels the words of countless shop girls. Although Brenda is empty-handed, she is not empty, but leaves the office wearing the new diaphragm. With no physical evidence of her successful birth control foray, Brenda is able to escape the interpellation that Dottie's brown bag forces upon her.

Brenda and Dottie represent one last controlling power on female sexuality: parental control. While Dottie has a less hostile relationship with her mother, both she and Brenda are largely influenced by what their parents, especially mothers, will think about their sexual behavior. When Brenda returns to Radcliffe, she leaves her diaphragm at home. Her mother finds it in a drawer in Brenda's bedroom, revealing the secret sexual nature of Neil and Brenda's relationship to her parents. According to her mother, the realization of their daughter's active sexuality, embodied by the diaphragm, has "broken her parents' hearts" (129). Barbara Frey Waxman reads Brenda as consciously leaving the diaphragm in order to end her relationship with Neil and "retreat to the safety of childhood's maternal protection" (101). However, this position does not consider Brenda's continual ambivalence towards the device. She never wanted the diaphragm and repeatedly indicates that her relationship is more meaningful if risky. Therefore, her decision to leave the diaphragm at home may be read as an attempt to rekindle the romance with Neil. Both Dottie and Brenda are adults, college age or older, and yet both are still controlled psychologically by their parents. As women, they are sexually children until handed from parent to husband. Their "modern" freedom as sexual beings is limited, despite the ability to escape pregnancy, by the disciplining force of guilt. The diaphragm marks them as wayward children, as "bad girls" rather than "honest women."

McCarthy and Roth play with literary genre and device to explore the serious intersection of contraceptive technology and heterosexual relationships. While the tone employed by McCarthy and Roth is humorous, the texts act to transmit technological information about the diaphragm and its role in controlling the female body. Indeed, other literary works have mentioned McCarthy as providing them with their first information about contraception. In Wendy Wasserstein's 1978 play, *Uncommon Women and Others*, the character Leilah reveals, "Do you know the first time I ever really understood about diaphragms or sex was from reading *The Group*. I remember when I was twelve taking it down from my parents' library shelf and rereading the passages about Dottie leaving her diaphragm on Washington Square" (28). As best sellers, the works of McCarthy and Roth contributed to a social conversation about sexuality and contraception at the same time that they complicated ideas about modern intimacy. Foregrounding contraception within sexuality, and sexuality within relationships, results in a reconsideration of courtship, romance, and marriage. Centered upon the contradictions inherent in birth control, these texts reinscribe troublesome assumptions about female sexual passivity even as they open space for the liberating power of contraception.

Conclusions

Lorraine Hansberry's *To Be Young, Gifted and Black*, based on her earlier letters, notebooks, and plays and published after her death at age thirty-five, demonstrates the continuing evolution of birth control in women's lives and in texts. Hansberry was born in 1930, and her realist plays contributed to the discussion of civil rights in the 1950s and 1960s.[13] Act I, Sequence 5 of the play corresponds with Hansberry's experience as an undergraduate at the University of Wisconsin. The character Candace represents Hansberry, an African American student with passionate political beliefs. When her friend Mariela announces that she is pregnant, a shocked Candace asks, "Doesn't he *wear* anything? Don't *you*?" (46). Candace clearly assumes that nonmarital sex is common at the university and that women protect themselves from pregnancy with birth control. This sexual freedom should be the right of women as well as men, Candace later argues with Monasse, a student from Ethiopia. "And you call yourself a revolutionary! (*He opens his mouth to speak—stammers—looks in vain for the referee.*) Well, I'll bet you at least one-half of the girls on this campus have them—diaphragms—and use them! And it's growing all the time—and, well, when the pill comes in, well . . . *all*

---

13. *To Be Young, Gifted and Black* was produced in 1969 and published in 1971.

the excuses will be over then! Women will be exactly as free as men" (48). Candace equates contraception with female sexuality, and the expression of female sexuality with equality between men and women. Birth control is an assumed right for this revolutionary African American woman. By attacking the sexual double standard and the code of silence (Monasse does not want to discuss birth control "with a young woman I respect" [48]), Candace prefigures the growing public conversation about contraception and its role in women's lives. Unfortunately, Candace's prophecy that with the birth control pill "women will be exactly as free as men" has proven overly optimistic.

Margaret Sanger wrote in 1920, "No woman can call herself free who does not own and control her own body" (94). However, as Roth, McCarthy, Hansberry, and others depict in fiction and nonfiction, birth control itself exists in a web of social control. Works by American authors intersected with the concerns of the birth control movement, exploring how the issues of economics, morality, female roles, and eugenics structured the reproductive lives of women and fictional narratives. The lens of the birth control movement provides a fascinating perspective for examining how seemingly contradictory arguments are employed to introduce a potentially radical social change so as to stretch, rather than rend, the social fabric. Although birth control was often explicitly absent in the texts, the prominence of contraception in the media and social conversation made that absence a site of exploration of consequence and possibility. The birth control movement shaped not only political debate and social roles in the years between world wars; it also shaped and was shaped by the textual discourse used to promote and subvert the cause.

Birth control enabled the development of the contraceptive text, interrupting the generic plots of fiction that tend to repeat marriage and motherhood as the most plausible roles for women. The failure of these texts to fulfill the true potential of reenvisioning female life-narratives indicates the degree to which the potential of contraception has been and still is limited by ideologies of gendered power. Birth control continues to be deployed in ways that oppress as well as free women, as a tool to reinscribe their sexual status and reproductive destiny. Contraceptive marketing, use, and access still interpellates women within economic and racial boundaries, rather than freeing them to complete control of their bodies. By examining the complex relationship between American literature, the social and political movement for birth control, and medical technology, we gain insight into the ways in which the rhetorical and aesthetic functions of literature merge and act upon public discourse.

Bibliography
••••

Aaron, Daniel. *Writers on the Left: Episodes in American Literary Communism.* New York: Harcourt, Brace & World, 1961.

Abbott, Leonard D. "Is William Sanger to Go to Jail?" *The Masses* September 1915: 19.

"Accident of Birth." *Fortune* February 1938: 83–114.

Adamic, Louis. "The Nation's Backbone." *Birth Control Review* August 1926: 252–53; September 1926: 282, 289.

Adams, Alice E. *Reproducing the Womb: Images of Childbirth in Science, Feminist Theory, and Literature.* Ithaca, NY: Cornell UP, 1994.

Adelman, Janet. *Suffocating Mothers: Fantasies of Maternal Origin in Shakespeare's Plays, Hamlet to The Tempest.* New York: Routledge, 1992.

Alcott, Louisa May. *Work.* 1873. New York: Penguin Classics, 1994.

"American Medicine Accepts Birth Control." *Birth Control Review* 4.9 (1937): 1–2.

Anderson, Sherwood. *Dark Laughter.* 1925. New York: Liveright, 1960.

"The Answer Box." *Birth Control Review* July 1930: 219.

"Are These Fit Fathers?" *Birth Control Review* November 1926: 338–39.

Armstrong, Nancy. "Introduction: Literature as Women's History." *Genre* 19 (Winter 1986): 347–69.

Arthur, Stacey L. "The Norplant Prescription: Birth Control, Woman Control, or Crime Control?" *UCLA Law Review* 40.1 (1992): 1–101.

Asbell, Bernard. *The Pill: A Biography of the Drug That Changed the World.* New York: Random House, 1998.

Ashley, Jessie. "The Law at Work." *Birth Control Review* February/March 1918: 3–4, 14.

Austin, Mary. *A Woman of Genius.* Garden City, NY: Doubleday, Page & Co., 1912.

Balay, Anne G. "'Hands Full of Living': Birth Control, Nostalgia, and Kathleen Norris." *American Literary History* 8.3 (1996): 471–95.

Balsamo, Anne. *Technologies of the Gendered Body: Reading Cyborg Women.* Durham, NC: Duke UP, 1997.

Banta, Martha. *Taylored Lives: Narrative Productions in the Age of Taylor, Veblen, and Ford.* Chicago: U of Chicago P, 1993.

Barnard, Seymour. "Philanthropy: A Comic Opera." *The Masses* March 1915: 15–16.
Barnes, Djuna. *Ryder.* New York: Horace Liveright, 1928.
Barns, Cornelia. "Remember, Mrs. Judd." *Birth Control Review* August 1919: 9.
Barrett, Wilton Agnew. "The Wash." *The Masses* April 1916: 19–20.
Barrineau, Nancy Warner. "Recontextualizing Dreiser: Gender, Class, and Sexuality in *Jennie Gerhardt.*" *Theodore Dreiser: Beyond Naturalism.* Ed. Miriam Gogol. New York: New York UP, 1995. 55–76.
Baskin, Alex. "Margaret Sanger, *The Woman Rebel*, and the Rise of the Birth Control Movement in the United States." *The Woman Rebel.* Ed. Alex Baskin. New York: Archives of Social History, 1976. i–xxii.
Bauman, Zygmunt. *Modernity and Ambivalence.* Ithaca, NY: Cornell UP, 1991.
Beattie, Ann. *Falling in Place.* New York: Random House, 1980.
Bederman, Gail. *Manliness & Civilization: A Cultural History of Gender and Race in the United States, 1880–1917.* Chicago: U of Chicago P, 1995.
Beer, Gillian. *The Romance.* London: Methuen, 1970.
Beisel, Nicola. *Imperiled Innocents: Anthony Comstock and Family Reproduction in Victorian America.* Princeton, NJ: Princeton UP, 1997.
Bender, Bert. *The Descent of Love: Darwin and the Theory of Sexual Selection in American Fiction, 1871–1926.* Philadelphia: U of Pennsylvania P, 1996.
———. "'His Mind Aglow': The Biological Undercurrent in Fitzgerald's *Gatsby* and Other Works." *Journal of American Studies* 32.3 (1998): 399–420.
Bennett, Joy, and Gabriella Hochmann. *Mary McCarthy: An Annotated Bibliography.* New York: Garland, 1992.
Berg, Allison Brooke. *Mothering the Race: Women's Narratives of Reproduction, 1890–1930.* Urbana: U of Illinois P, 2002.
Biggs, Lindy. *The Rational Factory: Architecture, Technology, and Work in America's Age of Mass Production.* Baltimore: Johns Hopkins UP, 1996.
"Birth Control." *The Masses* April 1916: 21.
"Birth Control Centers in the United States." *Birth Control Review* 3.7 (1936): Back Cover.
"The Birth Control Fight." *The Blast* July 1, 1916: 5.
"The Birth Control Primer." *Birth Control Review* January 1929: 3.
Bloch, Ivan. Rev. of *An American Tragedy*, by Theodore Dreiser, and *Dark Laughter*, by Sherwood Anderson. *Birth Control Review* 10.9 (Sept. 1926): 279–80.
Blossom, Frederick A. "Birth Control." *Birth Control Review* February 1917: 12.
Boeckmann, Cathy. *A Question of Character: Scientific Racism and the Genres of American Fiction, 1892–1912.* Tuscaloosa: U of Alabama P, 2000.
Boone, Joseph Allen. *Tradition Counter Tradition: Love and the Form of Fiction.* Chicago: U of Chicago P, 1987.
Booth, Wayne C. *The Rhetoric of Fiction.* 1961. 2d ed. Chicago: U of Chicago P, 1983.
Borell, Merriley. "Biologists and the Promotion of Birth Control Research, 1918–1938." *Journal of the History of Biology* 20.1 (1987): 51–87.
Bossard, James H. S. "The New Public Relief and Birth Control." *Birth Control Review* May 1934: 1.

Boughton, Alice C. "What 7309 'Mothers' Want." *Birth Control Review* January 1933: 8–11, 26–27.

Boyer, Paul S. *Purity in Print: Book Censorship in America from the Gilded Age to the Computer Age.* 1968. 2d ed. Madison: U of Wisconsin P, 2002.

Boyle, Kay. *My Next Bride.* 1934. New York: Penguin Books, 1986.

———. *Plagued by the Nightingale.* 1931. Crosscurrents/Modern Fiction. Ed. Harry T. Moore. Carbondale: Southern Illinois UP, 1966.

Boyle, Mary. *Re-Thinking Abortion: Psychology, Gender, Power and the Law.* New York: Routledge, 1997.

Brackett, Elizabeth. "Morning-After Pill Protest." *NewsHour with Jim Lehrer.* PBS. WTTW-Chicago. 30 June 2005.

"Breaking Up the Home." *Birth Control Review* July 1928: 208–9.

Brightman, Carol. *Writing Dangerously: Mary McCarthy and Her World.* New York: Clarkson Potter, 1992.

Brinnin, John Malcolm. *The Third Rose: Gertrude Stein and Her World.* Gloucester, MA: Peter Smith, 1968.

Brodie, Janet Farrell. *Contraception and Abortion in Nineteenth-Century America.* Ithaca, NY: Cornell UP, 1994.

Bromley, Dorothy Dunbar, and Florence Britten. *Youth and Sex: A Study of 1300 College Students.* New York, 1938.

Browder, Clifford. *The Wickedest Woman in New York: Madame Restell, the Abortionist.* Hamden, CT: Anchor Books, 1988.

Brown-Guillory, Elizabeth, ed. *Women of Color: Mother-Daughter Relationships in 20th Century Literature.* Austin: U of Texas P, 1996.

Buhle, Mari Jo. *Women and American Socialism, 1870–1920.* Urbana: U of Illinois P, 1981.

Buhle, Paul. *Marxism in the United States: Remapping the History of the American Left.* London: Verso, 1987.

Bullough, Vern L. "A Brief Note on Rubber Technology and Contraception: The Diaphragm and the Condom." *Technology and Culture* 22.1 (1981): 104–11.

Burke, Carolyn. *Becoming Modern: The Life of Mina Loy.* New York: Farrar, Straus and Giroux, 1996.

———. "The New Poetry and the New Woman: Mina Loy." *Coming to Light: American Women Poets in the Twentieth Century.* Ed. Diane Wood Middlebrook and Marilyn Yalom. Ann Arbor: U of Michigan P, 1985. 37–57.

Burrill, Mary. "They That Sit in Darkness." *Birth Control Review* September 1919: 5–8.

Burstein, Janet. *Writing Mothers, Writing Daughters: Tracing the Maternal in Stories by American Jewish Women.* Urbana: U of Illinois P, 1996.

Caldwell, Ben. "Top Secret or a Few Million after B.C." *The Drama Review* 12.4 (1968): 47–50.

Caldwell, Erskine. *Tobacco Road and God's Little Acre.* New York: Nelson Doubleday, 1961.

Calverton, V. F. *The Bankruptcy of Marriage.* London: John Hamilton, Ltd., 1929.

———. *Sex Expression in Literature.* New York: Boni & Liveright, 1926.

Carby, Hazel. *Reconstructing Womanhood: The Emergence of the Afro-American Woman Novelist.* New York: Oxford UP, 1987.

Carmon, Walt. "Daughter of Earth." *New Masses* October 1930: 17–18.

Carter, Elmer A. "Eugenics for the Negro." *Birth Control Review* June 1932: 169–70.

Carter, Julian B. "Birds, Bees, and Venereal Disease: Toward an Intellectual History of Sex Education." *Journal of the History of Sexuality* 10.2 (2001): 213–49.

Castro, Joy. "'My Little Illegality': Abortion, Resistance, and Women Writers on the Left." *The Novel and the American Left: Critical Essays on Depression-Era Fiction.* Ed. Janet Galligani Casey. Iowa City: U of Iowa P, 2004. 16–34.

Chamberlain, K. R. "Breed! We Need Men." *Birth Control Review* 1.3 (1917): 5.

Chambers, Dianne. "Female Roles and National Identity in Kay Boyle's *Plagued by the Nightingale* and Edith Wharton's *Madame de Treymes.*" *Critical Essays on Kay Boyle.* Ed. Marilyn Elkins. New York: G. K. Hall and Co., 1997. 241–61.

Chandrasekhar, S. *"A Dirty, Filthy Book": The Writings of Charles Knowlton and Annie Besant on Reproductive Physiology and Birth Control and an Account of the Bradlaugh-Besant Trial.* Berkeley: U of California P, 1981.

Chapelier, Emile. "To Working Girls." *The Woman Rebel* April 1914: 12.

Chen, Constance M. *"The Sex Side of Life": Mary Ware Dennett's Pioneering Battle for Birth Control and Sex Education.* New York: The New Press, 1996.

Chesler, Ellen. *Woman of Valor: Margaret Sanger and the Birth Control Movement in America.* New York: Simon and Schuster, 1992.

Chodorow, Nancy. *The Reproduction of Mothering.* Berkeley: U of California P, 1978.

Clark, Suzanne. *Sentimental Modernism: Women Writers and the Revolution of the Word.* Bloomington: Indiana UP, 1991.

Clarke, Adele E. *Disciplining Reproduction: Modernity, American Life Sciences, and "the Problems of Sex."* Berkeley: U of California P, 1998.

Coiner, Constance. *Better Red: The Writing and Resistance of Tillie Olsen and Meridel Le Sueur.* New York: Oxford UP, 1995.

———. "Literature of Resistance: The Intersection of Feminism and the Communist Left in Meridel Le Sueur and Tillie Olsen." *Radical Revisions: Rereading 1930s Culture.* Ed. Bill Mullen and Sherry Lee Linkon. Urbana: U of Illinois P, 1996. 144–66.

Collins, Patricia Hill. "Shifting the Center: Race, Class, and Feminist Theorizing about Motherhood." *Representations of Motherhood.* Ed. Donna Bassin, Margaret Honey, and Meryle Mahrer Kaplan. New Haven, CT: Yale UP, 1994. 56–74.

Connell, Richard. "Weeds." *Birth Control Review* March 1922: 38–39; April 1922: 61–62.

"The Control of Births." *The New Republic* 6 March 1915: 114–15.

Coolidge, Mary. *Why Women Are So.* New York: Henry Holt, 1912.

Coontz, Stephanie. *Marriage, A History: From Obedience to Intimacy, or How Love Conquered Marriage.* New York: Viking, 2005.
Cooper, Helen M., Susan Merrill Squier, Adrienne Auslander Munich. "Arms and the Woman: The Con[tra]ception of the War Text." *Arms and the Woman: War, Gender, and Literary Representation.* Ed. Susan Merrill Squier, Helen M. Cooper, and Adrienne Auslander Munich. Chapel Hill: U of North Carolina P, 1989. 9–24.
Corea, Gena. *The Hidden Malpractice.* New York: Jove/HbJ Book, 1977.
Cornillon, Susan Koppelman. "The Fiction of Fiction." *Images of Women in Fiction.* Ed. Susan Koppelman Cornillon. Bowling Green, OH: Bowling Green State U Popular P, 1972. xx–xx. 113–30.
Cosslett, Tess. *Women Writing Childbirth: Modern Discourses in Motherhood.* Manchester: Manchester UP, 1994.
Cott, Nancy. *The Grounding of Modern Feminism.* New Haven, CT.: Yale UP, 1987.
Craig, John M. "'The Sex Side of Life': The Obscenity Case of Mary Ware Dennett." *Frontiers* 15.3 (1995): 145–66.
Cuddy, Lois A., and Claire M. Roche, eds. *Evolution and Eugenics in American Literature and Culture, 1880–1940: Essays on Ideological Conflict and Complicity.* Lewisburg, PA: Bucknell UP, 2003.
"The Curse of Abortion." *Birth Control Review* November 1929: 307.
Daly, Brenda O., and Maureen T. Reddy. *Narrating Mothers: Theorizing Maternal Subjectivities.* Knoxville: U of Tennessee P, 1991.
Dash, Irene. "The Literature of Birth and Abortion." *Regionalism and the Female Imagination* 3.1 (1977): 8–13.
David, Paul A., and Warren C. Sanderson. "The Emergence of a Two-Child Norm among American Birth-Controllers." *Population and Development Review* 13.1 (1987): 1–41.
Davis, Katherine Bemont. *Factors in the Sex Lives of Twenty-Two Hundred Women.* New York: Harper & Brothers Publishers, 1929.
Davison, Richard Allan. "Charles G. Norris, Margaret Sanger and *Seed.*" *Frank Norris Studies* 23 (Spring 1997): 1–3.
———. "Sinclair Lewis, Charles G. Norris, and Kathleen Norris: An Early Friendship." *Modern Fiction Studies* 31.3 (1985): 503–10.
Dawahare, Anthony. "Modernity and 'Village Communism' in Depression-Era America: The Utopian Literature of Meridel Le Sueur." *Criticism* 39.3 (1997): 409–31.
Dawkins, Laura. "From Madonna to Medea: Maternal Infanticide in African American Women's Literature of the Harlem Renaissance." *Literature Interpretation Theory* 15 (2004): 223–40.
Dawson, Deborah A., Denise J. Meny, and Jeanne Clare Ridley. "Fertility Control in the United States before the Contraceptive Revolution." *Family Planning Perspectives* 12 (1986): 76–86.
Day, Dorothy. *The Eleventh Virgin.* New York: Boni, 1924.
———. *The Long Loneliness: The Autobiography of Dorothy Day.* 1952. San Francisco, Harper & Row, 1981.
de Grazia, Edward. *Girls Lean Back Everywhere: The Law of Obscenity and the*

Assault on Genius. New York: Random House, 1992.

D'Emilio, John, and Estelle B. Freedman. *Intimate Matters: A History of Sexuality in America.* 1986. 2d ed. Chicago: U of Chicago P, 1997.

DeLillo, Don. *Underworld.* New York: Scribner, 1997.

Dell, Floyd. "The Outline of Marriage." *Birth Control Review Series:* 10.1 (January 1926): 8–9; 10.2 (February 1926): 47–48; 10.3 ((March 1926): 83–84; 10.4 (April 1926): 129–30; 10.5 (May 1926): 156–57; 10.6 (June 1926): 191.

Delmar, Vina. *Bad Girl.* New York: Grosset & Dunlap, 1928.

Dennett, Mary Ware. *Birth Control Laws: Shall We Keep Them, Change Them, or Abolish Them?* New York: Grafton Press, 1926.

"Do Women Want Children?" *Birth Control Review* 13.8 (March 1929): 80–81.

Douglas, Ann. *Terrible Honesty: Mongrel Manhattan in the 1920s.* New York: Farrar Straus & Giroux, 1995.

Doyle, Laura M. *Bordering on the Body: The Racial Matrix of Modern Fiction and Culture.* New York: Oxford UP, 1994.

Dreiser, Theodore. *An American Tragedy.* 1925. New York: Signet, 1964.

———. *Jennie Gerhardt.* 1911. Ed. James L. W. West III. New York: Penguin, 1992.

———. *Sister Carrie.* 1900. New York: Signet, 1980.

———. "A Word Concerning Birth Control." *Birth Control Review* April 1921: 5–6, 12–13.

DuBois, W. E. B. "Black Folk and Birth Control." *Birth Control Review* June 1932: 166–67.

———. "The Browsing Reader: Review of *Home to Harlem.*" *Crisis* 35 (1928): 202.

———. *Darkwater: Voices from Within the Veil.* New York: Harcourt, Brace and Howe, 1920.

———. "Opinion" *Crisis* October 1922: 248.

———. *Writings: The Suppression of the African Slave-Trade, The Souls of Black Folk, Dusk of Dawn, Essays and Articles.* New York: Library of America, 1996.

DuCille, Ann. *The Coupling Convention: Sex, Text, and Tradition in Black Women's Fiction.* New York: Oxford UP, 1993.

Dugdale, Richard L. *The Juke's: A Study in Crime, Pauperism, Disease, and Heredity.* New York: Putnam's Press, 1875.

Dunbar-Nelson, Alice. "Woman's Most Serious Problem." *The Works of Alice Dunbar-Nelson.* Vol. 2. Ed. Gloria T. Hull. New York: Oxford UP, 1988. 287–92.

DuPlessis, Rachel Blau. "'Seismic Orgasm': Sexual Intercourse, Gender Narratives, and Lyric Ideology in Mina Loy." *Studies in Historical Change.* Ed. Ralph Cohen. Charlottesville: UP of Virginia, 1992. 264–91.

———. *Writing beyond the Ending: Narrative Strategies of Twentieth-Century Women Writers.* Bloomington: Indiana UP, 1985.

Duvall, John N. *Faulkner's Marginal Couple: Invisible, Outlaw, and Unspeakable Communities.* Austin: U of Texas P, 1990.

Eastman, Max. "Revolutionary Birth Control." *The Masses* July 1915: 21–22.

"Editorial." *Birth Control Review* September 1923: 219.

Eldred, Janet Carey. "Faulkner's Still Life: Art and Abortion in *The Wild Palms*." *Faulkner Journal* 4.1–2 (Fall–Spring 1988–89): 139–58.

Eliot, T. S. *The Waste Land*. 1922. *The Heath Anthology of American Literature*. Vol. 2. Ed. Paul Lateur. 3d ed. Boston: Houghton Mifflin Company, 1998. 1411–1426.

Ellis, Havelock. "The Love Rights of Women." *Birth Control Review* June 1918: 3–6.

———. "A Research in Marriage." *Birth Control Review* May 1929: 125–26.

English, Daylanne Kathryn. "Gertrude Stein and the Politics of Literary-Medical Experimentation." *Literature and Medicine* 16.2 (1997): 188–209.

———. *Unnatural Selections: Eugenics in American Modernism and the Harlem Renaissance*. U of North Carolina P, 2004.

———. "W. E. B. DuBois's Family Crisis." *American Literature* 72.2 (2000): 291–319.

Epstein, Joseph. "Mary McCarthy in Retrospect." *Commentary* May 1993: 41–47.

Epstein, Julia. *Altered Conditions: Disease, Medicine, and Storytelling*. New York: Routledge, 1995.

Estabrook, Arthur H. *The Jukes in 1915*. Washington: The Carnegie Institute, 1916.

Falk, Candace Serena. *Love, Anarchy, and Emma Goldman*. New Brunswick, NJ: Rutgers UP, 1984. Revised ed, 1990.

"Family Problems." *Birth Control Review* March 1926: 88–89.

"Family Trees Which Should Not Bear Fruit." *Birth Control Review* January 1927: 16–17.

"Family Values in Margaret Sanger's Time." *Margaret Sanger Papers Newsletter* 4 (Winter 1992/93).

Faulkner, William. *As I Lay Dying*. 1930. New York: Vintage Books, 1987.

———. *If I Forget Thee, Jerusalem*. 1939. New York: Vintage Books, 1995.

———. *The Sound and the Fury*. 1929. New York: Vintage Books, 1987.

Fauset, Jessie Redmon. *The Chinaberry Tree: A Novel of American Life & Selected Writings*. 1931. Boston: Northeastern UP, 1995.

———. *Plum Bun: A Novel without a Moral*. 1928. Introduction by Deborah E. MacDowell. Boston: Beacon, 1990.

———. *There Is Confusion*. 1924. Foreword by Thadious M. Davis. Boston: Northeastern UP, 1989.

Field, Sara Bard. "A Birth-Control Meditation." *The Blast* December 15, 1916: 7.

Fishbein, Leslie. *Rebels in Bohemia: The Radicals of The Masses, 1911–1917*. Chapel Hill: U of North Carolina P, 1982.

Fishkin, Shelley Fisher. "Dreiser and the Discourse of Gender." *Theodore Dreiser: Beyond Naturalism*. Ed. Miriam Gogol. New York: New York UP, 1995. 1–30.

Fitzgerald, F. Scott. *The Beautiful and the Damned*. 1925. New York: Charles Scribner's Sons, 1950.

———. *The Great Gatsby*. 1925. New York: Scribner Classic, 1992.

Fitzgerald, Richard. *Art and Politics: Cartoonists of "The Masses" and "Libera-*

tor." Westport, CT: Greenwood, 1973.

Flamiano, Dolores. "The Birth of a Notion: Media Coverage of Contraception, 1915–1917." *Journalism and Mass Communication Quarterly* 75.3 (1998): 560–71.

Fleissner, Jennifer L. *Women, Compulsion, Modernity: The Moment of American Naturalism.* Chicago: U of Chicago P, 2004.

Fontana, Susan Sipple. "Eugenics and the Epidemic of Motherhood: The Politics of Reproduction in American Women's Fiction of the 1920s and 1930s." PhD diss., Miami University, 1994.

Forbes, Helen. "The Hunky Woman." *The Masses* May 1916: 12–13.

Foucault, Michel. *Discipline and Punish: The Birth of the Prison.* Trans. Alan Sheridan. New York: Vintage, 1979.

France, Alan W. "Reconsideration: Roth's 'Goodbye, Columbus' and the Limits of Commodity Culture." *MELUS* 15.4 (1988): 83–89.

Franzwa, Helen H. "Female Roles in Women's Magazine Fiction, 1940–1970." *Woman: Dependent or Independent Variable?* Ed. Rhoda Kessler Unger and Florence L. Denmark. New York: Psychological Dimensions, Inc., 1975. 42–53.

Frazier, E. Franklin. "The Negro and Birth Control." *Birth Control Review* March 1933: 68–70.

"Friend." "Hymn of the Unborn Babe." *Birth Control Review* July 1918: 16.

Gabaldon, Diana. *Outlander.* New York: Dell, 1991.

Gainor, J. Ellen. "*Chains of Dew* and the Drama of Birth Control." *Susan Glaspell: Essays on Her Theater and Fiction.* Ed. Linda Ben-Zvi. Ann Arbor: U of Michigan P, 1995. 165–93.

Gammel, Irene. "Sexualizing the Female Body: Dreiser, Feminism, and Foucault." *Theodore Dreiser: Beyond Naturalism.* Ed. Miriam Gogol. New York: New York UP, 1995. 31–54.

Garrett, Elizabeth H. "Birth Control's Business Baby." *New Republic* 17 January 1934: 269–72.

Gerould, Katherine Fullerton. "Feminine Fiction." *Saturday Review of Literature* 11 April 1936: 3+.

Gessler, Clifford. "Pregnancy." *Birth Control Review* December 1930: 352.

Gibson, Lydia. "The Boss's wife can buy information to limit her family." *The Blast* 1.5 (12 February 1916): cover.

Gilman, Charlotte Perkins. *The Crux.* 1911. Durham, NC: Duke UP, 2003.

———. *Herland.* 1915. New York: Pantheon, 1979.

Glasgow, Ellen. *Barren Ground.* 1925. New York: Hill and Wang, 1957.

Glaspell, Susan. *Chains of Dew.* Unpublished play, Library of Congress, 1920.

Glicksberg, Charles I. *The Sexual Revolution in Modern American Literature.* The Hague, Netherlands: Martinus Nijhoff, 1971.

Goddard, Henry H. *The Kallikak Family: A Study in the Heredity of Feeble-Mindedness.* New York: Macmillan, 1912.

Gogol, Miriam. "Introduction." *Theodore Dreiser: Beyond Naturalism.* Ed. Miriam Gogol. New York: New York UP, 1995. vii–xvii.

Goldberg, Carey. "Insurance for Viagra Spurs Coverage for Birth Control." *New York Times* 30 June 1999: A1.

Goldman, Emma. "Emma Goldman's Defense." *The Masses* June 1916: 27.

———. "Love and Marriage." *The Woman Rebel* March 1914: 3.

———. "Woman's Suffrage." 1914. *Red Emma Speaks: An Emma Goldman Reader*. Ed. Alix Kates Shulman. 3d ed. New York: Humanity Books, 1998. 190–203.

Goldstein, Sidney E. "Control of Parenthood as a Moral Problem—The Case for and against Birth Control." *Birth Control Review* October 1922: 195–97, 206.

Gordon, Linda. "Black and White Visions of Welfare: Women's Welfare Activism, 1890–1945." *Journal of American History* 78.2 (1991): 559–90.

———. *The Moral Property of Women: A History of Birth Control Politics in America*. 3d ed. Urbana: U of Illinois P, 2002.

———. "The Politics of Birth Control, 1920–1949: The Impact of Professionals." *International Journal of Health Services* 5.2 (1975): 253–77.

———. "The Politics of Population: Birth Control and the Eugenics Movement." *Radical America* 8.4 (1974): 61–98.

———. *Woman's Body, Woman's Right: A Social History of Birth Control in America*. New York: Grossman, 1976.

Gossel, Patricia Peck. "Packaging the Pill." In *Manifesting Medicine: Bodies and Machines*. Ed. Robert Bud, Bernard Finn, and Helmuth Trischler. Amsterdam: Harwood Academic Publishers, 1999. 105–21.

Grant, Madison. *The Passing of the Great Race; or, the Racial Basis of European History*. New York: Scribner, 1916.

Gray, Harriet. "The Scrub Woman." *Birth Control Review* June 1919: 13, 19.

Grimke, Angelina. "The Closing Door." *Birth Control Review* September 1919: 10–14; October 1919: 8–12.

———. "Goldie." *Birth Control Review* November 1920: 7–11; December 1920: 10–14.

———. *Rachel: A Play in Three Acts*. 1920. College Park, MD: McGrath, 1969.

———. "*Rachel*: The Reason and Synopsis by the Author." *Competitor* 1.1 (1920): 51–52.

Grossmann, Atina. *Reforming Sex: The German Movement for Birth Control and Abortion Reform, 1920–1950*. New York: Oxford UP, 1995.

Guest, May Pierce. "A Way Out." *Birth Control Review* May 1922: 83–85; June 1922: 108–10; July 1922: 131–33; August 1922: 153–54, 161.

Hagood, Margaret Jarman. *Mothers of the South: Portraiture of the White Tenant Farm Woman*. 1939. Charlottesville: UP of Virginia, 1977.

Haire, Norman. "Sterilization of the Unfit." *Birth Control Review* February 1922: 10–11.

Hale, Nancy. *The Prodigal Women*. New York: Charles Scribner's Sons, 1942.

Haller, Mark H. *Eugenics: Hereditarian Attitudes in American Thought*. New Brunswick, NJ: Rutgers UP, 1984.

Haman, Coralie. "Children: A Playlet." *Birth Control Review* September 1923: 230–37.

Hamilton, Alice. "Poverty and Birth Control." *Birth Control Review* August 1925: 226–28.

Hankins, F. H. "Eugenics and Birth Control." *Birth Control Review* June 1931: 170–71.

Hanna, A. C. "The Menace of the Feebleminded." *Birth Control Review* January 1927: 14–15.

Hansberry, Lorraine. *To Be Young, Gifted and Black: A Portrait of Lorraine Hansberry in Her Own Words.* Adapted by Robert Nemiroff. New York: Samuel French, Inc., 1971.

Hansen, Elaine Tuttle. *Mother without Child: Contemporary Fiction and the Crisis of Motherhood.* Berkeley: U of California P, 1997.

Harper, John Paull. "Be Fruitful and Multiply: Origins of Legal Restrictions to Planned Parenthood in Nineteenth-Century America." *Women of America: A History.* Ed. Carol Ruth Berkin and Mary Beth Norton. Boston: Houghton Mifflin, 1979. 245–69.

Hart, Hornell. "Harmony in Marriage." *Birth Control Review* November 1927: 292.

Hart, Jamie. "Who should have the children? Discussions of Birth Control among African-American Intellectuals, 1920–1939." *Journal of Negro History* 79.1 (1994): 71–84.

Hartley, C. Gasquoine. "Marriage and Birth Control." *Birth Control Review* April 1928: 112.

Hartmann, Susan M. *The Home Front and Beyond: American Women in the 1940s.* Boston: Twayne, 1982.

Hauck, Christina. "Why Do the Ramsays Have So Many Children?: Birth Control and *To the Lighthouse.*" *Virginia Woolf: Emerging Perspectives.* Ed. Mark Hussey and Vara Neverow. Jefferson City, MO: Pace UP, 1994.

Hemingway, Ernest. *A Farewell to Arms.* 1929. New York: Scribner Classic, 1986.

———. "Hills Like White Elephants." 1927. *Ernest Hemingway: The Short Stories.* New York: Simon & Schuster, 1995. 273–78.

———. *The Torrents of Spring: A Romantic Novel in Honor of the Passing of a Great Race.* 1926. New York: Scribner, 1972.

Henke, Suzette A. "Sexuality and Silence in Women's Literature." *Power, Gender, Values.* Ed. Judith Genova. Edmonton, AB: Academic Printing & Publishing, 1987. 45–62.

Henninger, Katherine. "'It's an Outrage': Pregnancy and Abortion in Faulkner's Fiction of the Thirties." *Faulkner Journal* 12.1 (1996): 23–41.

Hickey, Florence Wayne. "The Stork and the Wolf." *Birth Control Review* April 1925: 109.

Himes, Norman. "Crime, Mental Deficiency, and Birth Control." *Birth Control Review* June 1931: 173–74.

———. *Medical History of Contraception.* 1936. New York: Gamut Press, 1963.

Hirsch, Marianne. *The Mother/Daughter Plot: Narrative, Psychoanalysis, Feminism.* Bloomington: Indiana UP, 1989.

Hoekstra, Ellen. "The Pedestal Myth Reinforced: Women's Magazine Fiction, 1900–1920." *New Dimensions in Popular Culture.* Ed. Russell B. Nye. Bowling Green, OH: Bowling Green State U Popular P, 1972. 43–58.

Hollenberg, Donna. "Abortion, Identity Formation, and the Expatriate Woman Writer: HD and Kay Boyle in the Twenties." *Critical Essays on Kay Boyle.* Ed. Marilyn Elkins. Boston: Twayne, 1997. 211–27.
Hollick, Frederick. *The Marriage Guide.* New York: T. W. Strong, 1850.
Holmes, John Haynes. "Marriage Today and in the Future." *Birth Control Review* June–October 1927.
Holmes, Sarah C. "Re-Examining the Political Left: Erskine Caldwell and the Doctrine of Eugenics." *Evolution and Eugenics in American Literature and Culture, 1880–1940: Essays on Ideological Conflict and Complicity.* Ed. Lois A. Cuddy and Claire M. Roche. Lewisburg, PA: Bucknell UP, 2003. 240–58.
Homans, Margaret. *Bearing the Word: Language and Female Experience in Nineteenth-Century Women's Writing.* Chicago: U of Chicago P, 1986.
Honey, Maureen. "Gotham's Daughters: Feminism in the 1920s." *American Studies* 31.1 (1990): 25–40.
Hopkins, Mary Alden. "Birth Control and Public Morals." *Harper's Weekly* 22 May 1915: 489–90.
———. "Control of Births." *Harper's Weekly* 10 April 1915: 342–43.
———. "Education and the Birth Rate." *Harper's Weekly* 31 July 1915: 103–4.
———. "The Falling Birth Rate." *Harper's Weekly* 12 June 1915: 567–68.
———. "Is Contraception Immoral?" *Harper's Weekly* 19 June 1915: 591–92.
———. "Opposition to Family Limitation." *Harper's Weekly* 18 September 1915: 274.
———. "Spacing Out Babies." *Harper's Weekly* 24 April 1915: 401–2.
———. "Swarming Families." *Harper's Weekly* 1 May 1915: 415–16.
———. "What Doctors Say of Birth Control." *Harper's Weekly* 16 October 1916: 380–82.
———. "What They Say About Birth Control." *Harper's Weekly* 23 October 1916: 404–5.
Hull, Gloria T. *Color, Sex, and Poetry: Three Women Writers of the Harlem Renaissance.* Bloomington: Indiana UP, 1987.
Hull, Helen. "Till Death—." *The Masses* January 1917: 5–6.
———. "Usury." *The Masses* September 1916: 5, 8–10.
"Increased Opportunities for Babies." *The Masses* November 1913: 9.
Irigaray, Luce. *This Sex Which Is Not One.* Trans. Catherine Porter. Ithaca, NY: Cornell UP, 1985.
Irish, Margaret H. "Childbirth—A Woman's Problem." *Working Woman* May 1933: 17.
Irving, Katrina. *Immigrant Mothers: Narratives of Race and Maternity, 1890–1925.* Urbana: U of Illinois P, 2000.
Irwin, Inez Haynes. "The Making of a Militant." *"These Modern Women": Autobiographical Essays from the Twenties.* Ed. Elaine Showalter. New York: Feminist Press, 1989. 34–39.
"Is Contraceptive Advice Necessary?" *Birth Control Review* May 1932: 142–43.
Jameson, Frederic. *The Political Unconscious: Narrative as a Socially Symbolic Act.* Ithaca, NY: Cornell UP, 1981.
Jensen, Joan M. "The Evolution of Margaret Sanger's *Family Limitation* Pam-

phlet, 1914–1921." *Signs* 6.3 (1981): 548–65.

Johns-Heine, Patricke, and Hans H. Gerth. "Values in Mass Periodical Fiction, 1921–1940." *Public Opinion Quarterly* 13 (1949): 105–13.

Johnson, Barbara. "Apostrophe, Animation, and Abortion." *Contemporary Literary Criticism: Literary and Cultural Studies.* Ed. Robert Con Davis and Ronald Schleifer. New York: Longman, 1998. 221–35.

Johnson, Charles S. "A Question of Negro Health." *Birth Control Review* June 1932: 167–68.

Johnson, Georgia Douglas. "Maternity." *Bronze: A Book of Verse.* Boston: B. J. Brimmer Company, 1922. 42.

———. "Motherhood." *Birth Control Review* November 1922: 229.

———. "Safe." 1929. *The Selected Works of Georgia Douglas Johnson.* Introduction by Claudia Tate. New York: G. K. Hall & Co, 1997. 377–84.

Johnson, John W. *Griswold v. Connecticut: Birth Control and the Constitutional Right of Privacy.* Lawrence: UP of Kansas, 2005.

Jones, Margaret C. *Heretics and Hellraisers: Women Contributors to* The Masses, *1911–1917.* Austin: U of Texas P, 1993.

"Judges with Small Families Jail Kitty Marion." *Birth Control Review* November 1918: 5.

Kael, Pauline. "The Making of *The Group.*" *Kiss Kiss Bang Bang.* Boston: Little, Brown & Co., 1965. 67–100.

Kapsalis, Terri. *Public Privates: Performing Gynecology from Both Ends of the Speculum.* Durham, NC: Duke UP, 1997.

Katz, Esther. "The History of Birth Control in the United States." *History of Medicine* 4.2–3 (1988): 81–101.

———, ed. *The Selected Papers of Margaret Sanger. Volume 1: The Woman Rebel, 1900–1928.* Urbana: U of Illinois P, 2003.

Katz, Michael B., and Mark J. Stern. "Fertility, Class, and Industrial Capitalism: Erie County, New York, 1855–1915." *American Quarterly* 33.1 (Spring 1981): 63–92.

Kaufman, Marc. "2 FDA Officials Urged to Resign Over Plan B." *Washington Post* 13 May 2004: A3.

Keely, Karen A. "The Pure Products of America: Eugenics and Narrative in the Age of Sterilization." PhD diss., University of California Los Angeles, 1999.

Kelley, Edith Summers. *Weeds.* 1923. New York: Feminist Press, 1996.

Kennedy, David M. *Birth Control in America: The Career of Margaret Sanger.* New Haven: Yale UP, 1970.

Kevles, Daniel J. *In the Name of Eugenics: Genetics and the Uses of Human Heredity.* New York: Alfred A. Knopf, 1985.

Kiernan, Frances. *Seeing Mary Plain: A Life of Mary McCarthy.* New York: W. W. Norton, 2000.

Kloepfer, Deborah Kelly. *The Unspeakable Mother.* Ithaca, NY: Cornell UP, 1989.

Knowlton, Charles. *Fruits of Philosophy.* 1832. Ed. Charles Bradlaugh and Annie Besant. 3d ed. New York: Arno Press, 1878.

Koloze, Jeff. "'We a people who give children life': Pedagogic Concerns of the Aborted Abortion in Lorraine Hansberry's *A Raisin in the Sun.*" *NAAAS—*

Together We Can Make It Work. Ed. Lemuel Berry, Jr. Houston, TX: National Association of African American Studies, 1997. 800–818.

Krupskaya, Nadezhda. "Sane Birth Control." *Sunday Worker Magazine* 19 July 1936: 2.

Kunzel, Regina. "Pulp Fictions and Problem Girls: Reading and Rewriting Single Pregnancy in the Postwar United States." *American Historical Review* 100.5 (1995): 1465–87.

Ladd-Taylor, Molly. *Mother-Work: Women, Child Welfare, and the State, 1890–1930*. Urbana: U of Illinois P, 1994.

———. "Saving Babies and Sterilizing Mothers: Eugenics and Welfare Politics in the Interwar United States." *Social Politics* (1997): 136–53.

Lane, Ann J. "Introduction." *Herland* by Charlotte Perkins Gilman. New York: Pantheon, 1979. v–xxiv.

Langner, Lawrence. "Wedded: A Social Comedy." *Little Review* November 1914: 8–18.

Larsen, Nella. *Quicksand*. *Quicksand and Passing*. Ed. Deborah E. McDowell. New Brunswick, NJ: Rutgers UP, 1988. 1–135.

Larson, Edward J. "'In the Finest, Most Womanly Way': Women in the Southern Eugenics Movement." *American Journal of Legal History* 39.2 (1995): 119–47.

Laughlin, Harry. "Analysis of America's Modern Melting Pot." *Hearings before the Committee on Immigration and Naturalization*. November 21, 1922. House of Representatives. U.S. 67th Congress, 3d Session. Washington: GPO, 1922.

Lauter, Paul. *From Walden Pond to Jurassic Park: Activism, Culture, & American Studies*. Durham, NC: Duke UP, 2001.

Le Sueur, Meridel. "Anunciation." *Ripening: Selected Work*. 2d ed. New York: Feminist Press, 1990.

———. *The Girl*. 1978. Rev. ed. Minneapolis: West End Press, 1990.

———. "Salvation Home." *New Masses: An Anthology of the Rebel Thirties*. Ed. Joseph North. New York: International Publishers, 1969. 125–28.

———. "Sequel to Love." 1935. *Writing Red: An Anthology of American Women Writers, 1930–1940*. Ed. Charlotte Nekola and Paula Rabinowitz. New York: Feminist Press, 1987. 36–38.

———. "Women on the Breadlines." *New Masses* January 1932: 5–7.

Leon, Juan. "A Literary History of Eugenic Terror in England and America." PhD diss., Harvard University, 1989.

———. "'Meeting Mr. Eugenides': T. S. Eliot and Eugenic Anxiety." *Yeats Eliot Review* 9.4 (1988): 169–77.

Lerner, Barron H. "Constructing Medical Indications: The Sterilization of Women with Heart Disease or Tuberculosis, 1905–1935." *Journal of the History of Medicine and Allied Sciences* 49.3 (1994): 362–79.

Lewin, Tamar. "Father Owing Child Support Loses a Right to Procreate." *New York Times* 12 July 2001: A14.

Lingeman, Richard. *Theodore Dreiser: An American Journey*. New York: John Wiley & Sons, 1993.

"Literary Censorship and the Novels of the Winter." *Current Opinion* November

1913: 353, 377–80.

Little, C. C. "Unnatural Selection and Its Resulting Obligations." *Birth Control Review* August 1926: 243–44, 257.

London, Jack. "Told in the Drooling Ward." *The Complete Short Stories of Jack London*. Vol. 3. Stanford, CA: Stanford UP, 1993. 1762–70.

Loos, Anita. "The Force of Heredity, and Nella: A Modern Fable with a Telling Moral for Eugenists." *Vanity Fair* February 1915: 42.

Lowe-Evans, Mary. *Crimes against Fecundity: Joyce and Population Control*. Syracuse, NY: Syracuse UP, 1989.

Loy, Mina. "The Feminist Manifesto." *The Lost Lunar Baedecker: Poems of Mina Loy*. Ed. Roger L. Conover. New York: Farrar Straus Giroux, 1996.

Ludmerer, Kenneth M. "Genetics, Eugenics, and the Immigration Restriction Act of 1924." *Bulletin of the History of Medicine* 46.1 (1972): 59–81.

Luhan, Mabel Dodge. *Intimate Memories: Movers and Shakers. Vol. III: Movers and Shakers*. New York: Harcourt, Brace and Company, 1936.

Luker, Kristin. *Abortion and the Politics of Motherhood*. Berkeley: U of California P, 1984.

Lynd, Robert S., and Helen Merrell Lynd. *Middletown: A Study in American Culture*. New York: Harcourt, Brace & Co., 1929.

Lyon, Janet. *Manifestoes: Provocations of the Modern*. Ithaca, NY: Cornell UP, 1999.

Lysander, George. "Birth Control." *Birth Control Review* April 1918: 4.

MacKinnon, Janice R., and Stephen R. MacKinnon. *Agnes Smedley: The Life and Times of an American Radical*. Berkeley: U of California P, 1988.

Mailer, Norman. "The Mary McCarthy Case." *New York Review of Books* 17 October 1963: 1–3.

Mansfield, Katherine. "The Mother." *Birth Control Review* November 1925: 317.

Marks, Lara V. *Sexual Chemistry: A History of the Contraceptive Pill*. New Haven, CT: Yale UP, 2001.

Masel-Walters, Lynne. "For the 'Poor Mute Mothers'? Margaret Sanger and *The Woman Rebel*." *Journalism History* 11.1–2 (1984): 3–10, 37.

Maurer, James H. "An Economic Necessity for the Workers." *Birth Control Review* April 1927: 107.

McCann, Carole R. *Birth Control Politics in the United States, 1916–1945*. Ithaca, NY: Cornell UP, 1994.

McCarthy, Mary. "Dottie Makes an Honest Woman of Herself." *Partisan Review* January/February 1954: 34–52.

———. *The Group*. 1954. New York: Signet Book, 1963.

———. "Letter to a Translator about *The Group*." *Encounter* 23.5 (1964): 69–76.

McFalls, Joseph A. Jr., and George S. Masnick. "Birth Control and the Fertility of the U.S. Black Population, 1880–1980." *Journal of Family History* 6.1 (1981): 89–106.

McKay, Claude. *Home to Harlem*. 1928. Foreword by Wayne F. Cooper. Boston: Northeastern UP, 1987.

McKay, Nellie. "'What Were They Saying?': Black Women Playwrights of the

Harlem Renaissance." *The Harlem Renaissance Re-Examined.* Ed. Victor Kramer. New York: AMS, 1987. 129–48.

McLaren, Angus. *A History of Contraception: From Antiquity to the Present Day.* Oxford: Basic Blackwell, 1990.

Meckel, Richard A. *Save the Babies: American Public Health Reform and the Prevention of Infant Mortality, 1850–1920.* Baltimore: Johns Hopkins UP, 1990.

Meckier, Jerome. "Aldous Huxley, Evelyn Waugh, and Birth Control in *Black Mischief.*" *Journal of Modern Literature* 23.2 (2000): 277–90.

Mehlman, Peter. "The Sponge." *Seinfeld.* Episode 119. NBC. 7 December 1995.

"The Menace of the Feebleminded." *Birth Control Review* January 1927: 14–15.

"A Menace to Marriage." *Birth Control Review* May 1927: 144–45.

"A Menace to Profit." *The Blast* February 26, 1916: 5.

Michaels, Walter Benn. *Our America: Nativism, Modernism, and Pluralism.* Durham, NC: Duke UP, 1995.

Miller, Sally M. *Race, Ethnicity, and Gender in Early Twentieth-Century American Socialism.* New York: Garland Publishing, 1996.

Model, Suzanne W. "Work and Family: Blacks and Immigrants from South and East Europe." *Immigration Reconsidered: History, Sociology, and Politics.* Ed. Virginia Yans-McLaughlin. New York: Oxford UP, 1990. 130–59.

Mohr, James C. *Abortion in America: The Origins and Evolution of National Policy.* New York, 1978.

Morawska, Eva. "The Sociology and Historiography of Immigration." *Immigration Reconsidered: History, Sociology, and Politics.* Ed. Virginia Yans-McLaughlin. New York: Oxford UP, 1990. 187–238.

"More Reasons for Birth Control." *Birth Control Review* February 1929: 35.

Moriarty, Colleen. "The Cost of Contraception." *Shape* June 1998: 24.

Morrison, Toni. *Beloved.* 1987. New York: Alfred A. Knopf, 1998.

———. *Song of Solomon.* 1977. *Sula, Song of Solomon, Tar Baby.* New York: Alfred A. Knopf, Inc., 1987.

Morrisson, Mark S. *The Public Face of Modernism: Little Magazines, Audiences, and Reception 1905–1920.* Madison: U of Wisconsin P, 2001.

Morton, Patricia. *Disfigured Images: The Historical Assault on Afro-American Women.* New York: Greenwood, 1991.

Mosher, Clelia Duel. *The Mosher Survey: Sexual Attitudes of Forty-five Victorian Women.* Ed. James Mahood and Kristine Wenburg. New York: Arno Press, 1980.

Mott, Frank Luther. *Golden Multitudes: The Story of Best Sellers in the United States.* New York: Macmillan, 1947.

Mullen, Kate. "The Pregnant Woman." *Birth Control Review* June 1925: 169–70, 190.

Mumford, Ethel Watts. "A Holiday—A Short Story." *Birth Control Review* August 1921: 6, 10.

Nearing, Scott, and Nellie M. S. Nearing. *Woman and Social Progress: A Discussion of the Biologic, Domestic, Industrial and Social Possibilities of American*

Women. New York: Macmillan, 1912.

New York v. Sanger, 222 NY 192, 118 NE 637 (Court of Appeals 1917), National Archives, Records of the U.S. Supreme Court, RG 267 (MSPME-CDS C15: 298).

Nickel, John. "Eugenics and the Fiction of Pauline Hopkins." *ATQ* 14.1 (2000): 47–60.

Niebuhr, Elisabeth. "The Art of Fiction." *Paris Review* 27 (1962): 71–72.

Nies, Betsy Lee. "Eugenic Fantasies: Racial Ideology in the Literature and Popular Culture of the 1920s." PhD diss., University of Florida, 1998.

Nimkoff, Meyer E. "Education for Marriage." *Birth Control Review* September 1931: 245–47.

Norris, Charles G. *Seed: A Novel of Birth Control.* New York: Triangle Books, 1930.

Norris, Kathleen. *Mother.* New York: Grosset & Dunlap, 1911.

Oakes, Angela. "Nature." *Birth Control Review* January 1926: 10–12.

Ogburn, William F. "Birth Control and Early Marriage." *Birth Control Review* December 1926: 363.

Olasky, Marvin. "Advertising Abortion during the 1830s and 1840s: Madame Restell Builds a Business." *Journalism History* 13.2 (1986): 49–55.

Olsen, Tillie. *Yonnondio: From the Thirties.* New York: Delacorte Press, 1974.

"One Hundred Contraceptive Clinics." *Birth Control Review* June 1936: 3.

O'Neill, Eugene. *Strange Interlude.* 1928. *Three Plays by Eugene O'Neill.* New York: Vintage Books, 1959. 60–222.

O'Neill, William L. *Echoes of Revolt: "The Masses," 1911–1917.* Chicago: Quadrangle Books, 1966.

Orwell, George. *Keep the Aspidistra Flying.* New York: Harvest, 1969.

Oudshoorn, Nelly. *Beyond the Natural Body: An Archeology of Sex Hormones.* London: Routledge, 1994.

Owen, Robert Dale. "Moral Physiology (1831)." *Birth Control and Morality in Nineteenth Century America: Two Discussions.* By Charles Knowlton and Robert Dale Owen. New York: Arno Press, 1972.

Pangborn, Edgar Wood. "Book Review of *Daughter of Earth* by Agnes Smedley." *Birth Control Review* 13.7 (1929): 196–97.

———. "The Probation in Literature." *Birth Control Review* January 1929: 13–14.

Parker, Dorothy. "Mr. Durant." 1924. *Dorothy Parker: Complete Stories.* Ed. Colleen Breese. New York: Penguin Books, 1995. 23–32.

———. "Mrs. Hofstadter on Josephine Street." 1934. *The Portable Dorothy Parker.* New York: Penguin, 1976. 155–64.

Parry, Sally E. "Boundary Ambiguity and the Politics of Abortion: Women's Choices in Ann Vickers and Kingsblood." *Sinclair Lewis: New Essays in Criticism.* Ed. James M. Hutchisson. Troy, NY: Whitson, 1997. 68–79.

Paul, Diane. "Eugenics and the Left." *Journal of the History of Ideas* 45.4 (1984): 567–90.

Peck, Diana. "Birth Control Review." *Women's Periodicals in the United States.* Ed. Kathleen L. Endres and Theres L. Lueck. Westport, CT: Greenwood Press, 1996. 28–38.

Peiss, Kathy. "'Charity Girls' and City Pleasures: Historical Notes on Working-Class Sexuality, 1880–1920." *Powers of Desire: The Politics of Sexuality.* Ed. Ann Snitow, Christine Stansell, and Sharon Thompson. New York: Monthly Review Press, 1983. 74–87.
Pernick, Martin S. *The Black Stork: Eugenics and the Death of "Defective" Babies in American Medicine and Motion Pictures since 1915.* New York: Oxford UP, 1996.
———. "Defining the Defective: Eugenics, Aesthetics, and Mass Culture in Early-Twentieth-Century America." *The Body and Physical Difference: Discourses of Disability.* Ed. David T. Mitchell and Sharon L. Snyder. Ann Arbor: U of Michigan P, 1997. 89–110.
Petchesky, Rosalind Pollack. *Abortion and Woman's Choice: The State, Sexuality, & Reproductive Freedom.* 1984. Revised ed. Boston: Northeastern UP, 1990.
Piccinino, Linda J., and William D. Mosher. "Trends in Contraceptive Use in the United States: 1982–1995." *Family Planning Perspectives* 30.1 (January/February 1998): 4–10, 46.
Piercy, Marge. *Sex Wars: A Novel of the Turbulent Post–Civil War Period.* New York: William Morrow, 2005.
"Plea for Birth Control on the Stage." *Survey* 27 November 1915: 199.
Popini, Alexander. "The Happy Home." *The Masses* April 1912: 4.
Poston, Carol H. "Childbirth in Literature." *Feminist Studies* 4.8 (1978): 18–31.
"Prevention or Abortion—Which?" *Birth Control Review* July 1923: 181–82.
Pringle, Henry F. "What the Women of America Think about Birth Control." *Ladies' Home Journal* March 1938: 14–15.
Pruette, L. L. "A Matter of Life and Death." *Birth Control Review* January 1920: 13–14.
Rabinow, Paul. *The Foucault Reader.* New York: Pantheon, 1984.
Rabinowitz, Paula. "Ending Difference/Different Endings: Class, Closure, and Collectivity in Women's Proletarian Fiction." *Genders* 8 (1990): 62–77.
———. *Labor and Desire: Women's Revolutionary Fiction in Depression America.* Chapel Hill: U of North Carolina P, 1991.
———. "Maternity as History: Gender and the Transformation of Genre in Meridel Le Sueur's *The Girl*." *Contemporary Literature* 29.4 (1988): 538–48.
———. "Women and U.S. Literary Radicalism." *Writing Red: An Anthology of American Women Writers, 1930–1940.* Ed. Charlotte Nekola and Paula Rabinowitz. New York: Feminist Press, 1987. 1–16.
Rado, Lisa. "The Case for Cultural/Gender/Modernism Studies." *Modernism, Gender, and Culture: A Cultural Studies Approach.* Ed. Lisa Rado. New York: Garland, 1997. 3–14.
Radway, Janice. *Reading the Romance: Women, Patriarchy, and Popular Literature.* Chapel Hill: U of North Carolina P, 1991.
"Raising Garbage Collectors for the Doctors." *Birth Control Review* April/May 1917: 13.
Rafter, Nicole Hahn, ed. *White Trash: The Eugenic Family Studies 1877–1919.* Boston: Northeastern UP, 1988.

Ramirez, Annette B., and Conrad Seipp. *Colonialism, Catholicism, and Contraception: A History of Birth Control in Puerto Rico*. Chapel Hill: U of North Carolina P, 1983.

Reagan, Leslie J. "'About to meet her maker': Women, Doctors, Dying Declarations, and the State's Investigation of Abortion, Chicago, 1867–1940." *Journal of American History* 77.4 (1991): 1240–64.

Reed, James. *The Birth Control Movement and American Society: "From Private Vice to Public Virtue."* Princeton, NJ: Princeton UP, 1983.

———. "The Birth Control Movement before *Roe v. Wade*." *The Politics of Abortion and Birth Control in Historical Perspective*. Ed. Donald T. Critchlow. University Park: Penn State UP, 1996. 22–52.

———. "Doctors, Birth Control, and Social Values: 1830–1970." *The Therapeutic Revolution: Essays in the Social History of American Medicine*. Ed. Morris J. Vogel and Charles E. Rosenberg. Philadelphia: U of Pennsylvania P, 1979. 109–33.

Reed, John. "Broadway Nights." *The Masses* May 1916: 19–20.

Reed, Miriam. *Margaret Sanger: Her Life in Her Words*. Fort Lee, NJ: Barricade, 2003.

Renner, Stanley. "Moving to the Girl's Side of 'Hills Like White Elephants.'" *Hemingway Review* 15.1 (1995): 27–41.

"Review of *Tobacco Road*." *Springfield Republican* April 24 1932: 7e.

"Review of *Tobacco Road*." *Forum* May 1932: 87.

Riddle, John M. *Contraception and Abortion from the Ancient World to the Renaissance*. Cambridge, MA: Harvard UP, 1992.

———. *Eve's Herbs: A History of Contraception and Abortion in the West*. Cambridge, MA: Harvard UP, 1997.

Rideout, Walter. *The Radical Novel in the United States, 1900–1954*. New York: Hill and Wang, 1956.

Riley, John Winchell, and Matilda White. "The Use of Various Methods of Contraception." *American Sociological Review* 5 (1940): 890–903.

Roberts, Dorothy E. "Crime, Race, and Reproduction." *Tulane Law Review* 67.1 (1993): 1945–77.

———. *Killing the Black Body: Race, Reproduction, and the Meaning of Liberty*. New York: Vintage Books, 1997.

Roberts, Nora Ruth. "Radical Women Writers of the Thirties and the New Feminist Response." *Left Curve* 17 (1993): 85–93.

———. *Three Radical Women Writers: Class and Gender in Meridel LeSueur, Tillie Olsen, and Josephine Herbst*. Gender and Genre in Literature Series. New York: Garland Publishing, 1996.

Roberts, Walter Adolphe. "Birth Control and the Revolution." *Birth Control Review* June 1917: 7.

Robinson, Caroline H. "Collegians' Race Suicide." *Birth Control Review* 17.2 (1933): 48–50.

Roche, Claire M. "Reproducing the Working Class: Tillie Olsen, Margaret Sanger, and American Eugenics." *Evolution and Eugenics in American Literature and Culture, 1880–1940: Essays on Ideological Conflict and Complicity*. Ed. Lois A. Cuddy and Claire M. Roche. Lewisburg, PA: Bucknell UP, 2003. 259–75.

Rodrique, Jessie M. "The Black Community and the Birth-Control Movement." *Passion and Power: Sexuality in History.* Ed. Kathy Peiss and Christina Simmons. Philadelphia: Temple UP, 1989. 138–54.

Rogers, Lou. "Mrs. Poor Patient." *Birth Control Review* June 1918: 5.

———. "Must She Always Plead in Vain?" *Birth Control Review* July 1919: cover.

———. "The New Vision." *Birth Control Review* December 1918: 8–9.

Roosevelt, Theodore. "The American Woman as a Mother." *Ladies' Home Journal* July 1905: 3–4.

Rose, June. *Marie Stopes and the Sexual Revolution*. London: Faber and Faber, 1992.

Rosen, Robyn L. *Reproductive Health, Reproductive Rights: Reformers and the Politics of Maternal Welfare, 1917–1940*. Columbus: The Ohio State UP, 2003.

———. "Federal Expansion, Fertility Control, and Physicians in the United States: The Politics of Maternal Welfare in the Interwar Years." *Journal of Women's History* 10.3 (1998): 53–73.

Roth, Philip. *Goodbye, Columbus, and Five Short Stories*. New York: Vintage Books, 1987.

Sanger, Margaret. "The Aim." *The Woman Rebel* March 1914: 1.

"Sanger on Trial: The Brownsville Clinic Testimony." *Margaret Sanger Papers Project Newsletter* 25 (Fall 2000). www.nyu.edu/projects/sanger/secure/newsletter/articles/sanger-on-trial.php.

———. *An Autobiography*. New York: W. W. Norton & Company, 1938.

———. *Family Limitation*. New York: Maisel, 1914.

———. *Happiness in Marriage*. New York: Basic Books, 1926.

———. "Impressions of the East Side." *New York Call*. Part I, September 3, 1911; Part 2, September 10, 1911.

———. *Motherhood in Bondage*. 1928. Elmsford, NY: Maxwell Reprint Company, 1956.

———. *My Fight for Birth Control*. 1931. New York: Maxwell Reprint Company, 1969.

———. *The Pivot of Civilization*. Elmsford, NY: Maxwell, 1922.

———. "Quotable Quote." *Margaret Sanger Papers Project Newsletter* 42 (Spring 2006): 4.

———. "The Soviet Union's Abortion Law." *Woman Today* December 1936: 8, 30.

———. "Suppression. *The Woman Rebel* June 1914: 25.

———. "What Every Girl Should Know." *New York Call*. 12-part series. November 17, 1912–March 2, 1913.

———. "When Should a Woman Avoid Having Children."*Birth Control Review* November 1918: 6–7.

———. "Why the Woman Rebel?" *The Woman Rebel* March 1914: 8.

———. *Woman and the New Race*. New York: Truth Publishing Company, 1920.

———. *Woman, Morality, and Birth Control*. New York: New York Publishing Company, 1922.

Sarch, Amy. "Those Dirty Ads! Birth Control Advertising in the 1920s and 1930s." *Critical Studies in Mass Communication* 14 (1997): 31–48.

Scanlon, Jennifer. *Inarticulate Longings: The Ladies' Home Journal, Gender, and the Promises of Consumer Culture.* New York: Routledge, 1995.

Schoen, Johanna. *Choice & Coercion: Birth Control, Sterilization, and Abortion in Public Health and Welfare.* Chapel Hill: U of North Carolina P, 2005.

Schreiner, Olive. "Breeding Men for Battle." *Birth Control Review* April/May 1917: 5.

Schwarz, Judith. *Radical Feminists of Heterodoxy: Greenwich Village, 1912–1940.* Norwich, VT: New Victoria, 1986.

Seitler, Dana. "Unnatural Selection: Mothers, Eugenic Feminism, and Charlotte Perkins Gilman's Regeneration Narratives." *American Quarterly* 55.1 (March 2003): 61–88.

Sewell, Lemuel T. "The Negro Wants Birth Control." *Birth Control Review* May 1933: 131.

"Sex O'Clock in America." *Current Opinion* August 1913: 113–14.

Sharistanian, Janet. "Afterword." *The Unpossessed* by Tess Schlesinger. Old Westbury, NY: Feminist Press, 1984. 359–86.

Shorto, Russell. "Contra-Contraception." *New York Times Magazine* 7 May 2006: 48+.

Showalter, Elaine. "Killing the Angel in the House: The Autonomy of Women Writers." *Antioch Review* 32.3 (1992): 338–53.

Shulman, Alix. *To the Barricades: The Anarchist Life of Emma Goldman.* New York: Thomas Y. Crowell Co., 1971.

Simmons, Christina. "'Modern Marriage' for African Americans, 1920–1940." *Canadian Review of American Studies* 30.3 (2000). http://www.utpjournals.com/product/cras/303/simmons.html (accessed February 23, 2007).

———. "Women's Power in Sex: Radical Challenges to Marriage in the Early-Twentieth-Century United States." *Feminist Studies* 29.1 (Spring 2003): 169–98.

Slesinger, Tess. *The Unpossessed.* Old Westbury, NY: Feminist Press, 1934.

Smedley, Agnes. "Babies and Imperialism in Japan." *Birth Control Review* 3.6 (1919): 6–8.

———. "Birth Control in Germany." *Birth Control Review* 13.3 (1929): 77–78.

———. *Daughter of Earth.* 1929. New York: Feminist Press, 1987.

———. "Margaret Sanger Comes to Berlin." *Birth Control Review* 12.2 (1928): 50–54, 66.

Smith-Rosenberg, Carol. *Disorderly Conduct: Visions of Gender in Victorian America.* New York: Alfred A. Knopf, 1985.

Solinger, Rickie. *Pregnancy and Power: A Short History of Reproductive Politics in America.* New York: New York UP, 2005.

———. *Wake Up Little Susie: Single Pregnancy and Race Before Roe v. Wade.* New York: Routledge, 1992.

Solley, John B. "Book Review of *Seed* by Charles G. Norris." *Birth Control Review* 14.11 (1930): 328–29.

Soloway, Richard A. "The 'Perfect Contraceptive': Eugenics and Birth Control Research in Britain and America in the Interwar Years." *Journal of Contem-*

porary History 30 (1995): 637–64.

Stamp, Shelley. "Taking Precautions, or Regulating Early Birth-Control Films." *A Feminist Reader in Early Cinema*. Ed. Jennifer M. Bean and Diane Negra. Durham, NC: Duke UP, 2002: 270–97.

Stansell, Christine. *American Moderns: Bohemian New York and the Creation of a New Century*. New York: Henry Holt, 2000.

Stavney, Anne. "'Mothers of tomorrow': The New Negro Renaissance and the Politics of Maternal Representation." *African American Review* 32.4 (1998): 533–61.

Stein, Gertrude. *Three Lives*. 1909. New York: Random House, 1936.

Stevenson, Sheryl. "Ryder as Contraception: *Barnes v. the Reproduction of Mothering*." *Review of Contemporary Fiction* 13.3 (1993): 97–106.

"Still Another Reason for Birth Control." *Birth Control Review* 13.3 (March 1929): 67.

Stoddard, Lothrop. *Revolt Against Civilization: The Menace of the Under Man*. New York: Scribners, 1922.

Stokes, Mason Boyd. *The Color of Sex: Whiteness, Heterosexuality, and the Fictions of White Supremacy*. Durham, NC: Duke UP, 2001.

Stone, Hannah M. "Birth Control in America." *Birth Control Review* 16.6 (1932): 188–89.

———. "Family Limitation and Family Health." *Birth Control Review* June 1928: 182–83.

Stone, Percy Norwood. "Consumation—The Story of a Woman's Soul." *Birth Control Review* October 1922: 202–3.

Stubbs, Katherine. "Mechanizing the Female: Discourse and Control in the Industrial Economy." *Differences: A Journal of Feminist Cultural Studies* 7.3 (1995): 141–64.

Suleiman, Susan Rubin. *Authoritarian Fictions: The Ideological Novel as a Literary Genre*. New York: Columbia UP, 1983.

Taggard, Genevieve. "Legend." *Birth Control Review* July 1925: 199.

———. "With Child." *Birth Control Review* December 1925: 344.

Taylor, Carol M. "W. E. B. DuBois's Challenge to Scientific Racism." *Journal of Black Studies* 11.4 (1981): 449–60.

Tilton, Benjamin T. "Birth Control as a Prevention of Abortion." *Birth Control Review* March 1925: 71.

Tone, Andrea. "Contraceptive Consumers: Gender and the Political Economy of Birth Control in the 1930s." *Journal of Social History* 29.3 (1996): 485–506.

———, ed. *Controlling Reproduction: An American History*. Wilmington, DE: Scholarly Resources, Inc., 1997.

———. *Devices and Desires: A History of Contraceptives in America*. New York: Hill & Wang, 2001.

Trask, Michael. *Cruising Modernism: Class and Sexuality in American Literature and Social Thought*. Ithaca, NY: Cornell UP, 2003.

Trent, James W. "To Cut and Control: Institutional Preservation and the Sterilization of Mentally Retarded People in the United States, 1892–1947." *Journal of Historical Sociology* 6.1 (1993): 56–73.

Trent, Lucia. "Breed, Women, Breed." *Birth Control Review* April 1930: 113.
Trouard, Dawn. "Mary McCarthy's Dilemma: The Double Bind of Satiric Elitism." *Perspectives on Contemporary Literature* 7 (1981): 98–109.
Troxell, John P. "Birth Control—A Labor Viewpoint." *Birth Control Review* April 1927: 106, 125.
"An Unofficial Questionnaire: Seventy College Girls Express Their Opinions." *Birth Control Review* 14.10 (1930): 286–87.
Ureles, Sonia. "Man's Law." *The Woman Rebel*. Vol. 1, no. 2 (April 1914): 1.
Urgo, Joseph. "Faulkner Unplugged: Abortopoesis and The Wild Palms." *Faulkner and Gender: Faulkner and Yoknapatawpha, 1994*. Ed. Donald M. Kartiganer and Ann J. Abadie. Jackson: U of Mississippi P, 1996. 252–72.
Vorse, Mary Heaton. "The Magnet." *Birth Control Review* March 1921: 8, 16.
Ware, Susan. *Holding Their Own: American Women in the 1930s*. Boston: Twayne, 1982.
Wasserstein, Wendy. *Uncommon Women and Others*. New York: Dramatists Play Service Inc., 1978.
Watkins, Elizabeth Siegel. *On the Pill: A Social History of Oral Contraceptives 1950–1970*. Baltimore: Johns Hopkins UP, 1998.
Waxman, Barbara Frey. "Jewish American Princess, Their Mothers, and Feminist Psychology: A Rereading of Roth's 'Goodbye, Columbus.'" *Studies in American Jewish Literature* 7.1 (1988): 90–104.
Weil, Dorothy. "A New Woman?" *The Masses* January 1916: 17–18.
Wellman, Rita. "On the Dump." *Birth Control Review* December 1918: 7, 10.
Wertz, Richard W., and Dorothy C. Wertz. *Lying-In: A History of Childbirth in America*. New Haven, CT: Yale UP, 1989.
Wheelock, Warren. "Mother and Child." *Birth Control Review* December 1931: cover.
White, Ray L. "Hemingway's Private Explanation of *The Torrents of Spring*." *Modern Fiction Studies* 13 (1967): 261–63.
White, Ray Lewis. *Sherwood Anderson's Memoirs: A Critical Edition*. Chapel Hill: U of North Carolina P, 1969.
Wiggam, Albert Edward. *The Fruit of the Family Tree*. Garden City, NY: Garden City Publishing Co., 1922.
Wilt, Judith. *Abortion, Choice, and Contemporary Fiction: The Armageddon of the Maternal Instinct*. Chicago: U of Chicago P, 1990.
Woollcott, Alexander. "The Play." *New York Times* 28 April 1922: 20.
Young, Arthur. "Hell on Earth." *The Masses* March 1915.
Zuckerman, Mary Ellen. *A History of Popular Women's Magazines in the United States, 1792–1995*. Westport, CT: Greenwood, 1998.

Index

abortion, 4, 9n10, 12, 150, 170; and birth control movement, 104–9; and fiction, 65, 106–8, 132, 151–56, 160, 163, 170, 171
Adamic, Louis: "The Nation's Backbone," 76
African American: authors, 70–71, 75–76, 93–96, 115–16, 142–43; and birth control, 71, 139n30, 140–41; clubwomen, 70; and eugenics, 139–43; and motherhood, 92–93
Alcott, Louisa May: Work, 114
American Medical Association, 14, 35–36, 168
Anderson, Margaret, 38–39
Anderson, Sherwood, 22; Dark Laughter and eugenics, 118, 118n17
Ashley, Jessie: "The Law at Work," 46–47
Austin, Mary: and Birth Control Review, 72; and Emma Goldman, 72; and Margaret Sanger, 72; A Woman of Genius, 71–72

Barnard, Seymour: "Philanthropy: A Comic Opera," 41
Barnes, Djuna, 99; and censorship, 104; Ryder, 102–4
Barns, Cornelia, 45, 74n14
Barrett, Wilton Agnew: "The Wash," 42–43
birth control, 4n4; in 1940, 154; in the 1800s, 12, 15, 178; abstinence as, 44, 44n17; acceptance of, 145; access to in ancient world, 10–11; and African American women, 71, 96, 189; associated with witchcraft, 11; available to married people, 70; as business, 2, 166; and censorship, 11–12, 13–14; class divide, 28, 40, 145, 148–49, 157, 180, 180n10; and consumerism, 2–3, 169, 181 187; and demographics, 150, 182; and the Depression, 145–49, 165, 165n17, 166, 166n18; diaphragm popularity, 176–77, 176n7; ease of use, 122, 122n23; gendered power relations, 184–85; and health, 86; insurance coverage of, 1, 1n1; Lysol as, 77, 77n16; and morality, 55, 70, 80; and physicians, 168; as preventing abortion, 14, 104–9, 104n20, 150; and Progressive Era reform, 24; and promiscuity, 4, 67; and prostitution, 25–26; and public health, 86, 149, 149n4; and "race suicide," 183; as a science, 77–78; as scientific motherhood, 88–89; and single women, 146, 181–82; and socialism/communism, 156, 156n10; and social activists, 40–41, 41n16; and social control, 189; and soldiers in WWI, 78, 78n17; and sterilization, 144, 144n36; usage of, 35–36, 36n13; variety of, 3; women's responsibility, 3, 11

birth control and the eugenics movement, 110n1, 111, 113, 113n9, 116–17, 124, 141, 141n33; *Are You Fit to Marry?*, 110, 144; and immigration, 111n4; in opposition, 121; leaders, 121; rhetoric of, 121–22

Birth Control Federation of America, 166

birth control knowledge: in ancient world, 10–11; and class divide, 12, 15, 16, 28, 35–37, 38, 41, 48–49; factors of decline, 11; gendered aspect of, 49; health consequences, 26–27; ignorance breeding fear, 71–72; and race, 48–49, 48n20

birth control and marriage, 11, 73–76, 82, 168–69; abuse and alcohol, 80–81, 81n18; African American support for, 71; fear and ignorance, 77; prostitution, 79–80; saving the relationship, 79

birth control and motherhood, 85–104; and race, 92–93

birth control movement, 4, 71; and African American activists, 93; and African American women, 70, 70n12, 70n13; and abortion, 104–5; audience in the 1920s, 54; and class divide, 35; and clinics, 113, 175–76; conservative shift of, 35, 51, 55, 168; contradictions in, 82, 108–9, 166; in other countries, 16n20; in mainstream press in 1920s, 59–60, 59n5; and female sexuality, 82–83; on "feminine hygiene" advertising, 77–78; and heteronormativity, 6, 6n7; and involuntary sterilization, 123; leaders of, 22–23, 23n4; and medical establishment, 77–78; and moral majority, 55, 61–62; and *Mother Earth*, 28; and Gregory Pincus, 169; and poverty, 22, 23, 25, 42–43; and race, 141, 141n34; scholarly attention to, 9, 9n10; and science, 141; and sexuality, 82–86; and socialism, 24, 24n5, 28, 32, 43; as social revolution, 21, 29, 35, 40–41; and traditional values, 83–84; and two-child norm, 86; and white-middle class women, 60; and *The Woman Rebel*, 28; and women's rights, 56

birth control opponents: birth control as murder, 98; birth control promoting prostitution, 78; motherhood as selflessness, 99

birth control in popular culture, 8; advertisements, 1–2, 14; and the Comstock Act, 77; and euphemisms, 76–77, 77n15; and *Seinfeld*, 8

birth control and poverty, 30, 32, 36–37, 71; effect on men, 43–44; charity, 40–41; and eugenics, 130. *See also* birth control movement: poverty

"Birth Control Primer": and morality, 80; and prevention of abortion, 105

Birth Control Review: advertising in, 60, 78; against abortion, 104–6; birth control and marriage, 54n3, 54, 61, 73–74, 75, 76; "Breaking Up the Home," 76; "Breed, Women, Breed" (Trent), 33–34; censorship of, 37–38, 49–50, 78; "Children" (Haman), 48–49; and class, 37–38, 46–48; "The Closing Door" (Grimke), 94; conservative shift, 51–52; "Consummation—The Story of a Woman's Soul" (Stone), 81; and the Depression, 146; "Do Women Want Children?," 88; "Enslaved Maternity," 104; and eugenics, 112n7, 112–13, 113n8, 121, 124–25; "Family Limitation and Family Health," 76; "Family Problems," 79; and marriage manuals, 55; founded, 35; funded by, 60; "Goldie" (Grimke), 94–95; "A Holiday" (Mumford), 73; "Hymn of the Unborn Babe," 91; idolization of motherhood, 91; "The Law at Work" (Ashley), 46–47; "Legend"

(Taggard) 74–75; "The Love Rights of Women" (Ellis), 54; "The Magnet" (Vorse), 74; and *The Masses*, 129–30; "A Matter of Life and Death" (Pruette), 73; "A Menace to Marriage," 76; "The Nation's Backbone" (Adamic), 75; "Nature" (Oakes), 79–80; "The Negro Wants Birth Control" (Sewell), 141 ; "On the Dump" (Wellman), 46; "The Pregnant Woman" (Mullen), 90; "Prevention or Abortion—Which?," 105; "The Probation in Literature" (Pangborn), 66; rhetoric of motherhood, 89, 90; "The Scrub Woman," 124; and Agnes Smedley, 158; and sterilization, 123; "The Stork and the Wolf" (Hickey), 147; "Still Another Reason for Birth Control—The Right of the Child to Be Welcome," 92; "They That Sit in Darkness" (Burrill), 47–48; "A Way Out" (Guest), 78–79; "Weeds" (Connell), 99n17, 125; "A Word Concerning Birth Control" (Dreiser), 62–63
birth rate, 15–16, 111
The Black Stork: and eugenics 110–11, 110n1, 139, 139n29
The Blast, 31, 35, 56; and birth control, 36, 38; and Emma Goldman, 35; and Lydia Gibson, 36; and Margaret Sanger, 35, 35n12
Blossom, Frederick, 105
Boyle, Kay: *My Next Bride*, 152–53; *Plagued by the Nightingale*, 134–35
Buck v. Bell (1927), 122
Burrill, Mary: "They That Sit in Darkness," 47–48

Caldwell, Ben: "Top Secret or a Few Million after B.C.," 143
Caldwell, Erskine: *Tobacco Road*, 130–31
Calverton, V. F.: *Bankruptcy of Marriage*, 55; *Sex Expression in Literature*, 5
Chamberlain, K. R.: "Breed! We Need Men," 31; "The Jones Family Group," 40
Chapelier, Emile: and birth control, 28; and *The Masses*, 40; "To Working Girls," 28
Chodorow, Nancy, 102
Clinical Research Bureau, 88, 121
Comstock, Anthony, 13; in literature, 17, 17n22
Comstock Act (1873), 13, 13n15; censoring literature, 13–14; challenges to, 15; effectiveness of, 15, 15n19; in literature, 39–40; and *Little Review*, 39; and *New York Call*, 26; defeat of, 149; rhetoric of ads that circumvented, 13–15
Connell, Richard: "Weeds," 99n17, 125
contraception. *See* birth control
contraceptive rhetoric: acceptance of female sexuality, 55; of African American community, 94; against abortion, 104–5; aligned with women's magazines, 62; as anticapitalistic, 29; and benefit of controlled pregnancies, 90–91; and child's rights, 92; of class war, 30; conservative, 70, 82, 83, 85, 123; contradictions of, 108–9; critiquing social system, 32; and economics, 29, 30, 42, 43, 74, 146–47; and eugenics, 111, 112, 112n7; 123; and health risk, 72–74, 92, 92n10; ideal of motherhood, 85, 85n1, 88, 89, 89n7, 92, 99, 166–67, 166n19; and machine imagery, 30, 30n9; and marriage, 61, 69–70, 73–74, 76, 82; and morality, 55, 69–70, 78, 106; as nostalgic, 86; and pathos, 73, 83; and socialism, 29; and social justice, 35; stops abuse and alcoholism, 80–81; unborn child's perspective, 91; in war time, 31–32; audience for, 54, 129
Coolidge, Mary: *Why Women Are So*, 100

The Crisis: birth control and motherhood, 93; and DuBois, 95; on eugenics and birth control, 141; "Motherhood" (Johnson, G. D.), 93

Day, Dorothy, 4; The Eleventh Virgin, 4–5; The Long Loneliness, 5n5
Dell, Floyd, 21, 21n2, 74n14
Delmar, Vina: and Bad Girl, 66
Dennett, Mary Ware: on contraceptive advertising, 77–78; as a birth control advocate, 20, 23n4, 26–27; and The National Birth Control League, 35
Dreiser, Theodore: An American Tragedy, 63–65, 107–8; banned, 63; as birth control advocate, 25–26, 62–63; and Birth Control Review, 62–63; critique of Comstock Act, 63; First American Birth Control Conference sponsor, 63; The Genius, 63; Jennie Gerhardt, 64, 64n8; on marriage and birth control, 62–66; realism and sexuality, 22; Sister Carrie, 63–64; "A Word Concerning Birth Control," 62–63
DuBois, W. E. B: birth control advocate, 92–93; "Black Folk and Birth Control," 141; The Crisis, 141; "Criteria of Negro Art," 95; on eugenics and birth control, 140–41
Dugdale, Robert L.: The Jukes: A Study in Crime, Pauperism, and Heredity, 114, 115
DuPlessis, Rachel Blau, 6; on Mina Loy, 118n16; on "writing beyond the ending," 67n9, 169n1, 174, 182

Eastman, Max, 21, 40
Eisenstadt v. Baird (1972), 70, 170
Eliot, T. S.: and eugenic anxiety, 127; The Waste Land 106–7, 127
Ellis, Havelock, 21–22, 54n3; "The Love Rights of Women," 54
Estabrook, Arthur H.: The Jukes, 114
eugenics, 111–12, 111n2, 111n3, 111n4; and the African American community, 115–16, 140–42; anti-immigration, 117, 119; in Barren Ground (Glasgow), 115–16; in The Chinaberry Tree (Fauset), 142–43; and class divide, 117, 132; in The Crux (Gilman), 114, 114n10; and family studies, 114–15, 114n11, 120, 120n21, 130; in "The Force of Heredity, and Nella" (Loos), 5; in The Great Gatsby (Fitzgerald), 119–21; and institutionalization, 126; language of, 115, 15n13; and Meridel Le Sueur, 131–33; and Mina Loy, 118; and Mother (K. Norris), 117; motives, 128, 128n26; negative, 121; and Plagued by the Nightingale (Boyle), 134–35; in Plum Bun (Fauset), 116; popularity of, 143–44; and popular culture, 113; and public health, 131; in Quicksand (Larsen), 142; and race, 130, 138–39, 139n30, 140, 142, 142n35, 143; "science" of, 121; in Seed (C. Norris), 135–38; and sexuality, 132–33; and sterilization, 130; and The Sound and the Fury (Faulkner), 124, 126–27; and Strange Interlude (O'Neill), 123; in Three Lives (Stein), 139–40; in Tobacco Road (E. Caldwell), 113, 130–31; in "Told in the Drooling Ward" (London), 125–26; in Torrents of Spring (Hemingway), 118–19; and The Waste Land (Eliot), 127–28; in Work (Alcott), 114. See also birth control and the eugenics movement

Farm Security Administration program (1936), 149
Faulkner, William: As I Lay Dying, 153–54; If I Forget Thee, Jerusalem, 8, 67, 154–56, 154n8; The Sound and the Fury, 124, 126–27
Fauset, Jessie Redmon, 70–71; The Chinaberry Tree, 71, 142–43; and eugenics, 142–43; Plum Bun, 54,

115–16; *There Is Confusion*, 54
Fitzgerald, F. Scott: on Anthony Comstock in *The Beautiful and the Damned*, 17; *The Great Gatsby*, 119–21
Forbes, Helen: "The Hunky Woman," 43
Freud: and sex education, 20, 20n1; *Three Essays on the Theory of Sexuality*, 20

Gibson, Lydia, 36
Gilman, Charlotte Perkins: *Herland*, 87, 87n6; and voluntary motherhood, 87
Glasgow, Ellen, 22; *Barren Ground* and eugenics, 115–16
Glaspell, Susan: and birth control movement, 67n11; *Chains of Dew*, 67–69
Goddard, Henry H.: *The Kallikak Family* and eugenic family studies, 120, 120n21
Goldman, Emma: and contraceptive rhetoric, 29; on the infant mortality rate, 50–51; as a leader of the birth control movement, 23n4; on marriage, 159; and *The Masses*, 50–51; and *Mother Earth*, 23–24; publicizing birth control information, 23–24; shifting away from birth control movement, 51; and *The Women Rebel*, 29; on women's rights, 56
Grant, Madison: *The Passing of the Great Race*, 115, 118–19
Gray, Harriet: "The Scrub Woman," 124
Greenwich Village: art and politics, 21–22, 21n2; and sexuality and marriage, 53
Grimke, Angelina Weld: depiction of African Americans, 70–71; "The Closing Door," 94; "Goldie," 94–95; on motherhood, 93; *Rachel*, 95–96
Griswold v. Connecticut (1965), 170
Guest, May Pierce: "A Way Out," 78–79

Hagood, Mary Jarman, 148–49
Hale, Nancy: *The Prodigal Women*, 171–73
Haman, Coralie: "Children: A Playlet," 48–49
Hansberry, Lorraine: *To Be Young, Gifted and Black*, 188–89
Hemingway, Ernest, 67; *A Farewell to Arms*, 102; "Hills Like White Elephants," 154; *The Torrents of Spring*, 118–19, 118n18
Himes, Norman: and history of birth control, 10–11; and eugenics, 113n8
Hull, Helen: "Till Death—," 44–45; "Usury," 58

infanticide, 93–94, 93n12, 96
involuntary sterilization, 111, 122–23, 123n24, 125, 128, 128n25, 132
Irwin, Inez Haynes, 73

Johnson, Georgia Douglas: "Maternity" and lynching, 96
Joyce, James: birth control and sexuality in *Ulysses*, 39, 39n15

Katz, Esther: on limitation of birth control statistics, 15n19, 16; and Margaret Sanger Papers Project, 23n4
Kelley, Edith Summers: eugenics, 116; pro-contraceptive narratives of motherhood, 99; *Weeds*, 100–101

Ladies' Home Journal: "The American Woman as a Mother" (Roosevelt), 60, 96–97; on birth control, 60; and eugenics, 113; "What the Women of America Think about Birth Control," 62
Langner, Lawrence: *Wedded: A Social Comedy*, 38–39, 58–59
Larsen, Nella, 75, 99; *Quicksand*, 8–9, 75–76, 101–2, 142
Le Sueur, Meridel: "Annunciation," 31; and the birth control move-

ment, 160–61; and the Communist Party, 160; and eugenics, 131; *The Girl*, 132–33, 158, 161–65; "Sequel to Love," 132–33; "Women on the Breadlines," 162, 162n16; on working women, 161
Little Review: birth control advocate, 38–39; and censorship, 39; and *The Masses*, 38–39; and *Ulysses*, 39
Lohman, Anna (Madame Restell), 14
London, Jack: "Told in the Drooling Ward," 125–26
Loos, Anita: "The Force of Heredity, and Nella: A Modern Fable with a Telling Moral for Eugenists," 114
Loy, Mina: and eugenics, 118, 118n16; "Feminist Manifesto," 118
Luhan, Mabel Dodge, 22
lynching, 93–94; anti-lynching dramas, 94–96

Marion, Kitty, 37–38
marriage: and childbirth 72; as norm, 82; and prostitution, 159. *See also* birth control and marriage
marriage manuals: conception and contraception in, 10, 10n11, 12–13, 54–55
The Masses, 21–22, 31; and birth control, 28, 28n8, 31, 40, 41, 42, 45–46; "Breed! We Need Men" (Chamberlain), 31; "Broadway Nights" (Reed), 43; critique of marriage, 56–57; and Emma Goldman, 50–51; "The Happy Home" (Popini), 28; "Hell on Earth" (Young), 129; "The Hunky Woman" (Forbes), 43; "The Jones Family Group" (Chamberlain), 40; and Max Eastman 40; "A New Woman?" (Weil), 57–58; "Philanthropy: A Comic Opera" (Barnard), 41; and poverty, 41, 42; "Till Death—" (Hull), 44–45; "Usury" (Hull), 58; "The Wash" (Barrett), 42–43
McCarthy, Mary: "Dottie Makes an Honest Woman of Herself,"
173–83; *The Group*, 174, 175n4, 180n11, 180n12, 183
McKay, Claude: *Home to Harlem*, 53, 78
Morrison, Toni: *Beloved*, 93n12; *Song of Solomon*, 143
mortality rate in childbirth, 26
motherhood: across racial lines, 93; childbirth as dehumanizing, 100–101; and class divide, 99–100; ideal in 1920s, 85; as natural desire, 88–89, 89n7, 99; as patriotic duty, 96–97, 97n15; and "race suicide," 96–97, 97n15, 117, 145; as selfless, 96; and unwanted children, 92, 92n10; unwed, 107n23; as voluntary, 109
Mullen, Kate: "The Pregnant Woman," 90
Muller v. State of Oregon (1908), 85
Mumford, Ethel Watts: "A Holiday," 73

naturalism, 18–19, 21
The New Republic, 55–56
The New Woman, 54–55
Norris, Charles G.: and Margaret Sanger, 136; *Seed*, 135–38
Norris, Kathleen: eugenics, 117; *Mother*, 24–25, 97–99

Oakes, Angela: "Nature," 79–80
Olsen, Tillie: *Yonnondio*, 157
O'Neill, Eugene: *Strange Interlude*, 123
Orwell, George: on Anthony Comstock in *Keep the Aspidistra Flying*, 17n22

Pangborn, Edgar Wood: "The Probation in Literature," 66
Parker, Dorothy: "Mr. Durant," 108; "Mrs. Hofstadter on Josephine Street," 115
the Pill: 1–2, 1n1, 1n2, 122n23, 169, 174
Planned Parenthood Federation of America, 168

Popini, Alexander: "The Happy Home," 28
Poynter, Beulah: *The Unborn*, 122
Progressive Era, 13
Pruette, L. L.: "A Matter of Life and Death," 73

realism, 22, 42, 157, 159, 167
Reed, John: "Broadway Nights," 43
Restell, Madame (Anna Lohman), 14
Robinson, Caroline H.: "Collegian's Race Suicide," 145
Roe v. Wade (1973), 170
Rogers, Lou, 32, 36–37, 50
Roosevelt, Theodore: "The American Woman as a Mother," 60, 96–96; on "race suicide," 117
Roth, Philip: "Goodbye, Columbus," 173, 183–87

Sanger, Margaret: arraignment, 27–28; and *Birth Control Review*, 22, 22n3, 35, 38, 149, 149n5; and "doctors only" bill, 50, 78, 146; and Emma Goldman, 22, 27, 51; and eugenics, 112–13, 112n6, 121; and *Family Limitation*, 27, 29, 176, 176n6; on female sexual satisfaction, 55; on "feminine hygiene" advertising, 77–78; First American Birth Control Conference, 63; first birth control clinic, 35; and Gregory Pincus, 1; *Happiness in Marriage*, 55; "Impressions of the East Side," 48, 48n19 ; and International Workers of the World, 29; leading birth control movement, 22–23, 23n4; and Mary Ware Dennett, 26, 77–78; and medical community, 78; on modern motherhood, 86; *Motherhood in Bondage*, 18, 104; *My Fight for Birth Control*, 27; and *New York Call*, 26; *Pivot of Civilization*, 112, 112n6, 122; portrayed by opponents, 70; prediction of Pill popularity, 2; publicizing birth control, 8, 8n9, 23–24; and socialism, 29, 35; as symbol 173, 185–86; and Theodore Dreiser, 26, 63; 1917 trial testimony, 17, 17n23; "What Every Child Should Know," 26; "What Every Mother Should Know," 26; "When Women Should Avoid Having Children," 30; *Woman and the New Race*, 32–33, 86, 90, 112; "Woman, Morality, and Birth Control," 92; and *The Woman Rebel*, 24, 27, 28, 30, 39–40, 56; *Woman Today*, 156, 156n10; *Working Woman*, 156, 156n10
Sanger, William: arrest, 28
Sewell, Lemuel T.: "The Negro Wants Birth Control," 141
sexuality: apart from reproduction, 7, 53; and motherhood, 54; and race, 53n2; recognition of in 1910s, 21
Sheppard-Towner Maternity and Infancy Act (1921), 86, 86n3
Slesinger, Tess, 150; *The Unpossessed*, 150–52
Smedley, Agnes: *Daughter of Earth*, 158–60, 160n14; and Emma Goldman, 158; and Margaret Sanger, 158
Stein, Gertrude: eugenics in *Three Lives*, 139–40; and racism, 139–40, 139n31; "The Gentle Lena," 76
Stoddard, Lothrop: *Revolt Against Civilization: The Menace of the Under Man*, 115, 119–20, 121, 140
Stone, Dr. Hannah M., 169
Stone, Percy Norwood: "Consummation—The Story of a Woman's Soul," 81

Taggard, Genevieve, 74n14, 91n9; "Legend," 74–75; "With Child," 91
Tilton, Benjamin T., 104–5
Trent, Lucia: "Breed, Women, Breed," 33–34

Ureles, Sonia: "Man's Law," 39–40
U.S. v. One Package of Japanese Pessaries (1936), 18, 146, 146n2, 168

"voluntary motherhood," 12
Vorse, Mary Heaton: "The Magnet," 74

Wasserstein, Wendy: *Uncommon Women and Others*, 188
Weber, Lois: *The Hand That Rocks the Cradle*, 72–73
Weil, Dorothy: critique of marriage, 57–58; "A New Woman?," 57–58
Wellman, Rita: "On the Dump," 46
Wells, H. G.: and *Birth Control Review*, 72
The Woman Rebel, 24, 27–28, 30, 39–40, 56; "Man's Law" (Ureles), 39–40

women's magazines: effect of advertisement revenue on content, 60; female sexuality in marriage, 62; fiction in, 60–61; motherhood as sacred, 98; positive portrayal of career women, 62; traditional values, 60, 62
women's rights: in the context of marriage, 56
women's suffrage and sexuality, 20
Woodhull, Victoria: and free love, 56

Young, Arthur: "Hell on Earth," 129

www.ingramcontent.com/pod-product-compliance
Lightning Source LLC
Chambersburg PA
CBHW020946230426
43666CB00005B/196